Practical Machine Learning with R and Python – Third Edition

Machine Learning in Stereo

This book is dedicated to my late Mom who instilled in me the qualities of tenacity and endurance and to my late Dad to whom I owe most of my grey cells.

This book is also dedicated to my wife Shanthi for the companionship and support through the years, and finally to my daughter Shreya who started an interesting chapter in my life.

Table of Contents

Preface

Plummeting hardware prices, more powerful processors and exploding data generation has led to the re-emergence of AI and associated technologies. Datascience, Machine Learning (ML), Deep Learning (DL), Probabilistic Graphical Models, NLP have moved from research labs to our humble homes. In the last couple of years, the buzz around these three technologies namely Datascience, Machine Learning and Deep Learning has been getting louder and louder, that it is impossible for seasoned professionals or those beginning their careers to ignore these technologies.

The two most popular languages for Datscience, ML and DL are R and Python. There is a never-ending battle between diehard fans of these languages, about which language is better suited for datascience or machine learning. In my opinion, rather than debate about which is superior or otherwise, why should one not become adept in both. So, instead of implementing ML algorithms in one of the languages, this book implements equivalent ML algorithms in both languages. In effect, it like learning Machine Algorithms in stereo!! The book is well suited for both the expert and the novice.

The first two chapters 'Essential R' and 'Essential Python for Datscience' distils the key programming constructs in both languages. A beginner needs to get familiar with these constructs with which he can later build his language vocabulary. The third chapter 'R vs Python: Different similarities and similar differences', highlights equivalent programming constructs in both languages. Anybody who is more familiar with one of the language, R or Python, can learn how to write equivalent code in the other language.

The next six chapters implement the most common Machine Learning algorithms in equivalent R and Python. The first chapter 'Regression of a continuous variable' touches upon univariate, multivariate, polynomial and knn regression. The second chapter 'Classification and Cross Validation', deals with logistic regression, knn classification, leave one out and K-fold cross validation in R and Python. The next chapter 'Regression techniques and regularization' addresses best-fit, forward-fit, backward-fit. This also includes regularization techniques like ridge regression and lasso. Chapter four 'SVMs, Decision Trees and Validation curves' deals with ML models like SVMs. Decisions tree. A closer look is taken at Validation ROC and AUC curves. Chapter five 'Splines, GAMs, Random Forests and Boosting ', discusses more advanced techniques like B-Splines, GAMs, random forest and boosting. The last chapter 'PCA, K-Means and Hierarchical Clustering' deals with unsupervised learning methods like K-means, PCA and hierarchical clustering.

All ML algorithms have equivalent code in R and Python. This book is largely based on the 2 MOOC courses that I completed over the last 2 years namely Statistical Learning, (https://lagunita.stanford.edu/courses/HumanitiesandScience/StatLearning/Winter2015

I hope this book can be used as a quick reference for ML algorithms. I also hope that equivalent implementations in R and Python will give a more multi-dimensional view of these algorithms enabling you to internalize the algorithms better.

Tinniam V. Ganesh

Introduction

This is the third edition of my book 'Practical Machine Learning in R and Python :Third edition - Machine Learning in stereo'. In the third edition, all code sections, are formatted using fixed-width font Consolas. This makes the R and Python output for dataframes or confusion matrix to be properly stacked one above the other. I have also fixed some of the typos. This makes the code much more elegant and readable.

In the second edition I added more content, added extensive comments to the code, besides including details of parameters in the Machine Learning function calls. In addition lots of effort went into formatting the code sections so that it is easy to go through the code flow.

Other books by Tinniam V Ganesh (available in Amazon as paperback and kindle versions)

1. Cricket analytics with Cricketr: Second Edition
2. Beaten by sheer pace!: Cricket analytics with yorkr
3. Deep Learning from first principles-Second Edition – In vectorized Python, R and Octave

1.   Essential R

1. Introduction

This chapter discusses 'Essential R', or in other words, the most important R constructs that you will use most often. I have tried to distil the key R phrases, which are used most frequently. With these statements it is possible to write quite complex code. Once you become familiar with these statements, you can progress to building up your repertoire in R.

You can download the associated code in this chapter as an R Markdown file from Github at https://github.com/tvganesh/PracticalMachineLearningWithRandPython

1.1 Installing R and R Studio

Install the latest R version from CRAN (https://cran.r-project.org/). Also, install RStudio (https://www.rstudio.com/products/rstudio/download/#download). RStudio is one of the best IDEs for developing in R

1.2 R basics

R is a very friendly language and flexible in many ways. We can start anywhere in the line, and continue onto the next line. There is no continuation character as in other languages, no statement delimiters. If you end a line with an operator you can continue to the next line. Also in R, the assignment is the "<-", though the '=' also works.

1.3 Variables

```
# Comments in R have a '#' as the start character. This line is a
comment.
c <- 5.26  # No variable definitions or declarations
c    # Display the value of c by writing the variable in a separate
line
## [1] 5.26
a <- 5 * 3 +    # No line continuation character, no statement
delimiters
     2/6
a
## [1] 15.33333
```

```
    c <- 4 + 2.679 +     # Start anywhere and continue to the next
line by ending the line with an operator
                23*7/8
```

Note: In R we can display the value of a variable, matrix, dataframe by typing it on a separate line as shown below

```
c
## [1] 26.804
```

1.4 Variable types

R has the following variable types

1.Character   2. Integer 3. Numeric 4. Logical 5. Complex 6. Raw

You can check the variable type by using the "class" command. This is a very useful command and often, we may need to check the variable type before trying to use it in computations/plots etc.

```
x<- "Hello world" # Can also use x= "Hello World"
x
## [1] "Hello world"
class(x)
## [1] "character"
y<-2.5
y
## [1] 2.5
class(y)
## [1] "numeric"
```

1.5. Vectors - All elements of same type

In a vector all elements are of the same type. If you create a vector with numeric and character values, then all elements will be converted to character. You can check the type of a variable by using 'class'

```
#2.  Vectors - All elements of same type
# Create a numeric vector. Note: Enter values within c(,,,)
myvector <- c(1,2,4,5,8,10,12)
#Display value of myvector
myvector
## [1]  1  2  4  5  8 10 12
myvector <- 2:12
myvector
```

```
## [1]  2  3  4  5  6  7  8  9 10 11 12
# Create a character vector
charVector <- c("one","two","three") # character vector
charVector
## [1] "one"    "two"    "three"
# Create a numeric vector myvector2
myvector2 <- c(5,7,9,12)
#Check the type of the vector2
class(myvector2)
## [1] "numeric"
# Concatenate myvector2 with a character vector
myvector2 <-c(myvector2,"the")
# Check the class again
class(myvector2)
## [1] "character"
class(myvector2[1])
## [1] "character"
```

You can get the length of the vector with

```
# Use length to determine the number of elements in vector
length(myvector)
## [1] 11
```

1.6 Sequences

Vectors can also be created by using the "seq" command.

```
# Creating vectors with sequences. In the example below, the sequence
starts at 5 and ends at 50 and is incremented by 5
myvector <- seq(5,50,by=5)
myvector
##  [1]  5 10 15 20 25 30 35 40 45 50
# Create a sequence between 6 & 43 with a period length of 7
seq(6,43,by=7)
## [1]  6 13 20 27 34 41
# This is useful when we want 7 equal intervals between 6 & 43
seq(6,43,length=7)
## [1]  6.00000 12.16667 18.33333 24.50000 30.66667 36.83333 43.00000
```

1.7 Repeating sequences

Repeating sequences can be created as below

```
a <- rep(5:9,times=3)
a
```

```
## [1] 5 6 7 8 9 5 6 7 8 9 5 6 7 8 9
b <- rep(3:7,len=2)
b
## [1] 3 4
```

1.8. To get help on any topic use '?' or help()

```
# Get help on any topic using '?'
?seq
## starting httpd help server ...
##   done
# You can also use help. This is commented to avoid displaying it
again.
#help(seq)
```

1.9 Finding index of value in sequence

A useful command is 'which' which returns the index where a value(s) are found

```
myvector <- c(1,2,4,5,8,4, 10,12)
# Use 'which' to get the index(indices) while checking for a value
which(myvector == 4)
## [1] 3 6
```

2.1 Matrix,lists and dataframes

Create 5 x 4 numeric matrix

```
# Create  5 x 4 numeric matrix
y<-matrix(1:20, nrow=5,ncol=4)
y
##      [,1] [,2] [,3] [,4]
## [1,]    1    6   11   16
## [2,]    2    7   12   17
## [3,]    3    8   13   18
## [4,]    4    9   14   19
## [5,]    5   10   15   20
class(y)
## [1] "matrix"
```

2.2 Lists

In lists the elements can be dissimilar. The list below has the following objects a)
Character variable b) character vector c) matrix and 4) numeric variable

11

```
w <- list(name="Fred", mynumbers=charVector, mymatrix=y, age=5.3)
# Display w
w
## $name
## [1] "Fred"
##
## $mynumbers
## [1] "one"    "two"    "three"
##
## $mymatrix
##      [,1] [,2] [,3] [,4]
## [1,]    1    6   11   16
## [2,]    2    7   12   17
## [3,]    3    8   13   18
## [4,]    4    9   14   19
## [5,]    5   10   15   20
##
## $age
## [1] 5.3
```

2.3 Data frames

A data frame is the most commonly used data type in R. Most data analysis is done on dataframes. Dataframes can be thought of as Excel sheets with rows and columns. Each column can be of a different type, but all elements in the column must be of the same type.

```
d <- c(1,2,3,4)
e <- c("red", "white", "red", NA)
f <- c(TRUE,TRUE,TRUE,FALSE)
mydataframe <- data.frame(d,e,f)
names(mydataframe) <- c("ID","Color","Passed") # variable names
mydataframe
##   ID Color Passed
## 1  1   red   TRUE
## 2  2 white   TRUE
## 3  3   red   TRUE
## 4  4  <NA>  FALSE
class(mydataframe)
## [1] "data.frame"
```

2.4 Subsetting

To subset vectors use the index to subscript into the vector

```
myvector <- seq(2,20,by=2)
myvector
```

```
## [1]  2  4  6  8 10 12 14 16 18 20
```

Get the 4th element in myvector. **Note:** In R, the indices start from 1 to N and not 0 to N-1 as is common in C,C++,Java or Python.

```
myvector[4]
## [1] 8
```

2.5 Get a range of elements, from the 3rd to 7th

```
s <- myvector[3:7]
s
## [1]  6  8 10 12 14
```

2.6 Subset based on a condition

```
myvector <- seq(2,20,by=2)
myvector
## [1]  2  4  6  8 10 12 14 16 18 20
# Find all values of myvector which are greater than 10
b <- myvector>10
# b is a logical vector of 'TRUE' and 'FALSE'
b
## [1] FALSE FALSE FALSE FALSE FALSE  TRUE  TRUE  TRUE  TRUE  TRUE
# Subset myvector with the logical vector
a <- myvector[b]
a
## [1] 12 14 16 18 20
```

It is possible to combine both in a single statement as shown below

```
# Subset myvector for values > 10
a <- myvector[ myvector > 10]
```

2.7 Exclude elements from vector

To leave out an element from a vector we can use the '-index' as below

```
# Remove the 2nd element from myvector
myvector[-2]
## [1]  2  6  8 10 12 14 16 18 20
```

2.8 Subsetting a vector based on a substring

```
m <- c("about","aboard","board","bus","cat","abandon")
a <- grep("ab",m)
a
## [1] 1 2 6
# String with "ab"
containsAB <- m[a]
# Or combine both statements into a single statement
containsAB <- m[grep("ab",m)]
containsAB
## [1] "about"   "aboard"   "abandon"
```

2.9 Operations on vectors

We can do arithmetic and logical operation on vectors

```
myvector <- seq(2,20,by=2)
myvector
##  [1]  2  4  6  8 10 12 14 16 18 20
# Arithmetic operations on vectors
myvector1 <- seq(3,30,by=3)
myvector1
##  [1]  3  6  9 12 15 18 21 24 27 30
# Addition of 2 vectors
a <- myvector + myvector1
a
##  [1]  5 10 15 20 25 30 35 40 45 50
# Product of 2 vectors
b <- myvector * myvector1
b
##  [1]   6  24  54  96 150 216 294 384 486 600
# Raising element to a power
myvector^3
##  [1]    8   64  216  512 1000 1728 2744 4096 5832 8000
#Logical operations on 2vectors
a <- myvector < myvector1
a
##  [1] TRUE TRUE TRUE TRUE TRUE TRUE TRUE TRUE TRUE TRUE
```

Arithmetic and logical operations between vectors can be performed, as long as the length of one of the vectors is a multiple of the other

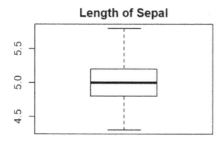

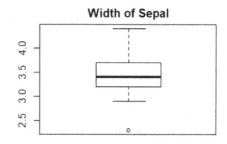

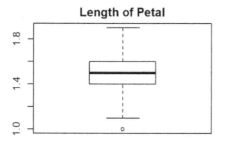

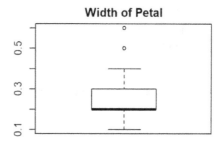

3.1 Accessing elements in matrix

We can access elements in a matrix by specifying the row and the column index. **Note:**
We can also specify the row and the column vector

```
y<-matrix(1:20, nrow=5,ncol=4)
y
##       [,1] [,2] [,3] [,4]
## [1,]    1    6   11   16
## [2,]    2    7   12   17
## [3,]    3    8   13   18
## [4,]    4    9   14   19
## [5,]    5   10   15   20
y[2,3]
## [1] 12
```

3.2 Matrix operations

Included below are some key matrix operations. R has several packages that deal with
matrices for various analysis. Some of the main operations are shown below

```
A <- matrix(1:9,nrow=3,ncol=3)
B <- matrix(seq(5,10,length=9),nrow=3,ncol=3)
```

3.3 Some key matrix operations

```
# Matrix addition
C <- A+B
C
##          [,1]    [,2]    [,3]
## [1,] 6.000 10.875 15.750
## [2,] 7.625 12.500 17.375
## [3,] 9.250 14.125 19.000
# Matrix subtraction
C <- A -B
C
##           [,1]    [,2]    [,3]
## [1,] -4.000 -2.875 -1.750
## [2,] -3.625 -2.500 -1.375
## [3,] -3.250 -2.125 -1.000
# Element wise matrix multiplication
C = A*B
C
##          [,1]  [,2]  [,3]
## [1,]  5.00 27.50 61.25
## [2,] 11.25 37.50 75.00
## [3,] 18.75 48.75 90.00
#Matrix multiplication
C = A %*% B
C
##           [,1]     [,2]     [,3]
## [1,]  71.250  93.75 116.250
## [2,]  88.125 116.25 144.375
## [3,] 105.000 138.75 172.500
```

3.4 Subsetting lists

Lists can be subsetted using an index and a double square bracket

```
w <- list(name="Fred", mynumbers=charVector, mymatrix=y, age=5.3)
w
## $name
## [1] "Fred"
##
## $mynumbers
## [1] "one"    "two"    "three"
##
## $mymatrix
##       [,1] [,2] [,3] [,4]
## [1,]    1    6   11   16
## [2,]    2    7   12   17
```

```
## [3,]    3    8    13    18
## [4,]    4    9    14    19
## [5,]    5   10    15    20
##
## $age
## [1] 5.3
# To access an object in a list , use [[]]e.g
w[[2]]
## [1] "one"    "two"    "three"
# You can further access the elements in the object depending on the
type
a = w[[2]] #a is a vector
a[2]
## [1] "two"
b=w[[3]]
b
##        [,1] [,2] [,3] [,4]
## [1,]    1    6    11    16
## [2,]    2    7    12    17
## [3,]    3    8    13    18
## [4,]    4    9    14    19
## [5,]    5   10    15    20
#
b[2,3]
## [1] 12
```

3.5. Subsetting dataframes

```
head(mtcars,3)
##                  mpg cyl disp  hp drat    wt  qsec vs am gear carb
## Mazda RX4       21.0   6  160 110 3.90 2.620 16.46  0  1    4    4
## Mazda RX4 Wag   21.0   6  160 110 3.90 2.875 17.02  0  1    4    4
## Datsun 710      22.8   4  108  93 3.85 2.320 18.61  1  1    4    1
# We can subset like matrices
# Dataframe 'df' are subsetted as
#df[row,column]/df[row vector,column vector]
mtcars[2,3]
## [1] 160
# We can also subset by providing the row & column vectors as  df[row
vector,column vector]
mtcars[2:5,3:6]
##                  disp  hp drat    wt
## Mazda RX4 Wag     160 110 3.90 2.875
## Datsun 710        108  93 3.85 2.320
## Hornet 4 Drive    258 110 3.08 3.215
## Hornet Sportabout 360 175 3.15 3.440
# If the row/row vector is not included then it means all rows
#Get all rows but only columns 3 to 7
```

17

```
a=mtcars[,3:7]
# Display only top 4 rows of a
head(a,4)
##                  disp  hp drat    wt  qsec
## Mazda RX4         160 110 3.90 2.620 16.46
## Mazda RX4 Wag     160 110 3.90 2.875 17.02
## Datsun 710        108  93 3.85 2.320 18.61
## Hornet 4 Drive    258 110 3.08 3.215 19.44
# If the column/column vector is not included then it means all rows
# Get all columns for rows 2 to 5
mtcars[2:5,]
##                  mpg cyl disp  hp drat    wt  qsec vs am gear
carb
## Mazda RX4 Wag    21.0   6  160 110 3.90 2.875 17.02  0  1    4
4
## Datsun 710       22.8   4  108  93 3.85 2.320 18.61  1  1    4
1
## Hornet 4 Drive   21.4   6  258 110 3.08 3.215 19.44  1  0    3
1
## Hornet Sportabout 18.7  8  360 175 3.15 3.440 17.02  0  0    3
2
```

3.6 Check column names

To check the column names of a dataframe we can either use names() or colnames()

```
names(mtcars)
##  [1] "mpg"  "cyl"  "disp" "hp"   "drat" "wt"   "qsec" "vs"   "am"
"gear"
## [11] "carb"
colnames(mtcars)
##  [1] "mpg"  "cyl"  "disp" "hp"   "drat" "wt"   "qsec" "vs"   "am"
"gear"
## [11] "carb"
```

3.7 Access a specific column by name

To access a column by name, use the $

```
mtcars$mpg
##  [1] 21.0 21.0 22.8 21.4 18.7 18.1 14.3 24.4 22.8 19.2 17.8 16.4
17.3 15.2
## [15] 10.4 10.4 14.7 32.4 30.4 33.9 21.5 15.5 15.2 13.3 19.2 27.3
26.0 30.4
## [29] 15.8 19.7 15.0 21.4
```

3.8 Find all rows where mpg >15

We can also subset based on a specific condition. To subset all rows of dataframe where mpg >15.0 we can use

```
a <- mtcars$mpg>15
a
##  [1]  TRUE  TRUE  TRUE  TRUE  TRUE  TRUE FALSE  TRUE  TRUE  TRUE
TRUE
## [12]  TRUE  TRUE  TRUE FALSE FALSE FALSE  TRUE  TRUE  TRUE  TRUE
TRUE
## [23]  TRUE FALSE  TRUE  TRUE  TRUE  TRUE  TRUE  TRUE FALSE  TRUE

#Subset the dataframe using this logical vector for the row vector.
# Leave the column empty
b <- mtcars[a,]
b
```

	mpg	cyl	disp	hp	drat	wt	qsec	vs	am	gear	carb
## Mazda RX4	21.0	6	160.0	110	3.90	2.620	16.46	0	1	4	4
## Mazda RX4 Wag	21.0	6	160.0	110	3.90	2.875	17.02	0	1	4	4
## Datsun 710	22.8	4	108.0	93	3.85	2.320	18.61	1	1	4	1
## Hornet 4 Drive	21.4	6	258.0	110	3.08	3.215	19.44	1	0	3	1
## Hornet Sportabout	18.7	8	360.0	175	3.15	3.440	17.02	0	0	3	2
## Valiant	18.1	6	225.0	105	2.76	3.460	20.22	1	0	3	1
## Merc 240D	24.4	4	146.7	62	3.69	3.190	20.00	1	0	4	2
## Merc 230	22.8	4	140.8	95	3.92	3.150	22.90	1	0	4	2
## Merc 280	19.2	6	167.6	123	3.92	3.440	18.30	1	0	4	4
## Merc 280C	17.8	6	167.6	123	3.92	3.440	18.90	1	0	4	4
## Merc 450SE	16.4	8	275.8	180	3.07	4.070	17.40	0	0	3	3
## Merc 450SL	17.3	8	275.8	180	3.07	3.730	17.60	0	0	3	3
## Merc 450SLC	15.2	8	275.8	180	3.07	3.780	18.00	0	0	3	3
## Fiat 128	32.4	4	78.7	66	4.08	2.200	19.47	1	1	4	1

	mpg	cyl	disp	hp	drat	wt	qsec	vs	am	gear	carb
## Honda Civic	30.4	4	75.7	52	4.93	1.615	18.52	1	1	4	2
## Toyota Corolla	33.9	4	71.1	65	4.22	1.835	19.90	1	1	4	1
## Toyota Corona	21.5	4	120.1	97	3.70	2.465	20.01	1	0	3	1
## Dodge Challenger	15.5	8	318.0	150	2.76	3.520	16.87	0	0	3	2
## AMC Javelin	15.2	8	304.0	150	3.15	3.435	17.30	0	0	3	2
## Pontiac Firebird	19.2	8	400.0	175	3.08	3.845	17.05	0	0	3	2
## Fiat X1-9	27.3	4	79.0	66	4.08	1.935	18.90	1	1	4	1
## Porsche 914-2	26.0	4	120.3	91	4.43	2.140	16.70	0	1	5	2
## Lotus Europa	30.4	4	95.1	113	3.77	1.513	16.90	1	1	5	2
## Ford Pantera L	15.8	8	351.0	264	4.22	3.170	14.50	0	1	5	4
## Ferrari Dino	19.7	6	145.0	175	3.62	2.770	15.50	0	1	5	6
## Volvo 142E	21.4	4	121.0	109	4.11	2.780	18.60	1	1	4	2

3.9 Subset on compound condition

To subset on a compound condition we need to assign the output to a logical vector. We can then subset all rows based on this logical vector.

```
a <- mtcars$mpg>15 & mtcars$mpg <25
a
## [1]  TRUE  TRUE  TRUE  TRUE  TRUE  TRUE FALSE  TRUE  TRUE  TRUE
TRUE
## [12]  TRUE  TRUE  TRUE FALSE FALSE FALSE FALSE FALSE FALSE  TRUE
TRUE
## [23]  TRUE FALSE  TRUE FALSE FALSE FALSE  TRUE  TRUE FALSE  TRUE

# Subset using the logical vector 'a' and select all columns (no
column vector)
c <- mtcars[a,]
c
##                   mpg cyl  disp  hp drat    wt  qsec vs am gear
carb
## Mazda RX4        21.0   6 160.0 110 3.90 2.620 16.46  0  1    4
4
## Mazda RX4 Wag    21.0   6 160.0 110 3.90 2.875 17.02  0  1    4
4
```

```
## Datsun 710         22.8  4 108.0  93 3.85 2.320 18.61  1  1    4
1
## Hornet 4 Drive     21.4  6 258.0 110 3.08 3.215 19.44  1  0    3
1
## Hornet Sportabout 18.7  8 360.0 175 3.15 3.440 17.02  0  0    3
2
## Valiant            18.1  6 225.0 105 2.76 3.460 20.22  1  0    3
1
## Merc 240D          24.4  4 146.7  62 3.69 3.190 20.00  1  0    4
2
## Merc 230           22.8  4 140.8  95 3.92 3.150 22.90  1  0    4
2
## Merc 280           19.2  6 167.6 123 3.92 3.440 18.30  1  0    4
4
## Merc 280C          17.8  6 167.6 123 3.92 3.440 18.90  1  0    4
4
## Merc 450SE         16.4  8 275.8 180 3.07 4.070 17.40  0  0    3
3
## Merc 450SL         17.3  8 275.8 180 3.07 3.730 17.60  0  0    3
3
## Merc 450SLC        15.2  8 275.8 180 3.07 3.780 18.00  0  0    3
3
## Toyota Corona      21.5  4 120.1  97 3.70 2.465 20.01  1  0    3
1
## Dodge Challenger   15.5  8 318.0 150 2.76 3.520 16.87  0  0    3
2
## AMC Javelin        15.2  8 304.0 150 3.15 3.435 17.30  0  0    3
2
## Pontiac Firebird   19.2  8 400.0 175 3.08 3.845 17.05  0  0    3
2
## Ford Pantera L     15.8  8 351.0 264 4.22 3.170 14.50  0  1    5
4
## Ferrari Dino       19.7  6 145.0 175 3.62 2.770 15.50  0  1    5
6
## Volvo 142E         21.4  4 121.0 109 4.11 2.780 18.60  1  1    4
2
```

4.1 Some common directory and file handling commands

Included below, are some common file and directory commands in R

Get the current working directory

```
getwd()
## [1] "C:/software/RandPythonBook/EssentialR/EssentialR-master"
```

Set the working directory. Note the forward slash

```
setwd("C:/software/R")
getwd()
## [1] "C:/software/R"
```

Go up one directory and then the current directory

```
setwd("..")
getwd()
## [1] "C:/software/RandPythonBook/EssentialR"
```

Show all objects in the environment

```
ls()
##  [1] "a"          "A"           "b"           "B"         "c"
##  [6] "C"          "charVector"  "containsAB"  "d"         "e"
## [11] "f"          "m"           "mydataframe" "myvector"
"myvector1"
## [16] "myvector2"  "s"           "w"           "x"         "y"
```

Remove a specific object for e.g. 'myvector which was created earlier from the environment

```
rm("myvector")
```

This is a particularly useful command. We will need to do this every now and then, so that we can start with a clean slate and don't have variables left by some previous operations

Remove all objects from the working environment

```
rm(list=ls())
```

Show contents of dir

```
dir()
##  [1] "EssentialR-1.html"  "EssentialR-1.Rmd"    "EssentialR-
1_cache"
##  [4] "EssentialR-1_files" "EssentialR.pptx"     "essentialR.R"
##  [7] "mytest2.R"          "README.md"           "RMarkdown.Rmd"
## [10] "tendulkar.csv"      "testdir"             "testRpackage"
## [13] "testShinyApp"
```

Other useful commands Create a directory

```
dir.create("testdir")
## Warning in dir.create("testdir"): 'testdir' already exists
```

Create a file

```
file.create("myTest.R")
## [1] TRUE
```

Check if file exists

```
file.exists("mytest.R")
## [1] TRUE
```

Rename a file

```
file.rename("mytest.R","mytest2.R")
## [1] TRUE
```

4.2 To print an object

```
myvector <- seq(2,20,by=2)
myvector
##  [1]  2  4  6  8 10 12 14 16 18 20
myvector
##  [1]  2  4  6  8 10 12 14 16 18 20
print(myvector)
##  [1]  2  4  6  8 10 12 14 16 18 20
```

4.3 For loops

There are 2 ways to write 'for' loops. **Important note**: One should avoid 'for' loops, as 'for' loops are very performance intensive. Try to use vectors instead of 'for' loops wherever possible

```
for(i in 1:5){
  print(i*5)
}
## [1] 5
## [1] 10
## [1] 15
## [1] 20
## [1] 25
for(i in seq_along(myvector)){
  print(myvector[i])
}
```

```
## [1] 2
## [1] 4
## [1] 6
## [1] 8
## [1] 10
## [1] 12
## [1] 14
## [1] 16
## [1] 18
## [1] 20
```

Avoid 'for' loops if possible. Try to use vector functions using sapply,lapply,tapply instead of 'for' loops. for loops are very performance intensive. Vectorized operations with sapply,lapply and tapply are orders of magnitude faster.

4.4 R functions. To create a function

A function definition is given below. The return value is usually the last statement of the function. In the function below the return is the value 'c'

```
product <- function(a, b){
  c <- a*b
  c
}
```

Invoke the function

```
product(7,12)
## [1] 84
product(13,18)
## [1] 234
```

4.5 Accessing elements in a dataframe

There are several datasets available that comes with R. The dataframe is a tabular form of data with many rows and columns. The type of data can vary from column to column but are the same in each column

```
data()
class(iris)
## [1] "data.frame"
```

Create a new data frame from iris. Iris is a small plant.
See https://en.wikipedia.org/wiki/Iris_(plant) Display the iris dataframe by typing it on a separate line

```
head(iris,5)
##   Sepal.Length Sepal.Width Petal.Length Petal.Width Species
## 1          5.1         3.5          1.4         0.2  setosa
## 2          4.9         3.0          1.4         0.2  setosa
## 3          4.7         3.2          1.3         0.2  setosa
## 4          4.6         3.1          1.5         0.2  setosa
## 5          5.0         3.6          1.4         0.2  setosa
```

4.6 Check the size of the dataframe

```
dim(iris)
## [1] 150   5
```

4.7 Check the 1st few rows of the data frame

```
head(iris)
##   Sepal.Length Sepal.Width Petal.Length Petal.Width Species
## 1          5.1         3.5          1.4         0.2  setosa
## 2          4.9         3.0          1.4         0.2  setosa
## 3          4.7         3.2          1.3         0.2  setosa
## 4          4.6         3.1          1.5         0.2  setosa
## 5          5.0         3.6          1.4         0.2  setosa
## 6          5.4         3.9          1.7         0.4  setosa
```

4.8 The str() function

A very useful command to check the class of all columns in a dataframe is the 'str'
command. The 'str' command lists the columns in the dataframe, their type and also
displays a few representative values from each column

```
str(iris)
## 'data.frame':    150 obs. of  5 variables:
##  $ Sepal.Length: num  5.1 4.9 4.7 4.6 5 5.4 4.6 5 4.4 4.9 ...
##  $ Sepal.Width : num  3.5 3 3.2 3.1 3.6 3.9 3.4 3.4 2.9 3.1 ...
##  $ Petal.Length: num  1.4 1.4 1.3 1.5 1.4 1.7 1.4 1.5 1.4 1.5 ...
##  $ Petal.Width : num  0.2 0.2 0.2 0.2 0.2 0.4 0.3 0.2 0.2 0.1 ...
##  $ Species     : Factor w/ 3 levels "setosa","versicolor",..: 1 1
1 1 1 1 1 1 1 1 ...
```

4.9 The summary() function

We could also use the 'summary' command to get an overall view of dataframe. However
the 'str' command is more powerful than the 'summary' command

```
summary(iris)
##   Sepal.Length    Sepal.Width     Petal.Length    Petal.Width
##   Min.   :4.300   Min.   :2.000   Min.   :1.000   Min.   :0.100
##   1st Qu.:5.100   1st Qu.:2.800   1st Qu.:1.600   1st Qu.:0.300
##   Median :5.800   Median :3.000   Median :4.350   Median :1.300
##   Mean   :5.843   Mean   :3.057   Mean   :3.758   Mean   :1.199
##   3rd Qu.:6.400   3rd Qu.:3.300   3rd Qu.:5.100   3rd Qu.:1.800
##   Max.   :7.900   Max.   :4.400   Max.   :6.900   Max.   :2.500
##          Species
##   setosa    :50
##   versicolor:50
##   virginica :50
##
##
##
```

5.1 Name of columns in dataframe

To check the column names of iris we can use one of the following. They are both same

```
colnames(iris)
## [1] "Sepal.Length" "Sepal.Width"  "Petal.Length" "Petal.Width"
## [5] "Species"
#or
names(iris)
## [1] "Sepal.Length" "Sepal.Width"  "Petal.Length" "Petal.Width"
## [5] "Species"
```

5.2 Check the type of each column

We often need to check the class of every column. We could do this one by one, or simply use

```
sapply(iris,class)
## Sepal.Length  Sepal.Width Petal.Length  Petal.Width      Species
##    "numeric"    "numeric"    "numeric"    "numeric"     "factor"
```

5.3 Inspect the dataframe

To inspect the data. Display top 6 and bottom 6 of the dataframe

```
head(iris,6)
##   Sepal.Length Sepal.Width Petal.Length Petal.Width Species
## 1          5.1         3.5          1.4         0.2  setosa
## 2          4.9         3.0          1.4         0.2  setosa
```

```
## 3           4.7          3.2          1.3          0.2   setosa
## 4           4.6          3.1          1.5          0.2   setosa
## 5           5.0          3.6          1.4          0.2   setosa
## 6           5.4          3.9          1.7          0.4   setosa
tail(iris,6)
##      Sepal.Length Sepal.Width Petal.Length Petal.Width   Species
## 145          6.7          3.3          5.7          2.5 virginica
## 146          6.7          3.0          5.2          2.3 virginica
## 147          6.3          2.5          5.0          1.9 virginica
## 148          6.5          3.0          5.2          2.0 virginica
## 149          6.2          3.4          5.4          2.3 virginica
## 150          5.9          3.0          5.1          1.8 virginica
```

5.4 Subset a dataframe

Display 1-6 rows and 2-4 columns. This similar to how we subsetted the matrix We can use df[row,column] or df[row vector, column vector]

```
iris[1:6,2:4]
##   Sepal.Width Petal.Length Petal.Width
## 1         3.5          1.4         0.2
## 2         3.0          1.4         0.2
## 3         3.2          1.3         0.2
## 4         3.1          1.5         0.2
## 5         3.6          1.4         0.2
## 6         3.9          1.7         0.4
```

Display all rows for columns 1:3. If the row/row vector is omitted then display all rows

```
df<-iris[,1:3]
#Display top 5 rows
head(df,5)
##   Sepal.Length Sepal.Width Petal.Length
## 1          5.1         3.5          1.4
## 2          4.9         3.0          1.4
## 3          4.7         3.2          1.3
## 4          4.6         3.1          1.5
## 5          5.0         3.6          1.4
```

Display all columns for rows 1:5. If the column/column vector is omitted then display all columns

```
iris[1:5,]
##   Sepal.Length Sepal.Width Petal.Length Petal.Width Species
## 1          5.1         3.5          1.4         0.2  setosa
## 2          4.9         3.0          1.4         0.2  setosa
## 3          4.7         3.2          1.3         0.2  setosa
```

```
## 4            4.6          3.1          1.5          0.2   setosa
## 5            5.0          3.6          1.4          0.2   setosa
```

5.5 Rename columns

To rename columns, we use the same function 'colnames' and assign to it a character vector as shown here

```
colnames(iris) <-
c("lengthOfSepal","widthOfSepal","lengthOfPetal","widthOfPetal","Spec
ies")
colnames(iris)
## [1] "lengthOfSepal" "widthOfSepal"  "lengthOfPetal" "widthOfPetal"
## [5] "Species"
```

5.6 View a dataframe

To view a dataframe use the 'View' command

```
#This has been commented but you can try this command in RStudio
#View(iris)
```

5.7 To subset based on a value in a column

```
a <- iris$Species == "setosa"
#Subset these rows. The "," indicates include all columns for these rows. Here
for the #row vector we use the logical vector and we leave out the column
vector, indicating #we will require all columns
b <- iris[a,]
#Check the dimemsion ofthe 'b' dataframe
dim(b)
## [1] 50  5
```

5.8 Refer by column

```
colnames(b)
## [1] "lengthOfSepal" "widthOfSepal"  "lengthOfPetal" "widthOfPetal"
## [5] "Species"
b$widthOfSepal
##  [1] 3.5 3.0 3.2 3.1 3.6 3.9 3.4 3.4 2.9 3.1 3.7 3.4 3.0 3.0 4.0
4.4 3.9
## [18] 3.5 3.8 3.8 3.4 3.7 3.6 3.3 3.4 3.0 3.4 3.5 3.4 3.2 3.1 3.4
4.1 4.2
```

```
## [35] 3.1 3.2 3.5 3.6 3.0 3.4 3.5 2.3 3.2 3.5 3.8 3.0 3.8 3.2 3.7
3.3
```

5.9 Compute the mean and standard deviation of column

```
meanSepal <- mean(b$widthOfSepal)
meanSepal
## [1] 3.428
sdSepal <- sd(b$widthOfSepal)
sdSepal
## [1] 0.3790644
```

A very useful function is 'sapply' with which we can apply a function across vectors. In the R statement below, we have 4 column vectors of iris and we apply the function 'mean' to each of these column vectors

6.0 sapply()

```
m <- sapply(iris[1:4],mean)
m
## lengthOfSepal  widthOfSepal lengthOfPetal  widthOfPetal
##      5.843333      3.057333      3.758000      1.199333
```

6.1 Boxplot

To take a quick look at a specific column the box plot is particularly useful. To take a look at the documentation for a boxplot type ?boxplot

```
#?boxplot
```

Create a boxplot for the length of the sepal column of the Iris dataframe. The title of the plot requires the use of the 'main=' argument

```
boxplot(b$lengthOfSepal,main="Length of Sepal")
```

Length of Sepal

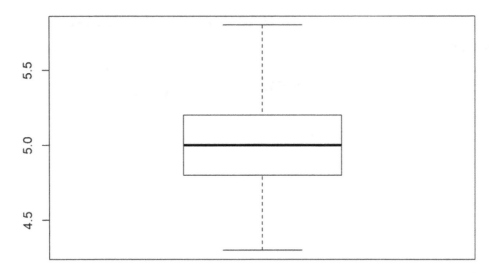

6.2 Display multiple plots

Often, we may need to display a boxplot for all the 4 numerical column vectors of Iris namely - widthOfSepal, lengthOfSepal, widthOfPetal & lengthOfPetal. The way to do this is to use the 'par' function with the 'mfrow' which specifies that we would like 4 plots in a 2 x 2 matrix setup. Draw all 4 plots. The 'mar=' parameter indicates the margins

```
par(mfrow=c(2,2)) # Set 2 rows x 2 columns
par(mar=c(4,4,2,2)) # Set the margins
boxplot(b$lengthOfSepal,main="Length of Sepal")
boxplot(b$widthOfSepal,main="Width of Sepal")
boxplot(b$lengthOfPetal,main="Length of Petal")
boxplot(b$widthOfPetal,main="Width of Petal")
```

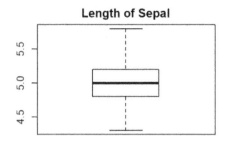

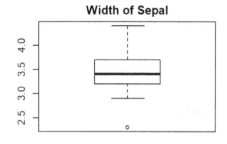

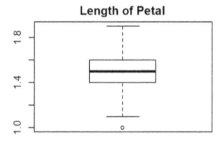

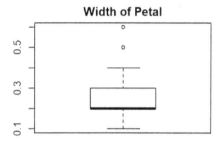

6.3 Reset the display

Reset the display with the following call. Otherwise you will get a 2 x 2 plots

```
dev.off()
## null device
##              1
```

6.4 Pairs plot

A useful function to check how data looks is pairs().This function will take pairs of columns and create a scatter plot. This will tell us how the columns are correlated

```
pairs(iris)
```

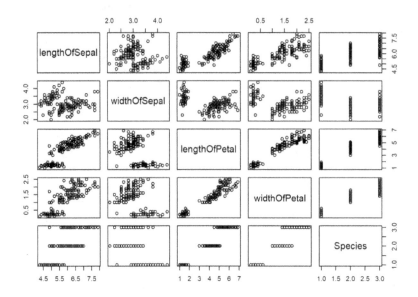

6.5 Cor() function

R also provides a way to compute the correlation numerically as follows. The output below shows that the length of Petal is positively correlated to width of Petal and length of Sepal

```
cor(iris[,1:4])
##              lengthOfSepal widthOfSepal lengthOfPetal
widthOfPetal
## lengthOfSepal     1.0000000   -0.1175698     0.8717538
0.8179411
## widthOfSepal     -0.1175698    1.0000000    -0.4284401    -
0.3661259
## lengthOfPetal     0.8717538   -0.4284401     1.0000000
0.9628654
## widthOfPetal      0.8179411   -0.3661259     0.9628654
1.0000000
```

6.6 Scatter plot

```
plot(iris$widthOfSepal,iris$lengthOfSepal)
```

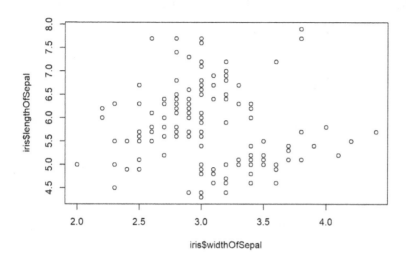

6.7 Add Title and Axis labels to plot

To the above plot add the x-axis & y-axis labels along with the title of the plot use xlab, ylab and main parameters

```
plot(iris$widthOfSepal,iris$lengthOfSepal, main="Iris - Length of
Sepal vs Width of Sepal", xlab="Sepal Width",  ylab="Sepal length")
```

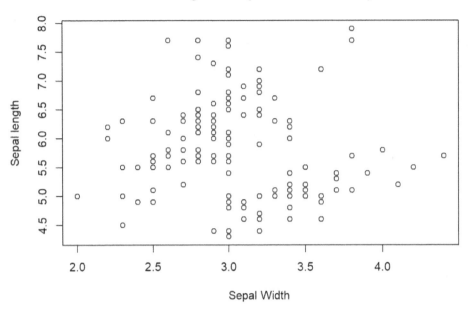

Iris - Length of Sepal vs Width of Sepal

6.8 Cleaning data

The IRIS data set is neat and tidy. However almost all real-world data is unclean, has many missing values, spaces for values or other junk characters. We must first 'clean' the data before applying any visualization or Machine Learning models on the data. (Check the help of read.csv using ?read.csv)

In the examples below I use a saved CSV file namely tendulkar.csv

6.9 Read the tendulkar dataframe

```
tendulkar= read.csv("tendulkar.csv",stringsAsFactors =
FALSE,na.strings=c(NA,"-"))
```

The 'summary' is a useful command for describing the overall content and structure of a dataframe

```
summary(tendulkar)
##       X              Runs              Mins              BF
##  Min.   :  1.0   Length:347        Min.   :  1.0   Min.   :  0.00
##  1st Qu.: 87.5   Class :character  1st Qu.: 33.0   1st Qu.: 22.00
##  Median :174.0   Mode  :character  Median : 82.0   Median : 58.50
```

```
## Mean    :174.0                       Mean    :125.5   Mean    : 89.75
## 3rd Qu.:260.5                         3rd Qu.:181.0   3rd Qu.:133.25
## Max.    :347.0                        Max.    :613.0   Max.    :436.00
##                                       NA's    :18     NA's    :19
##       X4s               X6s               SR               Pos
## Min.   : 0.000    Min.   :0.0000    Min.   :  0.00    Min.   :2.00
## 1st Qu.: 1.000    1st Qu.:0.0000    1st Qu.: 38.09    1st Qu.:4.00
## Median : 4.000    Median :0.0000    Median : 52.25    Median :4.00
## Mean   : 6.274    Mean   :0.2097    Mean   : 51.79    Mean   :4.24
## 3rd Qu.: 9.000    3rd Qu.:0.0000    3rd Qu.: 65.09    3rd Qu.:4.00
## Max.   :35.000    Max.   :4.0000    Max.   :166.66    Max.   :7.00
## NA's   :19        NA's   :18        NA's   :20        NA's   :18
##   Dismissal              Inns           Opposition           Ground
## Length:347        Min.   :1.000    Length:347          Length:347
## Class :character  1st Qu.:1.000    Class :character    Class
:character
## Mode  :character  Median :2.000    Mode  :character    Mode
:character
##                   Mean    :2.376
##                   3rd Qu.:3.000
##                   Max.    :4.000
##                   NA's    :1
##   Start.Date
## Length:347
## Class :character
## Mode  :character
##
##
##
##
```

The 'str' command is another command to get an overall description of the dataframe.

```
str(tendulkar)
## 'data.frame':    347 obs. of  13 variables:
## $ X          : int  1 2 3 4 5 6 7 8 9 10 ...
## $ Runs       : chr  "15" "DNB" "59" "8" ...
## $ Mins       : int  28 NA 254 24 124 74 193 1 50 324 ...
## $ BF         : int  24 NA 172 16 90 51 134 1 44 266 ...
## $ X4s        : int  2 NA 4 1 5 5 6 0 3 5 ...
## $ X6s        : int  0 NA 0 0 0 0 0 0 0 0 ...
## $ SR         : num  62.5 NA 34.3 50 45.5 ...
## $ Pos        : int  6 NA 6 6 7 6 6 6 6 6 ...
## $ Dismissal  : chr  "bowled" NA "lbw" "run out" ...
## $ Inns       : int  2 4 1 3 1 1 3 2 3 1 ...
## $ Opposition : chr  "v Pakistan" "v Pakistan" "v Pakistan" "v
Pakistan" ...
## $ Ground     : chr  "Karachi" "Karachi" "Faisalabad" "Faisalabad"
...
```

```
## $ Start.Date: chr  "15 Nov 1989" "15 Nov 1989" "23 Nov 1989" "23
Nov 1989" ...
```

Check the names of the columns for the dataframe 'tendulkar'

```
colnames(tendulkar)
##  [1] "X"          "Runs"      "Mins"       "BF"        "X4s"
##  [6] "X6s"        "SR"        "Pos"        "Dismissal" "Inns"
## [11] "Opposition" "Ground"    "Start.Date"
```

Check the dimensions of the tendulkar dataframe.

```
dim(tendulkar)
## [1] 347  13
```

Display top 5 and bottom 5 rows

```
head(tendulkar)
##     X Runs Mins  BF X4s X6s    SR Pos Dismissal Inns Opposition
Ground
## 1 1   15   28  24   2   0 62.50   6    bowled    2 v Pakistan
Karachi
## 2 2  DNB   NA  NA  NA  NA    NA  NA      <NA>    4 v Pakistan
Karachi
## 3 3   59  254 172   4   0 34.30   6       lbw    1 v Pakistan
Faisalabad
## 4 4    8   24  16   1   0 50.00   6   run out    3 v Pakistan
Faisalabad
## 5 5   41  124  90   5   0 45.55   7    bowled    1 v Pakistan
Lahore
## 6 6   35   74  51   5   0 68.62   6       lbw    1 v Pakistan
Sialkot
##      Start.Date
## 1 15 Nov 1989
## 2 15 Nov 1989
## 3 23 Nov 1989
## 4 23 Nov 1989
## 5  1 Dec 1989
## 6  9 Dec 1989
```

```
tail(tendulkar)
##         X Runs Mins  BF X4s X6s    SR Pos Dismissal Inns
Opposition
## 342 342   37  125  81   5   0 45.67   4    caught    2   v
Australia
## 343 343   21   71  23   2   0 91.30   4   run out    4   v
Australia
```

36

```
## 344 344   32   99  53    5    0 60.37    4        lbw    2   v
Australia
## 345 345    1    8   5    0    0 20.00    4        lbw    4   v
Australia
## 346 346   10   41  24    2    0 41.66    4        lbw    2 v West
Indies
## 347 347   74  150 118   12    0 62.71    4     caught    2 v West
Indies
##        Ground  Start.Date
## 342   Mohali 14 Mar 2013
## 343   Mohali 14 Mar 2013
## 344    Delhi 22 Mar 2013
## 345    Delhi 22 Mar 2013
## 346  Kolkata  6 Nov 2013
## 347   Mumbai 14 Nov 2013
```

As mentioned before if we want to check the class of all columns we can use the sapply() function to get the types of all columns

```
sapply(tendulkar,class)
##             X         Runs         Mins           BF          X4s
X6s
##     "integer"  "character"    "integer"    "integer"    "integer"
"integer"
##            SR          Pos     Dismissal          Inns    Opposition
Ground
##     "numeric"    "integer"  "character"    "integer"  "character"
"character"
##    Start.Date
## "character"
```

7.0 View the data frame

To view a dataframe in RStudio you can use the View(df)

#View(tendulkar)

Real world data will require a lot of cleaning before you can use it

```
# Remove all rows which have DNB (Did Not Bat) in the 'Runs' column,
# or in other words select rows which do not have the 'DNB' value.
#This is given by the '!=' or not 'equal
# to' #logical operator. Assign the result to a logical vector a
a <- tendulkar$Runs != "DNB"
head(a,3)
## [1]  TRUE FALSE  TRUE
```

```
#Now subset all rows based on the logical vector 'a',
tendulkar <- tendulkar[a,]
dim(tendulkar)
## [1] 330  13

# Next remove all rows with TDNB (Team Did Not bat)
c <- tendulkar$Runs != "TDNB"
tendulkar <- tendulkar[c,]

# Further remove all rows which have 'absent' in the Runs column and
# subset as before
d <- tendulkar$Runs != "absent"
tendulkar <- tendulkar[d,]

# Check the size of the tendulkar dataframe
dim(tendulkar)
## [1] 329  13

# Finally remove the "*"" indicating 'not out
tendulkar$Runs <- gsub("\\*","",tendulkar$Runs)

# Check the size of the cleaned tendulkar dataframe
dim(tendulkar)
## [1] 329  13
```

7.1 Complete cases

Another useful function for cleaning data is complete.cases. Check the documentation on 'complete.cases()'

```
#?complete.cases
# Check if all rows are complete
c <- complete.cases(tendulkar)

#Subset the rows which are complete
tendulkar <- tendulkar[c,]
```

Check the size of the tendulkar dataframe after all the above steps (a) to (e) for cleaning

```
dim(tendulkar)
## [1] 327  13
head(tendulkar,10)
##      X Runs Mins  BF X4s X6s    SR Pos Dismissal Inns   Opposition
## 1    1   15   28  24   2   0 62.50   6    bowled    2   v Pakistan
## 3    3   59  254 172   4   0 34.30   6       lbw    1   v Pakistan
## 4    4    8   24  16   1   0 50.00   6   run out    3   v Pakistan
## 5    5   41  124  90   5   0 45.55   7    bowled    1   v Pakistan
```

```
## 6    6    35   74  51    5   0 68.62    6     lbw   1     v Pakistan
## 7    7    57  193 134    6   0 42.53    6  caught   3     v Pakistan
## 8    8     0    1   1    0   0  0.00    6  caught   2 v New Zealand
## 9    9    24   50  44    3   0 54.54    6  caught   3 v New Zealand
## 10  10    88  324 266    5   0 33.08    6  caught   1 v New Zealand
## 11  11     5   15  13    1   0 38.46    6  caught   2 v New Zealand
##             Ground   Start.Date
## 1         Karachi  15 Nov 1989
## 3      Faisalabad  23 Nov 1989
## 4      Faisalabad  23 Nov 1989
## 5          Lahore   1 Dec 1989
## 6         Sialkot   9 Dec 1989
## 7         Sialkot   9 Dec 1989
## 8     Christchurch  2 Feb 1990
## 9     Christchurch  2 Feb 1990
## 10         Napier   9 Feb 1990
## 11       Auckland  22 Feb 1990
```

We can now do any sort of data analysis on the clean data using the many R packages that R comes with.

7.2 Base plot

R, by default, comes with some plotting ability. This is known as 'base plot'. Base plotting is easy to do. In the plot below, the function plot(x,y)

plot(tendulkar$BF,tendulkar$Runs)

39

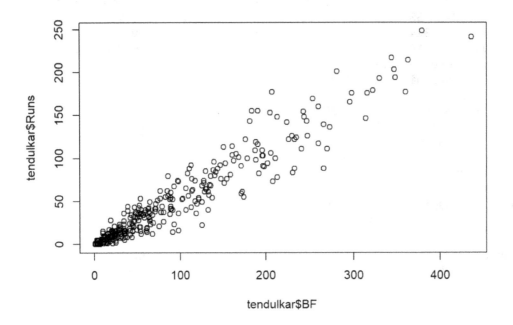

To add a title, and x and y labels, we need to invoke the plot function with additional parameters viz. 'xlab' for the X-axis label, 'ylab' for the Y-Axis label and 'main' to specify the plot title

```
plot(tendulkar$BF, tendulkar$Runs,pch=18, main="Tendulkar Runs scored
vs Balls Faced",
    xlab="Balls Faced", ylab='Runs')
```

Tendulkar Runs scored vs Balls Faced

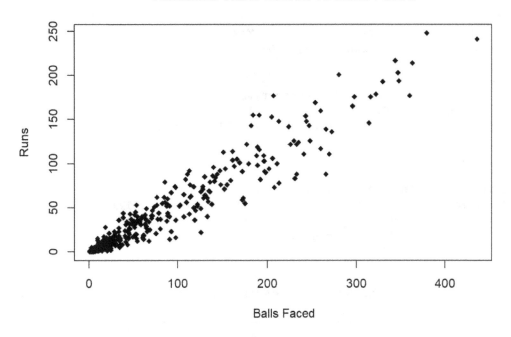

We can also fit a linear regression model between the Runs scored and the Balls faced by Tendulkar with the 'lm' call. To know more about 'ln' use ?lm

#?lm

7.3 Fit a linear regression line

Compute and plot a linear regression line Here Runs = a0 + a1 * BF

```
fit <-lm(tendulkar$Runs ~tendulkar$BF)
fit
##
## Call:
## lm(formula = tendulkar$Runs ~ tendulkar$BF)
##
## Coefficients:
##   (Intercept)   tendulkar$BF
##       -1.3572        0.5556
plot(tendulkar$Runs ~tendulkar$BF,xlab="Balls
Faced",ylab="Runs",main="Tendulkar's Runs vs Balls Faced")
summary(fit)
##
```

```
## Call:
## lm(formula = tendulkar$Runs ~ tendulkar$BF)
##
## Residuals:
##     Min      1Q  Median      3Q     Max
## -58.420  -5.976   0.246   5.913  63.358
##
## Coefficients:
##               Estimate Std. Error t value Pr(>|t|)
## (Intercept) -1.357213   1.198929  -1.132    0.258
## tendulkar$BF  0.555553   0.009552  58.164   <2e-16 ***
## ---
## Signif. codes:  0 '***' 0.001 '**' 0.01 '*' 0.05 '.' 0.1 ' ' 1
##
## Residual standard error: 15.11 on 325 degrees of freedom
## Multiple R-squared:  0.9124,  Adjusted R-squared:  0.9121
## F-statistic:  3383 on 1 and 325 DF,  p-value: < 2.2e-16
abline(fit,lty=5,lwd=3,col="blue")
```

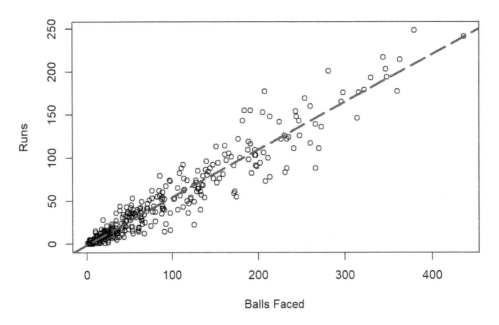

Tendulkar's Runs vs Balls Faced

7.4 Draw the histogram

```
#Plot the histogram of runs for Tendulkar
df = tendulkar
```

42

```
hist(as.numeric(df$Runs), main="Tendulkar's frequency of runs vs  run
ranges",
     xlab="Runs")
```

```
abline(v=median(df$Runs),col="blue",lwd=3.0)
abline(v=mean(df$Runs),col="red",lwd=3.0)
## Warning in mean.default(df$Runs): argument is not numeric or
logical:
## returning NA
```

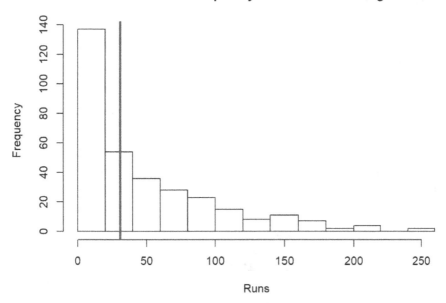

Tendulkar's frequency of runs vs run ranges

7.5 dplyr package

A look package dplyr. One of the most useful package for manipulating data in data frames

```
# Install package if necessary
#install.packages("dplyr")
#Call the library to the package to include dplyr
library(dplyr)
## Warning: package 'dplyr' was built under R version 3.4.2
##
## Attaching package: 'dplyr'
## The following objects are masked from 'package:stats':
##
```

```
##      filter, lag
## The following objects are masked from 'package:base':
##
##      intersect, setdiff, setequal, union
# Select columns
colnames(tendulkar)
##  [1] "X"          "Runs"      "Mins"      "BF"        "X4s"
##  [6] "X6s"        "SR"        "Pos"       "Dismissal" "Inns"
## [11] "Opposition" "Ground"    "Start.Date"
# Key functions select, filter, arrange, pipe,mutate, summarise

# Subset specific columns by name of column using 'select'. Note
there is no '$' sign or quotes to refer to # columns
df1 <- select(tendulkar, Runs,Mins,BF)

head(df1)
##    Runs Mins  BF
## 1    15   28  24
## 3    59  254 172
## 4     8   24  16
## 5    41  124  90
## 6    35   74  51
## 7    57  193 134

# This can be also written as below, where %>% is known as the 'pipe'
df1 <- tendulkar %>% select(Runs,Mins,BF)


# Subset rows, using 'filter' where the Runs > 50 and < 101
df2 <- filter(tendulkar,Runs>50 & Runs < 101)
## Warning: package 'bindrcpp' was built under R version 3.4.1

head(df2,5)
##  [1] X           Runs        Mins        BF         X4s         X6s
##  [7] SR          Pos         Dismissal   Inns       Opposition  Ground
## [13] Start.Date
## <0 rows> (or 0-length row.names)
# Also as
# df2 <- tendulkar %>% filter(Runs>50 & Runs < 101)
```

7.6 Clean the dataframe with dplyr

```
# Using dplyr to clean the Tendulkar dataframe
tendulkar= read.csv("tendulkar.csv",stringsAsFactors =
FALSE,na.strings=c(NA,"-"))

dim(tendulkar)
## [1] 347  13
```

```
#Remove rows for which Tendulkar$Runs was "DNB"
tendulkar <- tendulkar %>% filter(Runs != "DNB")

dim(tendulkar)
## [1] 330  13

#Remove rows for which Tendulkar$Runs was "TDNB"
tendulkar <-  tendulkar %>% filter(Runs != "TDNB")

dim(tendulkar)
## [1] 329  13

#Remove rows for which Tendulkar was "absent"
tendulkar <- tendulkar %>% filter(Runs != "absent")

#Finally we remove '*' as before
tendulkar$Runs <- gsub("\\*","",tendulkar$Runs)
class(tendulkar$Runs)
## [1] "character"
tendulkar$Runs <- as.numeric(tendulkar$Runs)

# Get only complete cases as before
c <- complete.cases(tendulkar)
tendulkar <- tendulkar[c,]
dim(tendulkar)
## [1] 327  13
```

7.7 Sort rows in descending order using 'arrange'

```
# There are more interesting conditions with which you can filter and
# select rows
# columns. Check the telated help with ?select & ?filter

# Use the arrange function to arrange columns in descending order of
# Runs
descRuns <- arrange(tendulkar,desc(Runs))

class(tendulkar$Runs)
## [1] "numeric"

head(descRuns)
##     X Runs Mins  BF X4s X6s    SR Pos Dismissal Inns    Opposition
## 1 201  248  552 379  35   0 65.43   4   not out    2   v Bangladesh
## 2 188  241  613 436  33   0 55.27   4   not out    1    v Australia
## 3 116  217  494 344  29   0 63.08   4    caught    1 v New Zealand
## 4 295  214  547 363  22   2 58.95   4    bowled    2    v Australia
## 5 290  203  516 347  23   1 58.50   4    caught    2   v Sri Lanka
## 6 132  201  392 281  27   0 71.53   4   not out    1    v Zimbabwe
```

```
##            Ground  Start.Date
## 1          Dhaka  10 Dec 2004
## 2         Sydney   2 Jan 2004
## 3      Ahmedabad  29 Oct 1999
## 4      Bangalore   9 Oct 2010
## 5 Colombo (SSC)  26 Jul 2010
## 6         Nagpur  25 Nov 2000
```

7.8 Create a new column with 'mutate'

```
# Create a new column with Strike rate
tendulkar <- tendulkar %>% mutate(StrikeRate=(Runs/BF)*100)
```

7.9 Group rows

```
a <- group_by(tendulkar, Ground)
head(a)
## # A tibble: 6 x 14
## # Groups:   Ground [4]
##       X  Runs  Mins    BF   X4s   X6s    SR   Pos Dismissal  Inns
##   <int> <dbl> <int> <int> <int> <int> <dbl> <int>     <chr> <int>
## 1     1    15    28    24     2     0 62.50     6    bowled     2
## 2     3    59   254   172     4     0 34.30     6       lbw     1
## 3     4     8    24    16     1     0 50.00     6   run out     3
## 4     5    41   124    90     5     0 45.55     7    bowled     1
## 5     6    35    74    51     5     0 68.62     6       lbw     1
## 6     7    57   193   134     6     0 42.53     6    caught     3
## # ... with 4 more variables: Opposition <chr>, Ground <chr>,
## #   Start.Date <chr>, StrikeRate <dbl>
```

8.1 Chain all dplyr columns

The following command in a single line does the follwoing
#1. Uses the data frame tendulkar (2nd parameter)
#2. Groups the runs scored by ground
#3. Computes the mean runs in each group
#4. Arranges in descending order

```
tendulkar1 <- tendulkar %>% group_by(Ground) %>% summarise(meanRuns=
mean(Runs)) %>%  arrange(desc(meanRuns))
```

```
# Plot the result as a barplot
barplot(tendulkar1$meanRuns,names=tendulkar1$Ground,las=2,ylab="Avera
ge Runs",
```

```
col=rainbow(length(tendulkar1$meanRuns)),main="Tendulkar's
average runs in Grounds",cex.names=0.8)
```

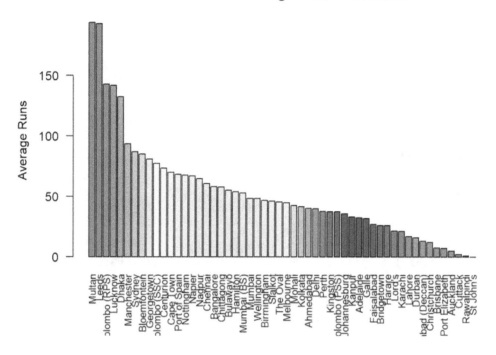

8.2 Grammar of Graphics - ggplot2

```
library(ggplot2)
## Warning: package 'ggplot2' was built under R version 3.4.2
p <- ggplot(tendulkar) + aes(x=Runs,y=BF) + geom_point()
p <- p + xlab("Runs") + ylab("Balls Faced") + ggtitle("Tendulkar -
Runs vs Balls Faced")
```

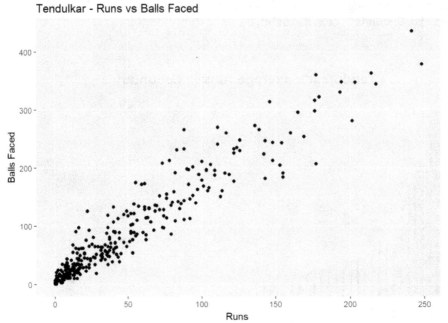

```
ggplot(tendulkar,aes(x=Runs,y=BF))+ geom_point() +  xlab("Runs") +
ylab("Balls Faced") + ggtitle("Tendulkar - Runs vs Balls Faced")
```

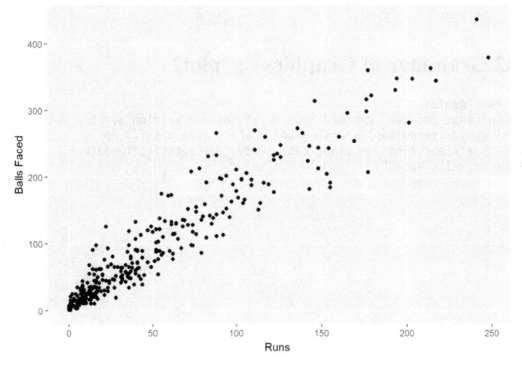

```
# Fit a smoothed regression line
ggplot(tendulkar,aes(x=Runs,y=BF))+ geom_point() +
geom_smooth(method="loess") +
  xlab("Runs") + ylab("Balls Faced") + ggtitle("Tendulkar - Runs vs
Balls Faced") +   theme(plot.title = element_text(size=16,
face="bold",hjust=0.5))+    theme(axis.text.x =
element_text(size=14,angle = 90, hjust = 1))
```

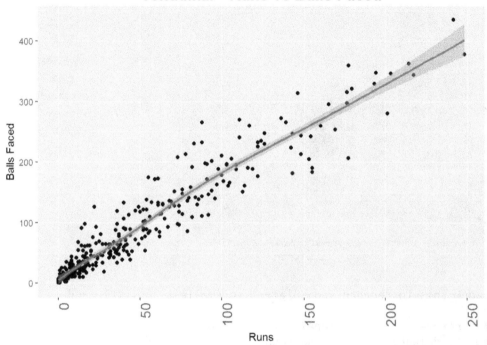

```
# Using dplyr and ggplot2
tendulkar1 <- tendulkar %>% group_by(Opposition) %>%
summarise(meanRuns= mean(Runs)) %>%    arrange(desc(meanRuns))

head(tendulkar1,10)
## # A tibble: 9 x 2
##        Opposition meanRuns
##            <chr>    <dbl>
## 1    v Bangladesh 91.11111
## 2      v Zimbabwe 65.57143
## 3     v Sri Lanka 56.68571
## 4   v West Indies 50.93750
## 5     v Australia 49.05405
## 6       v England 47.83019
## 7   v New Zealand 41.97368
## 8      v Pakistan 39.14815
## 9 v South Africa 38.68889
```

```
ggplot(tendulkar1,aes(x=Opposition,y=meanRuns,fill=Opposition)) +
    geom_bar(stat="identity")
```

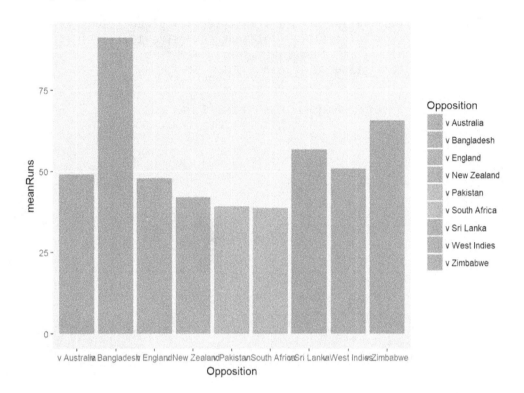

```
# Rework this to reorder from biggest to smallest and title and
labels
# Also rotate the x axis labels by 90 degrees
ggplot(tendulkar1,aes(x=reorder(Opposition,-
meanRuns),y=meanRuns,fill=Opposition)) +
    geom_bar(stat="identity") +
    ggtitle("Tendulkar's Mean Runs against opposition") +
    xlab("Opposition") + ylab("Mean Runs")+
    theme(axis.text.x = element_text(size=14,angle = 90, hjust = 1))
```

8.3 Going back to the Iris example- Plotting with base plot

```
names(iris)
## [1] "lengthOfSepal" "widthOfSepal"  "lengthOfPetal" "widthOfPetal"
## [5] "Species"
# Rename columns, if needed, to something more is easy to refer to
colnames(iris) <-
c("lengthOfSepal","widthOfSepal","lengthOfPetal","widthOfPetal","Spec
ies")
```

```
colnames(iris)
## [1] "lengthOfSepal" "widthOfSepal"  "lengthOfPetal" "widthOfPetal"
## [5] "Species"
setosa <- iris %>% filter(Species == "setosa")
#Correlation between columns
pairs(setosa)
```

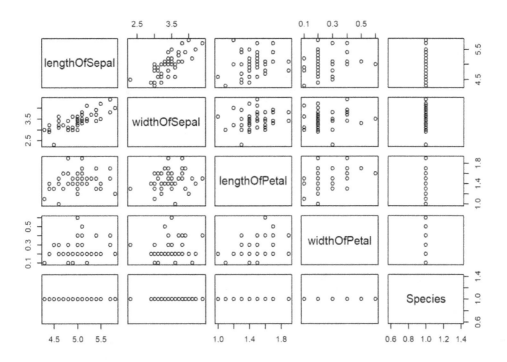

```
a <- setosa %>% select(lengthOfSepal,widthOfSepal)
plot(a$lengthOfSepal,a$widthOfSepal,xlab="Length of
Sepal",ylab="Width of Sepal",
    main="Length vs Width of Sepal of Setosa")
l <-lm(a$widthOfSepal~a$lengthOfSepal)
abline(l,lty=5,lwd=3,col="blue")
```

Length vs Width of Sepal of Setosa

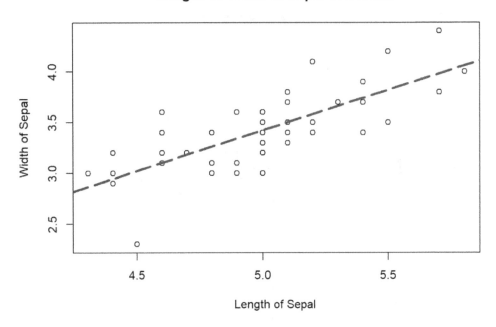

Plot IRIS with ggplot2

```
str(iris)
## 'data.frame':    150 obs. of  5 variables:
##  $ lengthOfSepal: num  5.1 4.9 4.7 4.6 5 5.4 4.6 5 4.4 4.9 ...
##  $ widthOfSepal : num  3.5 3 3.2 3.1 3.6 3.9 3.4 3.4 2.9 3.1 ...
##  $ lengthOfPetal: num  1.4 1.4 1.3 1.5 1.4 1.7 1.4 1.5 1.4 1.5 ...
##  $ widthOfPetal : num  0.2 0.2 0.2 0.2 0.2 0.4 0.3 0.2 0.2 0.1 ...
##  $ Species      : Factor w/ 3 levels "setosa","versicolor",..: 1 1
1 1 1 1 1 1 1 1 ...
# This can be with ggplot as follows for all species
ggplot(iris,aes(x=lengthOfSepal,y=widthOfSepal,colours=Species)) +
geom_point() +
  geom_smooth(method="loess") + facet_wrap(~Species) +
  xlab("Length of Sepal") + ylab("Width of Sepal")
```

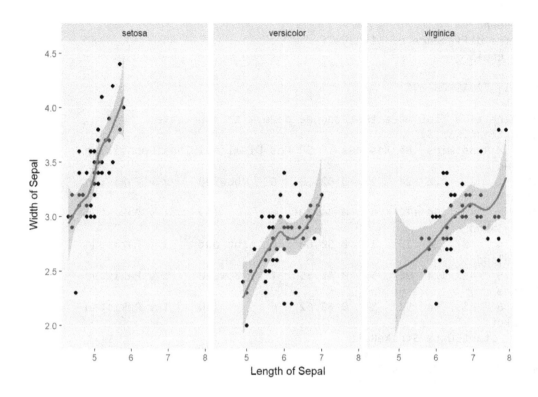

8.4 Package lubridate.

```
# This package is useful for handling date files in most
formats #dmy,ymd,dmyhhmmss,dd-mm-yy hh:mm:ss

#install.packages9"lubridate")
library(lubridate)
## Warning: package 'lubridate' was built under R version 3.4.2
##
## Attaching package: 'lubridate'
## The following object is masked from 'package:base':
##
##     date
start<-ymd("20110604")
day(start)
## [1] 4
month(start)
## [1] 6
year(start)
## [1] 2011

end=mdy("08-04-2011")
timespan <- end-start
```

```
timespan
## Time difference of 61 days
c <- end+5
c
## [1] "2011-08-09"

# There is a  lot more that can be done with lubridate
head(tendulkar,5)
##   X Runs Mins  BF X4s X6s    SR Pos Dismissal Inns Opposition
Ground
## 1 1   15   28  24   2   0 62.50   6    bowled    2 v Pakistan
Karachi
## 2 3   59  254 172   4   0 34.30   6       lbw    1 v Pakistan
Faisalabad
## 3 4    8   24  16   1   0 50.00   6   run out    3 v Pakistan
Faisalabad
## 4 5   41  124  90   5   0 45.55   7    bowled    1 v Pakistan
Lahore
## 5 6   35   74  51   5   0 68.62   6       lbw    1 v Pakistan
Sialkot
##     Start.Date StrikeRate
## 1 15 Nov 1989   62.50000
## 2 23 Nov 1989   34.30233
## 3 23 Nov 1989   50.00000
## 4  1 Dec 1989   45.55556
## 5  9 Dec 1989   68.62745

# Creating a moving average of runs for Tendulkar with ggplot
runs <- tendulkar %>% select(Runs,Start.Date)
runs$Start.Date <- dmy(runs$Start.Date)
head(runs)
##   Runs Start.Date
## 1   15 1989-11-15
## 2   59 1989-11-23
## 3    8 1989-11-23
## 4   41 1989-12-01
## 5   35 1989-12-09
## 6   57 1989-12-09
ggplot(runs,aes(x=Start.Date,y=Runs)) + geom_line(colour="darkgrey")
+  geom_smooth(method="loess") + ggtitle("Tendulkar's moving average
of runs") +    theme(plot.title = element_text(size=16,
face="bold",hjust=0.5))
```

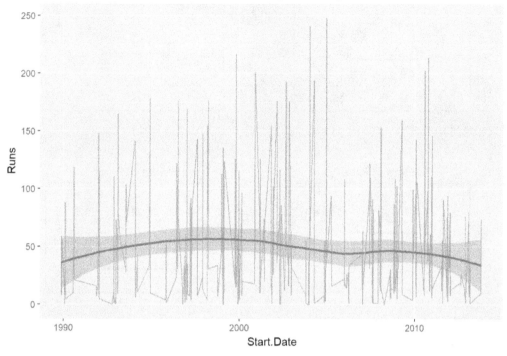

Tendulkar's moving average of runs

8.5 Other useful compact statements with dplyr and ggplot2

Plot Tendulkar runs by ground

Length of Sepal

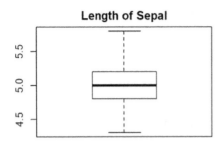

Width of Sepal

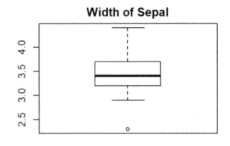

Length of Petal

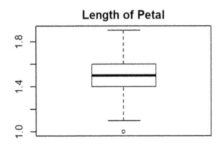

Width of Petal

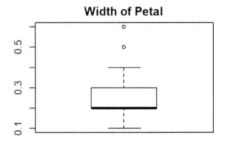

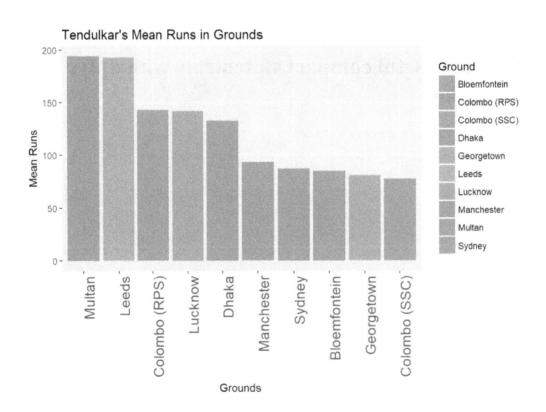

8.6 Plotting Error bar

Plot Tendulkar runs against opposition with error bar

```
# The x axis labels are rotated by 90 degrees
tendulkar1 <- tendulkar %>% group_by(Opposition) %>%
  summarise(meanRuns= mean(Runs),sdRuns=sd(Runs)) %>%
  arrange(desc(meanRuns))
top10 <- head(tendulkar1,10)
top10
## # A tibble: 9 x 3
##         Opposition meanRuns    sdRuns
##              <chr>    <dbl>     <dbl>
## 1    v Bangladesh 91.11111 75.98428
## 2      v Zimbabwe 65.57143 60.52935
## 3     v Sri Lanka 56.68571 53.52062
## 4    v West Indies 50.93750 48.11273
## 5      v Australia 49.05405 53.52656
## 6        v England 47.83019 47.51710
## 7    v New Zealand 41.97368 46.83986
## 8       v Pakistan 39.14815 45.21207
## 9 v South Africa 38.68889 45.55008
ggplot(top10,aes(x=reorder(Opposition,- meanRuns), y= meanRuns, fill=
Opposition)) +   geom_bar(stat="identity") +   geom_errorbar
(width=.1, aes(ymin=meanRuns-sdRuns,
ymax=meanRuns+sdRuns)) +   ggtitle("Tendulkar's Mean Runs against
opposition") +   xlab("Opposition") + ylab("Mean Runs") +
theme(axis.text.x = element_text(size=14,angle = 90, hjust = 1))
```

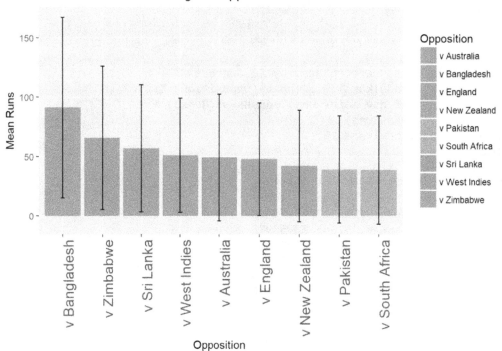

Tendulkar's Mean Runs against opposition

2.   Essential Python for Datascience

Introduction

To get started in Python, I would suggest that you install Anaconda (https://www.anaconda.com/download/). Anaconda installs most of the necessary packages for you to get started off. You can use either Jupyter notebook or the Spyder IDE for Python development

This chapter focuses on some of the most Essential Python constructs, that you will tend to use very often while performing data analysis. While Python for Datascience has several complex statements, this chapter distils some of the most commonly used statements. If you become adept in these, you can slowly build your Python vocabulary as you become more and more conversant with the language.

Download the associated code in this chapter as an R Markdown file from Github at https://github.com/tvganesh/PracticalMachineLearningWithRandPython

1.1 Basic directory operations

```
#To perform file or directory operation import the 'os' module
import os
# Change to a specific directory
os.chdir("C:\\software\\RandPythonBook\\EssentialR\\EssentialR-
master")

# Get current working directory
dir=os.getcwd()
print(dir)
## C:\software\RandPythonBook\EssentialR\EssentialR-master

import os
# List all files in a directory
files=os.listdir("C:\\software\\RandPythonBook\\EssentialR\\Essential
R-master")
print(files)
## ['EssentialR-1.html', 'EssentialR-1.Rmd', 'EssentialR-1_cache',
'EssentialR-1_files', 'EssentialR.pptx', 'essentialR.R', 'mytest2.R',
'README.md', 'RMarkdown.Rmd', 'tendulkar.csv', 'testdir',
'testRpackage', 'testShinyApp']
```

1.2. Tuples, lists and dictionaries

The 3 basic data types in Python are

- Tuple
- List
- Dictionary

Tuples: Tuples are immutable python objects which are enclosed within parenthesis. Immutability implies that objects cannot be added or removed to tuples. Hence, we cannot add or remove elements from tuples. However the entire tuple can be removed using the del() commands

List: Lists are a sequence of dissimilar objects enclosed within square brackets. Objects can be added to lists using append () and deleted using remove()

Dictionary: Dictionaries are name(key)-value pair enclosed within curly braces. The name- value pairs are separated using a ':'. The keys must be unique in the dictionary

The length of tuples, lists and dictionaries can be obtained with the len() # Tuples are enclosed in parentheses

```
mytuple=(1,3,7,6,"test")
print(mytuple)

# Lists are enclosed in square bracket
mylist = [1, 2, 7, 4, 12]

#Dictionary - These are like name-value pairs
mydict={'Name':'Ganesh','Age':54,'Occupation':'Engineer'}
print(mydict)
print(mydict['Age'])

# No of elements in tuples, lists and dictionaries can be got with
len()
print("Length of tuple=",len(mytuple))
print("Length of list =", len(mylist))
print("Length of dictionary =",len(mydict))
## (1, 3, 7, 6, 'test')
## {'Age': 54, 'Name': 'Ganesh', 'Occupation': 'Engineer'}
## 54
## ('Length of tuple=', 5)
## ('Length of list =', 5)
## ('Length of dictionary =', 3)
```

1.3. Accessing elements in tuples, lists and dictionaries

To access elements in tuples, lists and dictionaries use an index. Indices in tuples, lists and dictionaries start at 0.

1.3.1 Accessing tuples

```
# Accessing tuples
mytuple=(1,3,7,6,"test")
mytuple[0]

#Slices 2nd upto 4th
print(mytuple[2:4])
## (7, 6)
```

1.3.2 Accessing lists

```
# Accessing Lists
mylist = [1, 2, 7, 4, 12]
# Add an object to a list
mylist.append(20)
print(mylist)

# Print 3rd element. Index starts from 0
print(mylist[2])

# Print a slice from the 4th to 6th
print(mylist[3:6])

#Print the 2nd last object
print(mylist[-2])
print(mylist[-5:-2])
## [1, 2, 7, 4, 12, 20]
## 7
## [4, 12, 20]
## 12
## [2, 7, 4]
```

1.3.3 Accessing dictionaries

```
# Accessing Dictionaries
mydict={'Name':'Ganesh','Age':54,'Occupation':'Engineer','Education':
'Masters'}
#Print all objects of mydict
```

```
print(mydict.items())

# Print the keys
print(mydict.keys())

#Print the value with key 'Age'
print(mydict['Age'])

## [('Age', 54), ('Education', 'Masters'), ('Name', 'Ganesh'),
('Occupation', 'Engineer')]
## ['Age', 'Education', 'Name', 'Occupation']
## 54
```

1.4. Type of a variable

To check a variable type use type()

```
#Create a real valued variable
a=5.4

# Print the type of 'a'
print(type(a))

# Create a string variable
b='A string'

# Print the type of b
print(type(b))

# Create a tuple
mytuple=(1,3,7,6,"test")

# Print the type of mytuple
print(type(mytuple))

#Create list
mylist = [1, 2, 7, 4, 12]

# Print the type of list
print(type(mylist))

#Create mydict
mydict={'Name':'Ganesh','Age':54,'Occupation':'Engineer'}

# Print type
print(type(mydict))

## <type 'float'>
```

```
## <type 'str'>
## <type 'tuple'>
## <type 'list'>
## <type 'dict'>
```

1.5. Accessing help

To get help on any python command use help()

```
#Help
import pandas as pd
help(len)

#help(dict)
## Help on built-in function len in module __builtin__:
##
## len(...)
##      len(object) -> integer
##
##      Return the number of items of a sequence or collection.
```

1.6. Numpy

NumPy is one of the most fundamental package for scientific computing with Python. Numpy includes the support for handling large, multi-dimensional arrays and matrices, along with a large collection of high-level mathematical functions to operate on these arrays.

```
import numpy as np
#Create a 1d numpy array
data1 = [6, 7.5, 8, 0, 1]
arr1 = np.array(data1)
print(arr1)
## [ 6.   7.5 8.   0.   1.]
```

1.6.1 1D array

```
#Create numpy array in a single line
import numpy as np
arr1= np.array([6, 7.5, 8, 0, 1])

#Print the array
print(arr1)
## [ 6.   7.5 8.   0.   1. ]
```

1.6.2 2D array

```
#Create a 2d numpy array
import numpy as np
data2 = [[1, 2, 3, 4], [5, 6, 7, 8]]
arr2 = np.array(data2)

# Print the 2d array
print(arr2)
## [[1 2 3 4]
##  [5 6 7 8]]
```

1.6.3 Dimension and shape of an aray

```
import numpy as np
data2 = [[1, 2, 3, 4], [5, 6, 7, 8]]
arr2 = np.array(data2)

# Get the dimension of the array
print(arr2.ndim)

#Display the shape of the array
print(arr2.shape)
## 2
## (2L, 4L)
```

1.6.4 Create a matrix of zeros

```
import numpy as np

#Create matrix of 3 x6 matrix of zeros
print(np.zeros((3, 6)))
## [[ 0.  0.  0.  0.  0.  0.]
##  [ 0.  0.  0.  0.  0.  0.]
##  [ 0.  0.  0.  0.  0.  0.]]
```

1.6.5 Create a matrix of ones

```
import numpy as np
#Create matrix of 4 x 2 matrix of ones
print(np.ones((4,2)))
## [[ 1.  1.]
##  [ 1.  1.]
##  [ 1.  1.]
##  [ 1.  1.]]
```

1.6.6 Some operations on numpy arrays

```python
import numpy as np
G=np.random.randn(2,3)
print(G)

# Print the mean of the array
print(G.mean())

#Print the variance
print(G.var())
## [[ 1.14456629  0.96770677  0.16422922]
##  [-0.27179377 -0.55363259  2.51734607]]
## 0.661403664579
## 1.06102381793
```

1.6.7 More operations on numpy arrays

```python
import numpy as np
#Operations between numpy arrays
arr = np.array([[1., 2., 3.], [4., 5., 6.]])
print(arr)

# Add  arrays
print(arr+arr)

# Subtract an array from another
print(arr - arr)

# Perform element wise multiplication of arrays
print(arr * arr)
## [[ 1.   2.   3.]
##  [ 4.   5.   6.]]
## [[ 2.   4.   6.]
##  [ 8.  10.  12.]]
## [[ 0.   0.   0.]
##  [ 0.   0.   0.]]
## [[ 1.   4.   9.]
##  [ 16.  25.  36.]]
```

1.6.8 Slicing numpy arrays

```python
import numpy as np
#Create an array from 0 to 10 using arange
arr = np.arange(10)
print(arr)
```

```
# Display the 6th element. Index starts at 0
print(arr[5])

#Display from 6th up to 8th
print(arr[5:8])
## [0 1 2 3 4 5 6 7 8 9]
## 5
## [5 6 7]
```

1.6.9 Math operations on numpy arrays

```
import numpy as np
#Create an array from 0 to 10 using arange
arr = np.arange(10)
arr[5:8] = 12
print(arr)

# You can apply operations over the entire array in a single command
print(np.sqrt(arr))
print(np.sin(arr))
## [ 0  1  2  3  4 12 12 12  8  9]
## [ 0.          1.          1.41421356  1.73205081  2.
3.46410162
##   3.46410162  3.46410162  2.82842712  3.          ]
## [ 0.          0.84147098  0.90929743  0.14112001 -0.7568025  -
0.53657292
##  -0.53657292 -0.53657292  0.98935825  0.41211849]
```

1.6.10 Creating sequences with numpy arrays

```
import numpy as np
# Generate sequences from start to stop and increase by step
seq1=np.arange(2,12,3)
print(seq1)

# Generate a sequence between a start and stop value with 5 equally
spaced values
seq2=np.linspace(start=2,stop=12,num=5)
print(seq2)
## [ 2  5  8 11]
## [ 2.   4.5  7.   9.5 12. ]
```

1.6.11 Creating random arrays

```
import numpy as np
# This is very useful when trying to simulate certain conditions
```

```
#Generating random arrays
# Generate random numbers from the uniform distribution
print(np.random.rand(2,4))

# Generate random numbers between 0 & 1 from the normal distribution
print(np.random.randn(2,4))

#Generate random integers
print(np.random.randint(3,5,size=6).reshape(2,3))
## [[ 0.29324042  0.8596953   0.71186787  0.32192382]
##  [ 0.51826054  0.55103282  0.20060528  0.47663985]]
## [[-0.41485532 -1.25092742 -1.00347057 -0.6682005 ]
##  [-1.50118065 -0.8756469  -0.58597376 -1.13507102]]
## [[4 3 4]
##  [3 4 4]]

import numpy as np
# Reshape as a 5 x 4 matrix
arr2d = np.arange(20)
print(arr2d)
arr2d = np.arange(20).reshape(5,4)
print(arr2d)

#Reshape same array as a 2 x 10 matrix
arr2d=arr2d.reshape(2,10)
print(arr2d.shape)
print(arr2d)
## [ 0  1  2  3  4  5  6  7  8  9 10 11 12 13 14 15 16 17 18 19]
## [[ 0  1  2  3]
##  [ 4  5  6  7]
##  [ 8  9 10 11]
##  [12 13 14 15]
##  [16 17 18 19]]
## (2L, 10L)
## [[ 0  1  2  3  4  5  6  7  8  9]
##  [10 11 12 13 14 15 16 17 18 19]]
```

1.6.12 Indexing and slicing arays

```
import numpy as np
arr2d = np.arange(20)
print(arr2d)
arr2d = np.arange(20).reshape(5,4)
print(arr2d)

# Print the element from 2nd row and 3rd column
print(arr2d[1,2])

# Slicing arr[startRow:endRow,startColumn:endColumn]
```

```
#Slice an array
print(arr2d[2:4,1:4])

#Slice from the 0th to 3 row and 2 column
print(arr2d[:3,2])

# Slice all rows but only columns 2 & 3
# Note if the row or column is not included it implies all rows or
all columns
print(arr2d[:,1:3])

# Display all rows and all columns
print(arr2d[:,:])
## [ 0  1  2  3  4  5  6  7  8  9 10 11 12 13 14 15 16 17 18 19]
## [[ 0  1  2  3]
##  [ 4  5  6  7]
##  [ 8  9 10 11]
##  [12 13 14 15]
##  [16 17 18 19]]
## 6
## [[ 9 10 11]
##  [13 14 15]]
## [ 2  6 10]
## [[ 1  2]
##  [ 5  6]
##  [ 9 10]
##  [13 14]
##  [17 18]]
## [[ 0  1  2  3]
##  [ 4  5  6  7]
##  [ 8  9 10 11]
##  [12 13 14 15]
##  [16 17 18 19]]
```

1.6.13 Computing sum, mean of arrays

```
import numpy as np
arr = np.random.randn(4, 8) # normally-distributed data

#Print the mean of the aray
print(arr.mean())
print(np.mean(arr))

# Print sum
print(arr.sum())
## -0.176506745027
## -0.176506745027
## -5.64821584087
```

68

1.7 Pandas

Pandas is a Python package which can handle labeled data, csv or tables extremely well.

1.7.1. Pandas Series

```
# Import the pandas module
import pandas as pd
obj = pd.Series([4, 7, -5, 3])
print(obj)

# Create a series and also set the indices
obj2 = pd.Series([4, 7, -5, 3], index=['d', 'b', 'a', 'c'])
print(obj2)

# Print the indices
print(obj2.index)

# Print the values
print(obj2.values)
print(obj2)
## 0    4
## 1    7
## 2   -5
## 3    3
## dtype: int64
## d    4
## b    7
## a   -5
## c    3
## dtype: int64
## Index([u'd', u'b', u'a', u'c'], dtype='object')
## [ 4  7 -5  3]
## d    4
## b    7
## a   -5
## c    3
## dtype: int64
```

1.7.2 Pandas dataframes

```
import numpy as np
import pandas as pd

# Create 3 arrays with state, year and population
data = {'state': ['Ohio', 'Ohio', 'Ohio', 'Nevada', 'Nevada'],
        'year': [2000, 2001, 2002, 2001, 2002],
```

```python
                'pop': [1.5, 1.7, 3.6, 2.4, 2.9]}
print(data)

# Create a dataframe
frame = pd.DataFrame(data)

# The dataframe has 3 columns state, year and pop
print(frame)

#Create frame2
frame2 = pd.DataFrame(data, columns=['year', 'state', 'pop', 'debt'],
                      index=['one', 'two', 'three', 'four', 'five'])
print(frame2)
## {'state': ['Ohio', 'Ohio', 'Ohio', 'Nevada', 'Nevada'], 'pop':
[1.5, 1.7, 3.6, 2.4, 2.9], 'year': [2000, 2001, 2002, 2001, 2002]}
##     pop   state  year
## 0   1.5    Ohio  2000
## 1   1.7    Ohio  2001
## 2   3.6    Ohio  2002
## 3   2.4  Nevada  2001
## 4   2.9  Nevada  2002
##        year   state  pop debt
## one    2000    Ohio  1.5  NaN
## two    2001    Ohio  1.7  NaN
## three  2002    Ohio  3.6  NaN
## four   2001  Nevada  2.4  NaN
## five   2002  Nevada  2.9  NaN
```

1.7.3 Pandas dataframes from arrays

```python
import numpy as np
import pandas as pd
# Create a dataframe from an array
arr2d = np.arange(20)

# Reshape array
arr = np.arange(20).reshape(4,5)
print(arr)

# Create dataframe
df=pd.DataFrame(arr)
print(df)
print(df.shape)
## [[ 0  1  2  3  4]
##  [ 5  6  7  8  9]
##  [10 11 12 13 14]
##  [15 16 17 18 19]]
##     0   1   2   3   4
## 0   0   1   2   3   4
```

```
## 1    5    6    7    8    9
## 2   10   11   12   13   14
## 3   15   16   17   18   19
## (4, 5)
```

1.7.4 Important commands on Pandas dataframes

There are 3 important commands which are used very often on dataframes

- shape() - Get the shape of the dataframe
- info() - Get the details of the dataframe
- columns - Get the names of the columns

```
import pandas as pd
data = {'state': ['Ohio', 'Ohio', 'Ohio', 'Nevada', 'Nevada'],
        'year': [2000, 2001, 2002, 2001, 2002],
        'pop': [1.5, 1.7, 3.6, 2.4, 2.9]}
frame2 = pd.DataFrame(data, columns=['year', 'state', 'pop', 'debt'],
                   index=['one', 'two', 'three', 'four', 'five'])
print(frame2)

# Important commands on pandas
print(frame2.shape)
print(frame2.info())
print(frame2.columns)
##          year    state   pop debt
## one      2000     Ohio   1.5  NaN
## two      2001     Ohio   1.7  NaN
## three    2002     Ohio   3.6  NaN
## four     2001   Nevada   2.4  NaN
## five     2002   Nevada   2.9  NaN
## (5, 4)
## <class 'pandas.core.frame.DataFrame'>
## Index: 5 entries, one to five
## Data columns (total 4 columns):
## year      5 non-null int64
## state     5 non-null object
## pop       5 non-null float64
## debt      0 non-null object
## dtypes: float64(1), int64(1), object(2)
## memory usage: 200.0+ bytes
## None
## Index([u'year', u'state', u'pop', u'debt'], dtype='object')
```

1.7.5 Indexing and slicing dataframes

```
import pandas as pd
```

```
data = {'state': ['Ohio', 'Ohio', 'Ohio', 'Nevada', 'Nevada'],
        'year': [2000, 2001, 2002, 2001, 2002],
        'pop': [1.5, 1.7, 3.6, 2.4, 2.9]}
print(data)
frame = pd.DataFrame(data)

# The iloc method allows you to use indices much like an array
# Display all rows and the 1st column
print(frame)
print(frame.iloc[1:3,1:3])
print(frame.shape)

# Display rows 2nd to 4th and column 3
print(frame.iloc[1:4,2:3])

#Display row with index=1
print(frame.loc[1:4])
## {'state': ['Ohio', 'Ohio', 'Ohio', 'Nevada', 'Nevada'], 'pop':
[1.5, 1.7, 3.6, 2.4, 2.9], 'year': [2000, 2001, 2002, 2001, 2002]}
##     pop   state  year
## 0   1.5    Ohio  2000
## 1   1.7    Ohio  2001
## 2   3.6    Ohio  2002
## 3   2.4  Nevada  2001
## 4   2.9  Nevada  2002
##    state  year
## 1   Ohio  2001
## 2   Ohio  2002
## (5, 3)
##    year
## 1  2001
## 2  2002
## 3  2001
##     pop   state  year
## 1   1.7    Ohio  2001
## 2   3.6    Ohio  2002
## 3   2.4  Nevada  2001
## 4   2.9  Nevada  2002
```

1.7.6 Read an CSV file

```
# Read csv
import os
import pandas as pd
os.chdir("C:\software\RandPythonBook\python-final")
# Read an XL file
tendulkar=pd.read_csv('tendulkar.csv',encoding = "ISO-8859-1")

# Display the top 5 rows
```

72

```
print(tendulkar.head())
##     Unnamed: 0 Runs Mins   BF 4s 6s    SR Pos Dismissal Inns
Opposition   \
## 0            1   15   28   24  2  0 62.50   6    bowled    2  v
Pakistan
## 1            2  DNB    -    -  -  -     -   -         -    4  v
Pakistan
## 2            3   59  254  172  4  0 34.30   6       lbw    1  v
Pakistan
## 3            4    8   24   16  1  0 50.00   6   run out    3  v
Pakistan
## 4            5   41  124   90  5  0 45.55   7    bowled    1  v
Pakistan
##
##          Ground    Start Date
## 0       Karachi   15 Nov 1989
## 1       Karachi   15 Nov 1989
## 2    Faisalabad   23 Nov 1989
## 3    Faisalabad   23 Nov 1989
## 4        Lahore    1 Dec 1989
```

1.7.7 Read an Excel file

```
# Read an XL
import pandas as pd
car=pd.read_excel('gascar.xls',sheetname='cardata')
print(car.head())
##    CTY    YR  LN_Gas_Car  LN_Y_Pop  LN_Pmg_Pgdp  LN_Car_Pop
## 0    1  1960    4.173244 -6.474277    -0.334548   -9.766840
## 1    1  1961    4.100989 -6.426006    -0.351328   -9.608622
## 2    1  1962    4.073177 -6.407308    -0.379518   -9.457257
## 3    1  1963    4.059509 -6.370679    -0.414251   -9.343155
## 4    1  1964    4.037689 -6.322247    -0.445335   -9.237739
```

1.7.8 Common operations on dataframes

Included below are some of the most common operations on dataframes

- head()
- tail()
- shape()
- columns
- info()

```
import os
import pandas as pd
tendulkar=pd.read_csv('tendulkar.csv',encoding = "ISO-8859-1")
```

```
# Display the shape of the dataframe - no of rows and no of columns
print(tendulkar.shape)

#Display the column names
print(tendulkar.columns)

# Describe the data frame. The columns and the data types of the
columns
print(tendulkar.info())
## (347, 13)
## Index([u'Unnamed: 0',        u'Runs',        u'Mins',        u'BF',
##                u'4s',        u'6s',        u'SR',        u'Pos',
##          u'Dismissal',        u'Inns', u'Opposition',        u'Ground',
##          u'Start Date'],
##        dtype='object')
## <class 'pandas.core.frame.DataFrame'>
## RangeIndex: 347 entries, 0 to 346
## Data columns (total 13 columns):
## Unnamed: 0     347 non-null int64
## Runs           347 non-null object
## Mins           347 non-null object
## BF             347 non-null object
## 4s             347 non-null object
## 6s             347 non-null object
## SR             347 non-null object
## Pos            347 non-null object
## Dismissal      347 non-null object
## Inns           347 non-null object
## Opposition     347 non-null object
## Ground         347 non-null object
## Start Date     347 non-null object
## dtypes: int64(1), object(12)
## memory usage: 35.3+ KB
## None
```

1.7.9 Common operations on dataframes

```
import pandas as pd
tendulkar=pd.read_csv('tendulkar.csv',encoding = "ISO-8859-1")

#Rename columns as you find appropriate
tendulkar.columns=['No', 'Runs', 'Mins', 'BF', '4s', '6s', 'SR',
'Pos',  'Dismissal', 'Inns', 'Opposition', 'Ground', 'Start Date']

# Print top 5 roes
print(tendulkar.head(5))
```

```
##      No Runs Mins    BF 4s 6s      SR Pos Dismissal Inns   Opposition
Ground   \
## 0    1   15   28    24  2  0  62.50   6    bowled    2  v Pakistan
Karachi
## 1    2  DNB    -     -  -  -      -   -           -    4  v Pakistan
Karachi
## 2    3   59  254   172  4  0  34.30   6       lbw    1  v Pakistan
Faisalabad
## 3    4    8   24    16  1  0  50.00   6   run out    3  v Pakistan
Faisalabad
## 4    5   41  124    90  5  0  45.55   7    bowled    1  v Pakistan
Lahore
##
##     Start Date
## 0  15 Nov 1989
## 1  15 Nov 1989
## 2  23 Nov 1989
## 3  23 Nov 1989
## 4   1 Dec 1989
```

1.8 Cleaning dataframes

```
import pandas as pd
tendulkar=pd.read_csv('tendulkar.csv',encoding = "ISO-8859-1")

# Cleanup of Runs column
# Remove rows which have DNB
tendulkar.Runs
print(tendulkar.shape)

# Check all rows in Runs which do not have 'DNB'
a=tendulkar.Runs !="DNB"
# Remove rows which have 'DNB'
tendulkar=tendulkar[a]
print(tendulkar.shape)

# Remove rows which have TDNB
b=tendulkar.Runs !="TDNB"
tendulkar=tendulkar[b]
print(tendulkar.shape)

# Remove the '-' character
c= tendulkar.BF != "-"
tendulkar=tendulkar[c]

# Remove the '*' character
tendulkar.Runs= tendulkar.Runs.str.replace(r"[*]","")
print(tendulkar.shape)
```

```
# Write to csv file
tendulkar.to_csv("tendulkar1.csv")
## (347, 13)
## (330, 13)
## (329, 13)
## (328, 13)
```

1.9 Filtering based on row values

```
import pandas as pd
tendulkar=pd.read_csv('tendulkar1.csv',encoding = "ISO-8859-1")
print(tendulkar.shape)

# Select specific columns from tendulkar dataframe
df1=tendulkar[['Runs','BF','Ground']]
print(df1.head())

# Select rwos that meet some condition
a=tendulkar['Ground']=='Karachi'
df2=tendulkar[a]
print(df2.head())

# Filter rows when Groud is Karachi
df2=tendulkar[tendulkar['Ground']=='Karachi']
print(df2.head())

# This line will give an error
b = tendulkar['Runs'] >50
tendulkar3 = tendulkar[b]
print(tendulkar3.head())
## (328, 14)
##     Runs   BF       Ground
## 0     15   24      Karachi
## 1     59  172    Faisalabad
## 2      8   16    Faisalabad
## 3     41   90        Lahore
## 4     35   51       Sialkot
##      Unnamed: 0  Unnamed: 0.1  Runs  Mins  BF  4s  6s     SR  Pos
Dismissal  \
## 0             0             1    15    28  24   2   0  62.50    6
bowled
## 203         216           217    23    49  29   5   0  79.31    4
bowled
## 204         217           218    26    74  47   5   0  55.31    4
bowled
##
##       Inns  Opposition   Ground   Start Date
## 0        2  v Pakistan  Karachi  15 Nov 1989
## 203      2  v Pakistan  Karachi  29 Jan 2006
```

76

```
## 204       4  v Pakistan  Karachi   29 Jan 2006
##        Unnamed: 0  Unnamed: 0.1   Runs   Mins   BF   4s   6s      SR  Pos
Dismissal   \
## 0                0             1     15     28   24    2    0   62.50    6
bowled
## 203            216           217     23     49   29    5    0   79.31    4
bowled
## 204            217           218     26     74   47    5    0   55.31    4
bowled
##
##         Inns  Opposition   Ground   Start Date
## 0          2  v Pakistan  Karachi   15 Nov 1989
## 203        2  v Pakistan  Karachi   29 Jan 2006
## 204        4  v Pakistan  Karachi   29 Jan 2006
##        Unnamed: 0  Unnamed: 0.1   Runs   Mins    BF   4s   6s      SR  Pos
Dismissal   \
## 1                2             3     59    254   172    4    0   34.30    6
lbw
## 5                6             7     57    193   134    6    0   42.53    6
caught
## 8                9            10     88    324   266    5    0   33.08    6
caught
## 12              14            15     68    216   136    8    0   50.00    6
caught
## 13              15            16    119    225   189   17    0   62.96    6
not out
##
##        Inns    Opposition      Ground    Start Date
## 1         1     v Pakistan   Faisalabad  23 Nov 1989
## 5         3     v Pakistan      Sialkot   9 Dec 1989
## 8         1   v New Zealand      Napier   9 Feb 1990
## 12        2      v England   Manchester   9 Aug 1990
## 13        4      v England   Manchester   9 Aug 1990
import pandas as pd
tendulkar=pd.read_csv('tendulkar1.csv',encoding = "ISO-8859-1")

# # 18. Filtering rows  and selecting columns
# Check the type of 'Runs' column (element 0)
print(type(tendulkar['Runs'][0]))
#Convert to numeric. Use tab to see options
tendulkar['Runs']=pd.to_numeric(tendulkar['Runs'])
tendulkar['BF']=pd.to_numeric(tendulkar['BF'])

# Check the type of 'Runs' column
print(type(tendulkar['Runs'][0]))
b=tendulkar['Runs']>50

# Select only rows where Tendulkar scored more than 50
df3=tendulkar[tendulkar['Runs']>50]
```

```
df3.head()
print(tendulkar.head(3))
## <type 'numpy.int64'>
## <type 'numpy.int64'>
##    Unnamed: 0  Unnamed: 0.1  Runs  Mins   BF  4s  6s     SR  Pos
Dismissal \
## 0           0             1    15    28   24   2   0  62.50    6
bowled
## 1           2             3    59   254  172   4   0  34.30    6
lbw
## 2           3             4     8    24   16   1   0  50.00    6
run out
##
##    Inns  Opposition      Ground   Start Date
## 0     2  v Pakistan     Karachi  15 Nov 1989
## 1     1  v Pakistan  Faisalabad  23 Nov 1989
## 2     3  v Pakistan  Faisalabad  23 Nov 1989
```

2.1 Operating on dates in Pandas

```
import pandas as pd
tendulkar=pd.read_csv('tendulkar1.csv',encoding = "ISO-8859-1")

# Operations on dates
tendulkar['Start Date']=pd.to_datetime(tendulkar['Start Date'])
tendulkar.head()
a=tendulkar['Start Date'] > '01-01-2005'
tendulkar5K=tendulkar[tendulkar['Start Date'] > '01-01-2005']
print(tendulkar5K.head())

# iloc can be used for slicing. Similar to handling numpy arrays
print(tendulkar.iloc[1:4,2:6])
# .loc is used to select rows by index
print(tendulkar.loc[[2,5]])
##       Unnamed: 0  Unnamed: 0.1  Runs  Mins   BF  4s  6s     SR  Pos
Dismissal \
## 192         202           203    94   301  202  11   0  46.53    4
caught
## 193         204           205    52   147  102   9   0  50.98    4
caught
## 194         205           206    52   117   91   9   0  57.14    4
caught
## 195         206           207    41    78   71   7   0  57.74    4
caught
## 196         207           208    16   140   98   2   0  16.32    4
caught
##
##      Inns  Opposition  Ground Start Date
## 192     2  v Pakistan  Mohali 2005-03-08
```

```
## 193      1  v Pakistan      Kolkata 2005-03-16
## 194      3  v Pakistan      Kolkata 2005-03-16
## 195      2  v Pakistan   Bangalore 2005-03-24
## 196      4  v Pakistan   Bangalore 2005-03-24
##    Runs  Mins   BF  4s
## 1    59   254  172   4
## 2     8    24   16   1
## 3    41   124   90   5
##    Unnamed: 0  Unnamed: 0.1  Runs  Mins   BF  4s  6s      SR  Pos
Dismissal  \
## 2            3               4     8    24   16   1   0   50.00    6
run out
## 5            6               7    57   193  134   6   0   42.53    6
caught
##
##    Inns  Opposition        Ground Start Date
## 2     3  v Pakistan   Faisalabad 1989-11-23
## 5     3  v Pakistan      Sialkot 1989-12-09
```

2.2 Remove NA values in a dataframe

```
import pandas as pd
tendulkar=pd.read_csv('tendulkar1.csv',encoding = "ISO-8859-1")

#Further clean up
tendulkar2=tendulkar.dropna()

# Print shape
print(tendulkar2.shape)
## (328, 14)
```

2.3 Compute the mean of a column

```
import pandas as pd
tendulkar=pd.read_csv('tendulkar1.csv',encoding = "ISO-8859-1")

#Compute mean of column
print(tendulkar['Runs'].mean())
## 48.506097561
```

2.4 Group rows by condition, compute mean and then sort

```
import pandas as pd
tendulkar=pd.read_csv('tendulkar1.csv',encoding = "ISO-8859-1")

# Group by ground and compute mean
a=tendulkar[['Runs','BF','Ground']].groupby('Ground').mean()
```

```python
# Sort by descending Runs
b=a.sort_values('Runs',ascending=False)

# Print top 3 rows
print(b.head(3))
tendulkar[['Runs','BF','Ground']].groupby('Ground').mean().sort_value
s('Runs',ascending=False)

print(tendulkar.head(3))
##                     Runs      BF
## Ground
## Multan           194.0   348.0
## Leeds            193.0   330.0
## Colombo (RPS)    143.0   247.0
##     Unnamed: 0  Unnamed: 0.1  Runs  Mins   BF  4s  6s     SR  Pos
Dismissal  \
## 0             0             1    15    28   24   2   0  62.50    6
bowled
## 1             2             3    59   254  172   4   0  34.30    6
lbw
## 2             3             4     8    24   16   1   0  50.00    6
run out
##
##     Inns  Opposition       Ground   Start Date
## 0      2  v Pakistan       Karachi  15 Nov 1989
## 1      1  v Pakistan    Faisalabad  23 Nov 1989
## 2      3  v Pakistan    Faisalabad  23 Nov 1989
```

2.5 Group rows by condition, compute mean and then sort

```python
import pandas as pd
tendulkar=pd.read_csv('tendulkar1.csv',encoding = "ISO-8859-1")

# Group rows by some criteria and perform an operation Groupby
a=tendulkar[['Runs','BF','Ground']].groupby('Ground').mean()

# Sort
b=a.sort_values('Runs',ascending=False)
print(b.head(4))

# Group by Ground, compute mean and sort descending
c=tendulkar[['Runs','BF','Ground']].groupby('Ground').mean().sort_val
ues('Runs',ascending=False)
print(c.head(3))

# Group by Opposition, compute mean and sort descending
d=tendulkar[['Runs','BF','Opposition']].groupby('Opposition').mean().
sort_values('Runs',ascending=False)
```

```
print(d.head(3))
# You can add all the commands in a single line
f=tendulkar[['Runs','BF','Ground']].groupby('Ground').mean().sort_val
ues('Runs',ascending=False)
print(f.head(3))

#Compute mean and average of Runs and Balls faced
g=tendulkar[['Runs','BF','Ground']].groupby('Ground').agg(['sum','mea
n','count'])
print(g.head(3))
##                   Runs     BF
## Ground
## Multan           194.0   348.0
## Leeds            193.0   330.0
## Colombo (RPS)    143.0   247.0
## Lucknow          142.0   224.0
##                   Runs     BF
## Ground
## Multan           194.0   348.0
## Leeds            193.0   330.0
## Colombo (RPS)    143.0   247.0
##                      Runs           BF
## Opposition
## v Bangladesh    91.111111    143.777778
## v Zimbabwe      65.571429    114.071429
## v Sri Lanka     56.685714    104.971429
##                   Runs     BF
## Ground
## Multan           194.0   348.0
## Leeds            193.0   330.0
## Colombo (RPS)    143.0   247.0
##              Runs                  BF
##              sum    mean count    sum    mean count
## Ground
## Adelaide     326   32.600    10    584  58.4000    10
## Ahmedabad    642   40.125    16   1281  80.0625    16
## Auckland       5    5.000     1     13  13.0000     1
```

2.6 Lambda operations

Lambda operations allow you to create small anonymous function which compute
something. We can then apply these 'lambda' function on a series or columns of a
dataframes

```
# Python - Operations on list
a =[5,2,3,1,7]
b =[1,5,4,6,8]
```

```
# Create a lambda function to add 2 numbers
add=lambda x,y:x+y

# Add all elements of lists a and b
print(list(map(add,a,b)))
#or
#Element wise addition with map & lambda
print(list(map(lambda x,y: x+y,a,b)))

#Element wise subtraction
print(list(map(lambda x,y: x-y,a,b)))

#Element wise product
print(list(map(lambda x,y: x*y,a,b)))

# Exponentiating the elements of a list
print(list(map(lambda x: x**2,a)))

sum = lambda x, y : x + y
print(sum(3,4))

# using lamda to compute a sauare
items = [1, 2, 3, 4, 5]
squared = list(map(lambda x: x**2, items))
print(squared)
## [6, 7, 7, 7, 15]
## [6, 7, 7, 7, 15]
## [4, -3, -1, -5, -1]
## [5, 10, 12, 6, 56]
## [25, 4, 9, 1, 49]
## 7
## [1, 4, 9, 16, 25]
```

2.7 Lambda operations on an entire column of a data frame

```
import pandas as pd
tendulkar=pd.read_csv('tendulkar1.csv',encoding = "ISO-8859-1")
tendulkar['4s']=pd.to_numeric(tendulkar['4s'])
tendulkar['4s'].apply(lambda x:4*x)
```

2.8 Lambda operations to convert from Celsius to Fahrenheit

```
# Convert Celsius to Fahrenheit
Celsius = [39.2, 36.5, 37.3, 37.8]
Fahrenheit = list(map(lambda x: (float(9)/5)*x + 32, Celsius))
print(Fahrenheit)
## [102.56, 97.7, 99.14, 100.03999999999999]
```

2.9 a Python functions

```python
# Use the def key word to define function
def product(x,y):
    value=x*y
    return(value)

# Invoke the function
product(8,9)
```

3.1 Plotting a scatterplot

```python
import matplotlib.pyplot as plt
# Scatter plot
import pandas as pd
tendulkar=pd.read_csv('tendulkar1.csv',encoding = "ISO-8859-1")

plt.scatter(tendulkar.BF,tendulkar.Runs)

# Set the title of plot
plt.suptitle('Tendulkars Runs vs Balls faced', fontsize=20)

# Set x and y axis labels
plt.xlabel('Balls faced', fontsize=18)
plt.ylabel('Runs', fontsize=16)
plt.savefig('fig1.png', bbox_inches='tight')
plt.show()
```

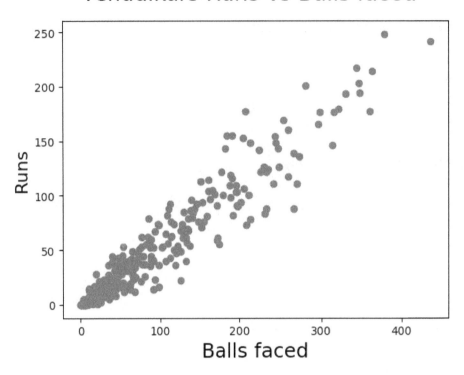

3.2 Plotting a histogram

```
#Histogram
import matplotlib.pyplot as plt

# Scatter plot
import pandas as pd
tendulkar=pd.read_csv('tendulkar1.csv',encoding = "ISO-8859-1")

#Create a histogram of runs
plt.hist(tendulkar['Runs'])

# Set title, x axis and y axis labels
plt.suptitle('Tendulkars histogram of Runs ', fontsize=20)
plt.xlabel('Frequency', fontsize=18)
plt.ylabel('Runs', fontsize=16)

# Save plot as png
plt.savefig('fig2.png', bbox_inches='tight')
plt.show()
```

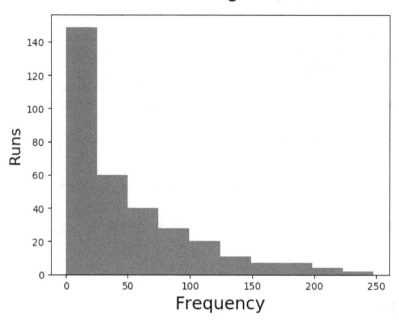

3.   R vs Python

A debate about which language is better suited for datascience, R or Python, can set off diehard fans of these languages into a tizzy. This chapter tries to look at some of the different similarities and similar differences between these languages. Largely, the ease or difficulty in learning R or Python is subjective. Some feel that R has a steeper learning curve than Python while others feel the opposite. This probably depends on the degree of familiarity with the language. Both R and Python do the same thing in just slightly different ways and syntaxes. The ease or the difficulty in the R/Python construct's largely is in the 'eyes of the beholder' nay, programmer' one could say.

To access the associated code in this chapter, you can download the R Markdown file from Github at
https://github.com/tvganesh/PracticalMachineLearningWithRandPython

1. R data types

R has the following data types

1.   Character
2.   Integer
3.   Numeric
4.   Logical
5.   Complex
6.   Raw

Python has several data types

1.   int
2.   float
3.   Long
4.   Complex and so on

2. R Vector vs Python List

A common data type in R is the vector. Python has a similar data type, the list

```
# R vectors
a<-c(4,5,1,3,4,5)

#Print 3rd element
```

```
print(a[3])
## [1] 1
print(a[3:4]) # R does not always need the explicit print.
## [1] 1 3

#R type of variable
print(class(a))
## [1] "numeric"

# Length of a
print(length(a))
## [1] 6

# Python lists
a=[4,5,1,3,4,5] #
print(a[2]) # Some python IDEs require the explicit print
print(a[2:5])

#Type of variable
print(type(a))

# Length of a
print(len(a))
## 1
## [1, 3, 4]
## <class 'list'>
## 6
```

2a. Other data types - Python

Python also has certain other data types like the tuple, dictionary etc. as shown below. R does not have as many of these data types; nevertheless, we can do everything that Python does equally well with R

```
# Python tuple
b = (4,5,7,8)
print(b)


#Python dictionary
c={'name':'Ganesh','age':54,'Work':'Professional'}
print(c)

#Print type of variable c
## (4, 5, 7, 8)
## {'name': 'Ganesh', 'age': 54, 'Work': 'Professional'}
```

2. Type of Variable

To know the type of the variable in R we use 'class', In Python the corresponding command is 'type'

```
#R - Type of variable
a<-c(4,5,1,3,4,5)
print(class(a))
## [1] "numeric"

#Python - Print type of tuple a
a=[4,5,1,3,4,5]
print(type(a))
b=(4,3,"the",2)
print(type(b))
## <class 'list'>
## <class 'tuple'>
```

3. Length

To know length in R, use length ()

```
#R - Length of vector
# Length of a
a<-c(4,5,1,3,4,5)
print(length(a))
## [1] 6
```

To know the length of a list,tuple or dict we can use len()

```
# Python - Length of list, tuple, dictionary etc
# Length of a
a=[4,5,1,3,4,5]
print(len(a))
# Length of b
b = (4,5,7,8)
print(len(b))
## 6
## 4
```

4. Accessing help

To access help in R we use the '?' or the 'help' function

```
#R - Help - To be done in R console or RStudio
```

```
#?sapply
#help(sapply)
```

Help in python on any topic involves

```
#Python help - This can be done on a (I)Python console
#help(len)
#?len
```

5. Subsetting

The key difference between R and Python concerning subsetting, is that in R the index starts at 1. In Python it starts at 0, much like C, C++ or Java To subset a vector in R we use

```
#R - Subset
a<-c(4,5,1,3,4,8,12,18,1)
print(a[3])
## [1] 1

# To print a range or a slice. Print from the 3rd to the 5th element
print(a[3:6])
## [1] 1 3 4 8
```

Python also uses indices. The difference in Python is that the index starts from 0

```
#Python - Subset
a=[4,5,1,3,4,8,12,18,1]
# Print the 4th element (starts from 0)
print(a[3])

# Print a slice from 4 to 6th element
print(a[3:6])
## 3
## [3, 4, 8]
```

6. Operations on vectors in R and operation on lists in Python

In R we can do many operations on vectors for e.g. element by element addition, subtraction, exponentiation, product etc. as show

```
#R - Operations on vectors
a<- c(5,2,3,1,7)
b<- c(1,5,4,6,8)
```

```
#Element wise Addition
print(a+b)
## [1]  6  7  7  7 15

#Element wise subtraction
print(a-b)
## [1]  4 -3 -1 -5 -1

#Element wise product
print(a*b)
## [1]  5 10 12  6 56

# Exponentiating the elements of a vector
print(a^2)
## [1] 25  4  9  1 49
```

In Python to do this on lists we need to use, the 'map' and the 'lambda' function as follows

```
# Python - Operations on list
a =[5,2,3,1,7]
b =[1,5,4,6,8]

#Element wise addition with map & lambda
print(list(map(lambda x,y: x+y,a,b)))

#Element wise subtraction
print(list(map(lambda x,y: x-y,a,b)))

#Element wise product
print(list(map(lambda x,y: x*y,a,b)))

# Exponentiating the elements of a list
print(list(map(lambda x: x**2,a)))
## [6, 7, 7, 7, 15]
## [4, -3, -1, -5, -1]
## [5, 10, 12, 6, 56]
## [25, 4, 9, 1, 49]
```

However, if we create numpy arrays from lists, then we can do the element wise addition, subtraction, product, etc. like R. Numpy is really a powerful module with many, many functions for matrix manipulations

```
import numpy as np
a =[5,2,3,1,7]
b =[1,5,4,6,8]
a=np.array(a)
```

```
b=np.array(b)

#Element wise addition
print(a+b)

#Element wise subtraction
print(a-b)

#Element wise product
print(a*b)

# Exponentiating the elements of a list
print(a**2)
## [ 6  7  7  7 15]
## [ 4 -3 -1 -5 -1]
## [ 5 10 12  6 56]
## [25  4  9  1 49]
```

7. Getting the index of element

To determine the index of an element which satisfies a specific logical condition in R, use 'which'. In the code below the index of element which is equal to 1 is 4

```
# R - Which
a<- c(5,2,3,1,7)
print(which(a == 1))
## [1] 4
```

In a Python array, we can use np.where to get the same effect. The index will be 3 as the index starts from 0

```
# Python - np.where
import numpy as np
a =[5,2,3,1,7]
a=np.array(a)
print(np.where(a==1))
## (array([3], dtype=int64),)
```

8. Data frames

R, by default comes with a set of in-built datasets. There are some datasets, which come with the SciKit- Learn package

```
# R
# To check built datasets use
#data() - In R console or in R Studio
```

```
#iris - Don't print to console
```

We can use the in-built data sets that come with Scikit package

```
#Python
import sklearn as sklearn
import pandas as pd
from sklearn import datasets
# This creates a sklearn bunch
data = datasets.load_iris()

# Convert to Pandas dataframe
iris = pd.DataFrame(data.data, columns=data.feature_names)
```

9. Working with dataframes

With R, you can work with dataframes directly. For more complex dataframe operations in R, there are convenient packages like dplyr, reshape2 etc. For Python we need to use the Pandas package. Pandas is quite comprehensive in the list of things we can do with data frames. The most common operations on a dataframe are

- Check the size of the dataframe
- Take a look at the top 5 or bottom 5 rows of dataframe
- Check the content of the dataframe

a) Size

In R use dim()

```
#R - Size
dim(iris)
## [1] 150   5
```

For Python use .shape

```
#Python - size
import sklearn as sklearn
import pandas as pd
from sklearn import datasets
data = datasets.load_iris()

# Convert to Pandas dataframe
iris = pd.DataFrame(data.data, columns=data.feature_names)
iris.shape
```

b) Top and bottom of dataframe

To know the top and bottom rows of a data frame we use head() & tail as shown below for R and Python

```
#R
head(iris,5)
##   Sepal.Length Sepal.Width Petal.Length Petal.Width Species
## 1          5.1         3.5          1.4         0.2  setosa
## 2          4.9         3.0          1.4         0.2  setosa
## 3          4.7         3.2          1.3         0.2  setosa
## 4          4.6         3.1          1.5         0.2  setosa
## 5          5.0         3.6          1.4         0.2  setosa

tail(iris,5)
##     Sepal.Length Sepal.Width Petal.Length Petal.Width   Species
## 146          6.7         3.0          5.2         2.3 virginica
## 147          6.3         2.5          5.0         1.9 virginica
## 148          6.5         3.0          5.2         2.0 virginica
## 149          6.2         3.4          5.4         2.3 virginica
## 150          5.9         3.0          5.1         1.8 virginica

#Python
import sklearn as sklearn
import pandas as pd
from sklearn import datasets
data = datasets.load_iris()
# Convert to Pandas dataframe
iris = pd.DataFrame(data.data, columns=data.feature_names)
print(iris.head(5))
print(iris.tail(5))
##    sepal length (cm)  sepal width (cm)  petal length (cm)  petal
width (cm)
## 0                5.1               3.5                1.4
0.2
## 1                4.9               3.0                1.4
0.2
## 2                4.7               3.2                1.3
0.2
## 3                4.6               3.1                1.5
0.2
## 4                5.0               3.6                1.4
0.2
##      sepal length (cm)  sepal width (cm)  petal length (cm)  petal
width (cm)
## 145                6.7               3.0                5.2
2.3
## 146                6.3               2.5                5.0
1.9
## 147                6.5               3.0                5.2
2.0
```

```
## 148                 6.2            3.4            5.4
2.3
## 149                 5.9            3.0            5.1
1.8
```

c) Check the contents of dataframe
To check the contents of a dataframe

```
#R
summary(iris)
##    Sepal.Length    Sepal.Width     Petal.Length    Petal.Width
##   Min.   :4.300   Min.   :2.000   Min.   :1.000   Min.   :0.100
##   1st Qu.:5.100   1st Qu.:2.800   1st Qu.:1.600   1st Qu.:0.300
##   Median :5.800   Median :3.000   Median :4.350   Median :1.300
##   Mean   :5.843   Mean   :3.057   Mean   :3.758   Mean   :1.199
##   3rd Qu.:6.400   3rd Qu.:3.300   3rd Qu.:5.100   3rd Qu.:1.800
##   Max.   :7.900   Max.   :4.400   Max.   :6.900   Max.   :2.500
##          Species
##   setosa    :50
##   versicolor:50
##   virginica :50
##
##
##

str(iris)
## 'data.frame':    150 obs. of  5 variables:
##  $ Sepal.Length: num  5.1 4.9 4.7 4.6 5 5.4 4.6 5 4.4 4.9 ...
##  $ Sepal.Width : num  3.5 3 3.2 3.1 3.6 3.9 3.4 3.4 2.9 3.1 ...
##  $ Petal.Length: num  1.4 1.4 1.3 1.5 1.4 1.7 1.4 1.5 1.4 1.5 ...
##  $ Petal.Width : num  0.2 0.2 0.2 0.2 0.2 0.4 0.3 0.2 0.2 0.1 ...
##  $ Species     : Factor w/ 3 levels "setosa","versicolor",..: 1 1
1 1 1 1 1 1 1 ...

#Python
import sklearn as sklearn
import pandas as pd
from sklearn import datasets
data = datasets.load_iris()
# Convert to Pandas dataframe
iris = pd.DataFrame(data.data, columns=data.feature_names)
print(iris.info())
## <class 'pandas.core.frame.DataFrame'>
## RangeIndex: 150 entries, 0 to 149
## Data columns (total 4 columns):
## sepal length (cm)    150 non-null float64
## sepal width (cm)     150 non-null float64
## petal length (cm)    150 non-null float64
## petal width (cm)     150 non-null float64
```

```
## dtypes: float64(4)
## memory usage: 4.8 KB
## None
```

d) Check column names

To check the column names

```
#R
names(iris)
## [1] "Sepal.Length" "Sepal.Width"  "Petal.Length" "Petal.Width"
## [5] "Species"

colnames(iris)
## [1] "Sepal.Length" "Sepal.Width"  "Petal.Length" "Petal.Width"
## [5] "Species"

#Python
import sklearn as sklearn
import pandas as pd
from sklearn import datasets
data = datasets.load_iris()
# Convert to Pandas dataframe
iris = pd.DataFrame(data.data, columns=data.feature_names)
#Get column names
print(iris.columns)
## Index(['sepal length (cm)', 'sepal width (cm)', 'petal length
(cm)',
##         'petal width (cm)'],
##       dtype='object')
```

e) Rename columns

In R, we can assign a vector to column names

```
#R
colnames(iris) <-
c("lengthOfSepal","widthOfSepal","lengthOfPetal","widthOfPetal","Spec
ies")
colnames(iris)
## [1] "lengthOfSepal" "widthOfSepal"  "lengthOfPetal" "widthOfPetal"
## [5] "Species"
```

In Python we can assign a list to columns

```
#Python
import sklearn as sklearn
import pandas as pd
from sklearn import datasets
data = datasets.load_iris()
```

```
# Convert to Pandas dataframe
iris = pd.DataFrame(data.data, columns=data.feature_names)
iris.columns =
["lengthOfSepal","widthOfSepal","lengthOfPetal","widthOfPetal"]
print(iris.columns)
## Index(['lengthOfSepal', 'widthOfSepal', 'lengthOfPetal',
'widthOfPetal'], dtype='object')
```

f) Subsetting dataframes

```
# R
#To subset a dataframe 'df' in R we use df[row,column] or df[row
vector,column vector]
#df[row,column]
iris[3,4]
## [1] 0.2

#df[row vector, column vector]
iris[2:5,1:3]
##   lengthOfSepal widthOfSepal lengthOfPetal
## 2           4.9          3.0           1.4
## 3           4.7          3.2           1.3
## 4           4.6          3.1           1.5
## 5           5.0          3.6           1.4
#If we omit the row vector, then it implies all rows or if we omit
the column vector
# then implies all columns for that row
iris[2:5,]
##   lengthOfSepal widthOfSepal lengthOfPetal widthOfPetal Species
## 2           4.9          3.0           1.4          0.2  setosa
## 3           4.7          3.2           1.3          0.2  setosa
## 4           4.6          3.1           1.5          0.2  setosa
## 5           5.0          3.6           1.4          0.2  setosa

# In R we can all specific columns by column names
iris$Sepal.Length[2:5]
## NULL

#Python
# To select an entire row we use .iloc. The index can be used with
the ':'. If
# .iloc[start row: end row]. If start row is omitted then it implies
the beginning of
# data frame, if end row is omitted then it implies all rows till end

#Python
import sklearn as sklearn
import pandas as pd
from sklearn import datasets
```

```
data = datasets.load_iris()
# Convert to Pandas dataframe
iris = pd.DataFrame(data.data, columns=data.feature_names)
print(iris.iloc[3])
print(iris[:5])

# In python we can select columns by column name as follows
print(iris['sepal length (cm)'][2:6])
#If you want to select more than 2 columns then you must use the
double '[[]]' since the
# index is a list itself
print(iris[['sepal length (cm)','sepal width (cm)']][4:7])
```

```
## sepal length (cm)    4.6
## sepal width (cm)     3.1
## petal length (cm)    1.5
## petal width (cm)     0.2
## Name: 3, dtype: float64
##     sepal length (cm)  sepal width (cm)  petal length (cm)  petal
width (cm)
## 0                5.1               3.5               1.4
0.2
## 1                4.9               3.0               1.4
0.2
## 2                4.7               3.2               1.3
0.2
## 3                4.6               3.1               1.5
0.2
## 4                5.0               3.6               1.4
0.2
## 2    4.7
## 3    4.6
## 4    5.0
## 5    5.4
## Name: sepal length (cm), dtype: float64
##     sepal length (cm)  sepal width (cm)
## 4              5.0               3.6
## 5              5.4               3.9
## 6              4.6               3.4
```

g) Computing Mean, Standard Deviation

```
#R
#Mean
mean(iris$lengthOfSepal)
## [1] 5.843333
#Standard deviation
sd(iris$widthOfSepal)
## [1] 0.4358663

#Python
```

```
#Mean
import sklearn as sklearn
import pandas as pd
from sklearn import datasets
data = datasets.load_iris()
# Convert to Pandas dataframe
iris = pd.DataFrame(data.data, columns=data.feature_names)
# Convert to Pandas dataframe
print(iris['sepal length (cm)'].mean())
#Standard deviation
print(iris['sepal width (cm)'].std())
## 5.843333333333335
## 0.4335943113621737
```

i) Boxplot

Boxplot can be produced in R, using baseplot

```
#R
boxplot(iris$lengthOfSepal)
```

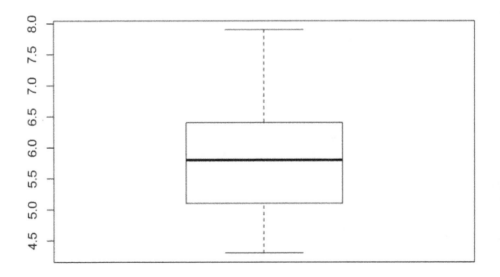

Matplotlib is a popular package in Python for plots

```
#Python
import sklearn as sklearn
import pandas as pd
import matplotlib.pyplot as plt
from sklearn import datasets
data = datasets.load_iris()

# Convert to Pandas dataframe
iris = pd.DataFrame(data.data, columns=data.feature_names)
img=plt.boxplot(iris['sepal length (cm)'])
plt.show(img)
```

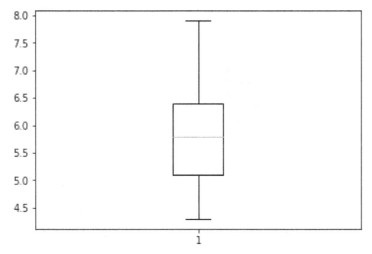

j) Scatterplot

```
#R
plot(iris$widthOfSepal,iris$lengthOfSepal)
```

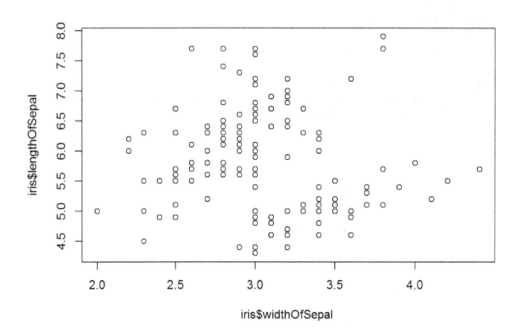

```
#Python
import matplotlib.pyplot as plt
import sklearn as sklearn
import pandas as pd
from sklearn import datasets
data = datasets.load_iris()

# Convert to Pandas dataframe
iris = pd.DataFrame(data.data, columns=data.feature_names)
img=plt.scatter(iris['sepal width (cm)'],iris['sepal length (cm)'])
#plt.show(img)
```

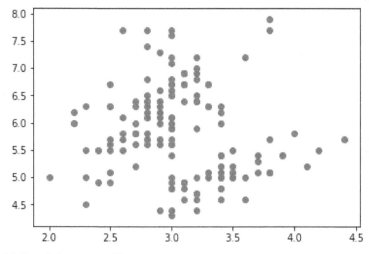

k) Read from csv file

```
#R
tendulkar= read.csv("tendulkar.csv",stringsAsFactors =
FALSE,na.strings=c(NA,"-"))

#Dimensions of dataframe
dim(tendulkar)
## [1] 347  13
names(tendulkar)
##  [1] "X"         "Runs"     "Mins"     "BF"        "X4s"
##  [6] "X6s"       "SR"       "Pos"      "Dismissal" "Inns"
## [11] "Opposition" "Ground"   "Start.Date"
```

Use pandas' read_csv() for Python

```
#Python
import pandas as pd
#Read csv
tendulkar= pd.read_csv("tendulkar.csv",na_values=["-"])
print(tendulkar.shape)
print(tendulkar.columns)
## (347, 13)
## Index(['Unnamed: 0', 'Runs', 'Mins', 'BF', '4s', '6s', 'SR', 'Pos',
##        'Dismissal', 'Inns', 'Opposition', 'Ground', 'Start Date'],
##        dtype='object')
```

l) Clean the dataframe in R and Python

The following steps are done for R and Python
1.Remove rows with 'DNB'

101

2.Remove rows with 'TDNB'
3.Remove rows with absent
4.Remove the "*" indicating not out
5.Remove incomplete rows with NA for R or NaN in Python
6.Do a scatter plot

```r
#R
# Remove rows with 'DNB'
a <- tendulkar$Runs != "DNB"
tendulkar <- tendulkar[a,]
dim(tendulkar)
## [1] 330  13

# Remove rows with 'TDNB'
b <- tendulkar$Runs != "TDNB"
tendulkar <- tendulkar[b,]

# Remove rows with absent
c <- tendulkar$Runs != "absent"
tendulkar <- tendulkar[c,]
dim(tendulkar)
## [1] 329  13

# Remove the "* indicating not out
tendulkar$Runs <- as.numeric(gsub("\\*","",tendulkar$Runs))
dim(tendulkar)
## [1] 329  13

# Select only complete rows - complete.cases()
c <- complete.cases(tendulkar)

#Subset the rows which are complete
tendulkar <- tendulkar[c,]
dim(tendulkar)
## [1] 327  13

# Do some base plotting - Scatter plot
plot(tendulkar$BF,tendulkar$Runs)
```

```python
#Python
import pandas as pd
import matplotlib.pyplot as plt
#Read csv
tendulkar= pd.read_csv("tendulkar.csv",na_values=["-"])
print(tendulkar.shape)

# Remove rows with 'DNB'
a=tendulkar.Runs !="DNB"
tendulkar=tendulkar[a]
print(tendulkar.shape)

# Remove rows with 'TDNB'
b=tendulkar.Runs !="TDNB"
tendulkar=tendulkar[b]
print(tendulkar.shape)

# Remove rows with absent
c= tendulkar.Runs != "absent"
tendulkar=tendulkar[c]
print(tendulkar.shape)

# Remove the "* indicating not out
tendulkar.Runs= tendulkar.Runs.str.replace(r"[*]","")

#Select only complete rows - dropna()
tendulkar=tendulkar.dropna()
print(tendulkar.shape)
```

```
tendulkar.Runs = tendulkar.Runs.astype(int)
tendulkar.BF = tendulkar.BF.astype(int)

#Scatter plot
plt.scatter(tendulkar.BF,tendulkar.Runs)
## (347, 13)
## (330, 13)
## (329, 13)
## (329, 13)
## (327, 13)
```

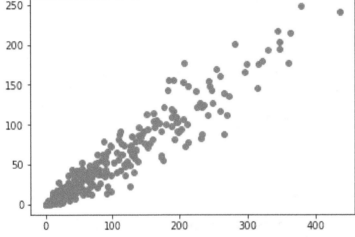

m) Chaining operations on dataframes

To chain a set of operations we need to use an R package like dplyr. We can also chain
The following operations are done on tendulkar data frame by dplyr for R and Pandas for
Python below

1. Group by ground
2. Compute average runs in each ground
3. Arrange in descending order

```
#R
library(dplyr)
tendulkar1 <- tendulkar %>% group_by(Ground) %>% summarise(meanRuns=
mean(Runs)) %>% arrange(desc(meanRuns))

head(tendulkar1,10)
## # A tibble: 10 × 2
##           Ground  meanRuns
##
## 1         Multan 194.00000
## 2          Leeds 193.00000
```

```
## 3   Colombo (RPS) 143.00000
## 4         Lucknow 142.00000
## 5           Dhaka 132.75000
## 6      Manchester  93.50000
## 7          Sydney  87.22222
## 8    Bloemfontein  85.00000
## 9      Georgetown  81.00000
## 10 Colombo (SSC)  77.55556
```

In Python this shown below. Initially the Tendulkar dataframe is created. Once the dataframe is created, like dplyr, in pandas we group by ground, compute the average and sort the output.

```python
#Python
import pandas as pd
#Read csv
tendulkar= pd.read_csv("tendulkar.csv",na_values=["-"])
print(tendulkar.shape)

# Remove rows with 'DNB'
a=tendulkar.Runs !="DNB"
tendulkar=tendulkar[a]

# Remove rows with 'TDNB'
b=tendulkar.Runs !="TDNB"
tendulkar=tendulkar[b]

# Remove rows with absent
c= tendulkar.Runs != "absent"
tendulkar=tendulkar[c]

# Remove the "* indicating not out
tendulkar.Runs= tendulkar.Runs.str.replace(r"[*]","")

#Select only complete rows - dropna()
tendulkar=tendulkar.dropna()

tendulkar.Runs = tendulkar.Runs.astype(int)
tendulkar.BF = tendulkar.BF.astype(int)

# Chaining commands in Pandas
tendulkar1=
tendulkar.groupby('Ground').mean()['Runs'].sort_values(ascending=False)

print(tendulkar1.head(10))
## (347, 13)
## Ground
## Multan          194.000000
```

```
## Leeds              193.000000
## Colombo (RPS)      143.000000
## Lucknow            142.000000
## Dhaka              132.750000
## Manchester          93.500000
## Sydney              87.222222
## Bloemfontein        85.000000
## Georgetown          81.000000
## Colombo (SSC)       77.555556
## Name: Runs, dtype: float64
```

9. Functions

a) R function definition

```
product <- function(a,b){
  c<- a*b
  c
}
product(5,7)
## [1] 35
```

```
b) Python function definition
def product(a,b):
  c = a*b
  return c

print(product(5,7))
## 35
```

Conclusion

This chapter discusses the many similarities between the 2 languages R and Python.

4. Regression of a continuous variable

Note: The next couple of chapters will include the implementations of many common Machine Learning algorithms in R and Python. For those, who know either language these implementations will help you enable to quickly ramp on the other language.

This chapter covers the following common Machine Learning Algorithms, which are used while performing a regression of a continuous target variable

- Univariate Regression
- Multivariate Regression
- Polynomial Regression
- K Nearest Neighbors Regression
-

The code includes the implementation in both R and Python.

While coding in R and Python I found that there were some aspects, which were more convenient in one language over the other. For example, plotting the fit in R is straightforward in R, while computing the R squared, splitting, as Train & Test sets etc. are available as built-in utilities in Python. In any case, these minor inconveniences can be easily be implemented in either language.

You can download the associated code in this chapter as an R Markdown file from Github at https://github.com/tvganesh/PracticalMachineLearningWithRandPython

R squared computation in R is computed as follows

$$RSS = \sum (y - yhat)^2$$
$$TSS = \sum (y - mean(y))^2$$
$$Rsquared - 1 - \frac{RSS}{TSS}$$

1.1a Univariate Regression – R code

Here a simple linear regression line is fitted between a single input feature and the target variable using R

```
# Source in the R function library
source("RFunctions.R")
```

```
# Read the Boston data file
df=read.csv("Boston.csv",stringsAsFactors = FALSE) # Data from MASS -
Statistical Learning

# Split the data into training and test sets (75:25)
train_idx <- trainTestSplit(df,trainPercent=75,seed=5)
train <- df[train_idx, ]
test <- df[-train_idx, ]

# Fit a linear regression line between 'Median value of owner
occupied homes' vs 'lower status of # population
fit=lm(medv~lstat,data=df)

# Display details of fit
summary(fit)
##
## Call:
## lm(formula = medv ~ lstat, data = df)
##
## Residuals:
##     Min      1Q  Median      3Q     Max
## -15.168  -3.990  -1.318   2.034  24.500
##
## Coefficients:
##             Estimate Std. Error t value Pr(>|t|)
## (Intercept) 34.55384    0.56263   61.41   <2e-16 ***
## lstat       -0.95005    0.03873  -24.53   <2e-16 ***
## ---
## Signif. codes:  0 '***' 0.001 '**' 0.01 '*' 0.05 '.' 0.1 ' ' 1
##
## Residual standard error: 6.216 on 504 degrees of freedom
## Multiple R-squared:  0.5441, Adjusted R-squared:  0.5432
## F-statistic: 601.6 on 1 and 504 DF,  p-value: < 2.2e-16

# Display the confidence intervals
confint(fit)
##                  2.5 %      97.5 %
## (Intercept) 33.448457 35.6592247
## lstat       -1.026148 -0.8739505

#Plot the lstat vs median value
plot(df$lstat,df$medv, xlab="Lower status (%)",ylab="Median value of
owned homes ($1000)", main="Median value of homes ($1000) vs Lowe
status (%)")

#Fit a straight line
abline(fit,lwd=3,col="red")
```

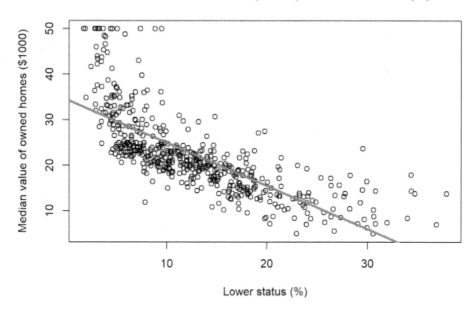

Median value of homes ($1000) vs Lower status (%)

```
#Compute the Rsquared values
rsquared=Rsquared(fit,test,test$medv)
sprintf("R-squared for uni-variate regression (Boston.csv) is : %f",
rsquared)
## [1] "R-squared for uni-variate regression (Boston.csv) is :
0.556964"
```

1.1b Univariate Regression – Python code

A simple regression line is fitted between a single feature variable and the output or target variable using Python.

```
import numpy as np
import pandas as pd
import os
import matplotlib.pyplot as plt
from sklearn.model_selection import train_test_split
from sklearn.linear_model import LinearRegression
#os.chdir("C:\\software\\machine-learning\\RandPython")

# Read the CSV file
df = pd.read_csv("Boston.csv",encoding = "ISO-8859-1")
```

```python
# Select the feature variable
X=df['lstat']

# Select the target
y=df['medv']

# Split into train and test sets (75:25)
X_train, X_test, y_train, y_test = train_test_split(X, y,random_state
= 0)
X_train=X_train.values.reshape(-1,1)
X_test=X_test.values.reshape(-1,1)

# Fit a linear model
linreg = LinearRegression().fit(X_train, y_train)

# Print the training and test R squared score
print('R-squared score (training):
{:.3f}'.format(linreg.score(X_train, y_train)))
print('R-squared score (test): {:.3f}'.format(linreg.score(X_test,
y_test)))
## R-squared score (training): 0.571
## R-squared score (test): 0.458

# Plot the linear regression line
fig=plt.scatter(X_train,y_train)

# Create a range of points. Compute yhat=coeff1*x + intercept and
plot
x=np.linspace(0,40,20)

#Plot a red linear regression line, add titles, x and y labels
fig1=plt.plot(x, linreg.coef_ * x + linreg.intercept_, color='red')
fig1=plt.title("Median value of homes ($1000) vs Lowe status (%)")
fig1=plt.xlabel("Lower status (%)")
fig1=plt.ylabel("Median value of owned homes ($1000)")
fig.figure.savefig('foo.png', bbox_inches='tight')
fig1.figure.savefig('foo1.png', bbox_inches='tight')
print "Finished"
## Finished
```

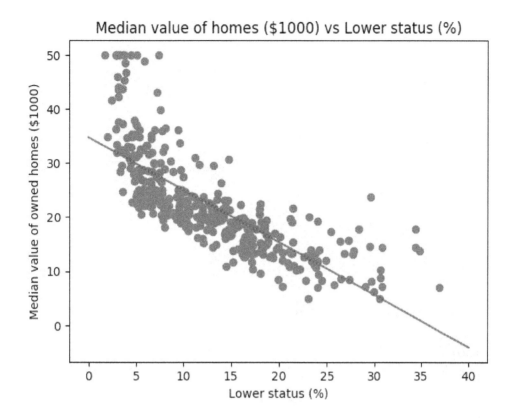

Median value of homes ($1000) vs Lower status (%)

1.2a Multivariate Regression – R code

The following code implements mulrivariate regression in R between several input/feature variables and the output/target variable

```
# Read crimes data
crimesDF <- read.csv("crimes.csv",stringsAsFactors = FALSE)

# Remove the 1st 7 columns which do not impact output
crimesDF1 <- crimesDF[,7:length(crimesDF)]

# Convert all to numeric
crimesDF2 <- sapply(crimesDF1,as.numeric)

# Check for NAs
a <- is.na(crimesDF2)

# Impute NAs to 0
crimesDF2[a] <-0

#Create as a dataframe
```

```
crimesDF2 <- as.data.frame(crimesDF2)

#Create a train/test split
train_idx <- trainTestSplit(crimesDF2,trainPercent=75,seed=5)
train <- crimesDF2[train_idx, ]
test <- crimesDF2[-train_idx, ]

# Fit a multivariate regression model between crimesPerPop and all
other features
fit <- lm(ViolentCrimesPerPop~.,data=train)

# Compute and print R Squared
rsquared=Rsquared(fit,test,test$ViolentCrimesPerPop)
sprintf("R-squared for multi-variate regression (crimes.csv)  is :
%f", rsquared)
## [1] "R-squared for multi-variate regression (crimes.csv)  is :
0.653940"
```

1.2b Multivariate Regression – Python code

The code below implements multi-variate regession between several feature variables and the target variable.

```
import numpy as np
import pandas as pd
import os
import matplotlib.pyplot as plt
from sklearn.model_selection import train_test_split
from sklearn.linear_model import LinearRegression

# Read the data using pandas
crimesDF =pd.read_csv("crimes.csv",encoding="ISO-8859-1")

#Remove the 1st 7 columns
crimesDF1=crimesDF.iloc[:,7:crimesDF.shape[1]]

# Convert all columns to numeric
crimesDF2 = crimesDF1.apply(pd.to_numeric, errors='coerce')

# Impute NA to 0s
crimesDF2.fillna(0, inplace=True)

# Select the X (feature vatiables - all)
X=crimesDF2.iloc[:,0:120]

# Set the target variable
y=crimesDF2.iloc[:,121]
```

```
# Create a train/ test split of data
X_train, X_test, y_train, y_test = train_test_split(X, y,random_state
= 0)

# Fit a multivariate regression model
linreg = LinearRegression().fit(X_train, y_train)

# Compute and print the R Square
print('R-squared score (training):
{:.3f}'.format(linreg.score(X_train, y_train)))
print('R-squared score (test): {:.3f}'.format(linreg.score(X_test,
y_test)))
## R-squared score (training): 0.699
## R-squared score (test): 0.677
```

1.3a Polynomial Regression – R

The code below in R and Python determine which polynomial provides the best fit.
Polynomials of degree 1, 2 & 3 are used and subsequently R squared is computed. It can
be seen that the quadratic model provides the best R squared score and hence the best fit

```
# Polynomial degree 1
df=read.csv("auto_mpg.csv",stringsAsFactors = FALSE) # Data from UCI
df1 <- as.data.frame(sapply(df,as.numeric))

# Select key columns from dataframe
df2 <- df1 %>% select(cylinder,displacement, horsepower,weight,
acceleration, year,mpg)

#Pick only rows which are complete
df3 <- df2[complete.cases(df2),]

# Split as train and test sets
train_idx <- trainTestSplit(df3,trainPercent=75,seed=5)
train <- df3[train_idx, ]
test <- df3[-train_idx, ]

# Polynomial of degree 1
fit <- lm(mpg~. ,data=train)

#Compute and print  R squared
rsquared1 <-Rsquared(fit,test,test$mpg)
sprintf("R-squared for Polynomial regression of degree 1
(auto_mpg.csv)  is : %f", rsquared1)
## [1] "R-squared for Polynomial regression of degree 1
(auto_mpg.csv)  is : 0.763607"
```

```
# 2nd order polynomial - Quadratic model on the data
x = as.matrix(df3[1:6])

# Make a  polynomial  of degree 2 for feature variables before split
df4=as.data.frame(poly(x,2,raw=TRUE))
df5 <- cbind(df4,df3[7])

# Split into train and test set
train_idx <- trainTestSplit(df5,trainPercent=75,seed=5)
train <- df5[train_idx, ]
test <- df5[-train_idx, ]

# Fit the quadratic model
fit <- lm(mpg~. ,data=train)

# Compute and print R squared
rsquared2=Rsquared(fit,test,test$mpg)
sprintf("R-squared for Polynomial regression of degree 2
(auto_mpg.csv)  is : %f", rsquared2)
## [1] "R-squared for Polynomial regression of degree 2
(auto_mpg.csv)  is : 0.831372"

#Polynomial of degree 3
x = as.matrix(df3[1:6])

# Make polynomial of degree 4  of feature variables before split
df4=as.data.frame(poly(x,3,raw=TRUE))
df5 <- cbind(df4,df3[7])
train_idx <- trainTestSplit(df5,trainPercent=75,seed=5)
train <- df5[train_idx, ]
test <- df5[-train_idx, ]

# Fit a model of degree 3
fit <- lm(mpg~. ,data=train)

# Compute and print R squared
rsquared3=Rsquared(fit,test,test$mpg)
sprintf("R-squared for Polynomial regression of degree 2
(auto_mpg.csv)  is : %f", rsquared3)
## [1] "R-squared for Polynomial regression of degree 2
(auto_mpg.csv)  is : 0.773225"
df=data.frame(degree=c(1,2,3),Rsquared=c(rsquared1,rsquared2,rsquared
3))

# Plot  how r-squared changes with increasing degree of polynomial
ggplot(df,aes(x=degree,y=Rsquared)) +geom_point() +
geom_line(color="blue") +  ggtitle("Polynomial regression - R squared
vs Degree of polynomial") +  xlab("Degree") + ylab("R squared")
```

Polynomial regression - R squared vs Degree of polynomial

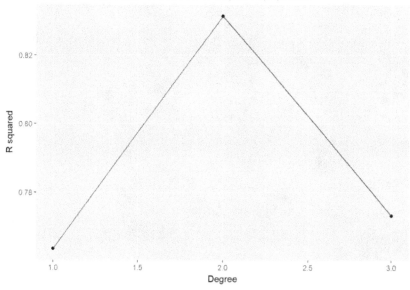

1.3a Polynomial Regression – Python

For Polynomial regression, polynomials of degree 1, 2 & 3 are used and then R squared is computed for the different degrees. It can be seen that the quadratic model provides the best R squared score and hence the best fit for Python

```
import numpy as np
import pandas as pd
import os
import matplotlib.pyplot as plt
from sklearn.model_selection import train_test_split
from sklearn.linear_model import LinearRegression
from sklearn.preprocessing import PolynomialFeatures

#Read the data using pandas
autoDF =pd.read_csv("auto_mpg.csv",encoding="ISO-8859-1")

# Select key columns
autoDF1=autoDF[['mpg','cylinder','displacement','horsepower','weight'
,'acceleration','year']]

# Convert selected columns to numeric
autoDF2 = autoDF1.apply(pd.to_numeric, errors='coerce')

# Drop NAs
autoDF3=autoDF2.dropna()
```

```python
autoDF3.shape

#Set the feature and target variables
X=autoDF3[['cylinder','displacement','horsepower','weight','accelerat
ion','year']]
y=autoDF3['mpg']

# Polynomial degree 1
X_train, X_test, y_train, y_test = train_test_split(X, y,random_state
= 0)

#Fit a degree 1 polynomial
linreg = LinearRegression().fit(X_train, y_train)

# Compute and print  R-squared on training data
print('R-squared score - Polynomial degree 1 (training):
:.3f}'.format(linreg.score(X_train, y_train)))

# Compute and print R squared  on test data
rsquared1 =linreg.score(X_test, y_test)
print('R-squared score - Polynomial degree 1 (test):
{:.3f}'.format(linreg.score(X_test, y_test)))

# Polynomial degree 2
poly = PolynomialFeatures(degree=2)

# Transform data to degree 2
X_poly = poly.fit_transform(X)

#Perform a train and test split on transformed data
X_train, X_test, y_train, y_test = train_test_split(X_poly,
y,random_state = 0)
linreg = LinearRegression().fit(X_train, y_train)

# Compute R squared on degree 2 fit on training data
print('R-squared score - Polynomial degree 2 (training):
:.3f}'.format(linreg.score(X_train, y_train)))

# Compute R squared on degree 2 fit on test data
rsquared2 =linreg.score(X_test, y_test)
print('R-squared score - Polynomial degree 2 (test):
{:.3f}\n'.format(linreg.score(X_test, y_test)))

#Polynomial degree 3
poly = PolynomialFeatures(degree=3)

# Transform data to  degree 3
X_poly = poly.fit_transform(X)
```

```python
#Perform a train/test split on transformed data
X_train, X_test, y_train, y_test = train_test_split(X_poly,
y,random_state = 0)

# Fit a 3rd degree polynomial on data
linreg = LinearRegression().fit(X_train, y_train)

# Compute and print R squared on training data
print('(R-squared score -Polynomial degree 3  (training): {:.3f}'
     .format(linreg.score(X_train, y_train)))

# Compute and print R squared  on test data
rsquared3 =linreg.score(X_test, y_test)
print('R-squared score Polynomial degree 3 (test):
{:.3f}\n'.format(linreg.score(X_test, y_test)))

#Plot how Rsquared changes with different polynomial degrees
degree=[1,2,3]
rsquared =[rsquared1,rsquared2,rsquared3]
fig2=plt.plot(degree,rsquared)
fig2=plt.title("Polynomial regression - R squared vs Degree of
polynomial")
fig2=plt.xlabel("Degree")
fig2=plt.ylabel("R squared")
fig2.figure.savefig('foo2.png', bbox_inches='tight')
print "Finished plotting and saving"
## R-squared score - Polynomial degree 1 (training): 0.811
## R-squared score - Polynomial degree 1 (test): 0.799
## R-squared score - Polynomial degree 2 (training): 0.861
## R-squared score - Polynomial degree 2 (test): 0.847
##
## (R-squared score -Polynomial degree 3 (training): 0.933
## R-squared score Polynomial degree 3 (test): 0.710
##
## Finished plotting and saving
```

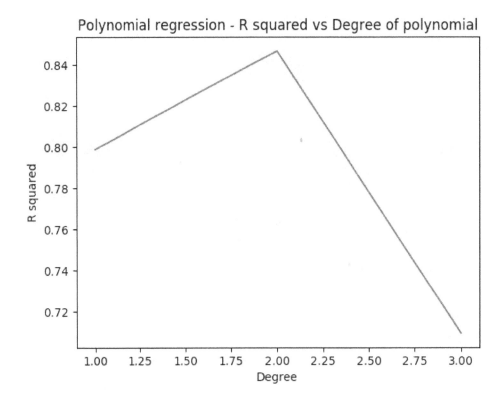

1.4 K Nearest Neighbors (KNN)

The code below implements KNN Regression for both R and Python. This is done for different neighbors. The R squared is computed in each case. This is repeated after performing feature scaling. The model fit is much better after feature scaling. Normalization refers to

$$X_{normalized} = \frac{X - min(X)}{max(X - min(X))}$$

Another technique that is used is 'Standardization; which is

$$X_{standardized} = \frac{X - mean(X)}{sd(X)}$$

1.4a K Nearest Neighbors (KNN) Regression – R(Unnormalized)

The R code below uses KNN regression in R and does not use feature scaling

```
# KNN regression requires the FNN package
library(FNN)

# Read the data and convert to data frame
df=read.csv("auto_mpg.csv",stringsAsFactors = FALSE) # Data from UCI
df1 <- as.data.frame(sapply(df,as.numeric))

# Select specific columns
df2 <- df1 %>% select(cylinder,displacement, horsepower,weight,
acceleration, year,mpg)

# Filter incomplete rows
df3 <- df2[complete.cases(df2),]

# Split the data frame as train and test
train_idx <- trainTestSplit(df3,trainPercent=75,seed=5)
train <- df3[train_idx, ]
test <- df3[-train_idx, ]

#  Select the feature variables
train.X=train[,1:6]
# Set the target for training
train.Y=train[,7]

# Set the feature and target variables in the test data
test.X=test[,1:6]
test.Y=test[,7]

# Initialize Rsquared as NULL
rsquared <- NULL

# Create a list of neighbors
neighbors <-c(1,2,4,8,10,14)

# Loop through the number of neighbors. Train different models for
different
# number of nearest neighbors and compute Rsquared
for(i in seq_along(neighbors)){
    # Perform a KNN regression fit
    knn=knn.reg(train.X,test.X,train.Y,k=neighbors[i])
    # Compute R sqaured
    rsquared[i]=knnRSquared(knn$pred,test.Y)
}

#Plot the Rsquared vs number of nearest neighbors
# Make a dataframe for plotting
df <- data.frame(neighbors,Rsquared=rsquared)
```

```
# Plot the number of neighors vs the R squared
ggplot(df,aes(x=neighbors,y=Rsquared)) + geom_point()
+geom_line(color="blue") + xlab("Number of neighbors") + ylab("R
squared") + ggtitle("KNN regression - R squared vs Number of
Neighors (Unnormalized)")
```

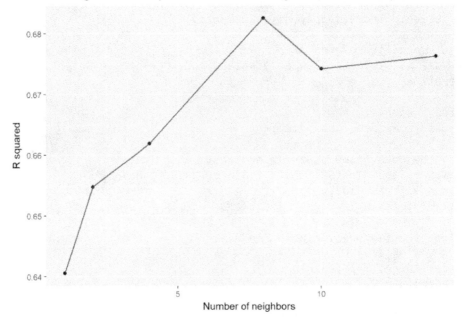

KNN regression - R squared vs Number of Neighors (Unnormalized)

1.4b K Nearest Neighbors (KNN) Regression – Python(Unnormalized)

The Python code below implements KNN regression in Python and does not use feature scaling.

```
import numpy as np
import pandas as pd
import os
import matplotlib.pyplot as plt
from sklearn.model_selection import train_test_split
from sklearn.linear_model import LinearRegression
from sklearn.preprocessing import PolynomialFeatures
from sklearn.neighbors import KNeighborsRegressor

# Read the data using pandas
autoDF =pd.read_csv("auto_mpg.csv",encoding="ISO-8859-1")
#Select the necessary columns
```

```python
autoDF1=autoDF[['mpg','cylinder','displacement','horsepower','weight'
,'acceleration','year']]

# Convert all columns to numeric
autoDF2 = autoDF1.apply(pd.to_numeric, errors='coerce')
autoDF3=autoDF2.dropna()
autoDF3.shape

# Set the feature and target variables
X=autoDF3[['cylinder','displacement','horsepower','weight','accelerat
ion','year']]
y=autoDF3['mpg']

# Perform a train/test split
X_train, X_test, y_train, y_test = train_test_split(X, y,
random_state = 0)
# Create a list of neighbors

# Compute R squared for different number of nearest neighbors
# Create an empty list
rsquared=[]

#Set the number of neighbors as a list
neighbors=[1,2,4,8,10,14]

# Loop through the neighbors and compute R squared
for i in neighbors:
        # Fit a KNN model
        knnreg = KNeighborsRegressor(n_neighbors = i).fit(X_train,
y_train)
        # Compute R squared
        rsquared.append(knnreg.score(X_test, y_test))
        print('R-squared test score: {:.3f}'
        .format(knnreg.score(X_test, y_test)))

# Plot the number of neighors vs the R squared
fig3=plt.plot(neighbors,rsquared)
fig3=plt.title("KNN regression - R squared vs Number of
neighbors(Unnormalized)")
fig3=plt.xlabel("Neighbors")
fig3=plt.ylabel("R squared")
fig3.figure.savefig('foo3.png', bbox_inches='tight')
print "Finished plotting and saving"
## R-squared test score: 0.527
## R-squared test score: 0.678
## R-squared test score: 0.707
## R-squared test score: 0.684
## R-squared test score: 0.683
## R-squared test score: 0.670
```

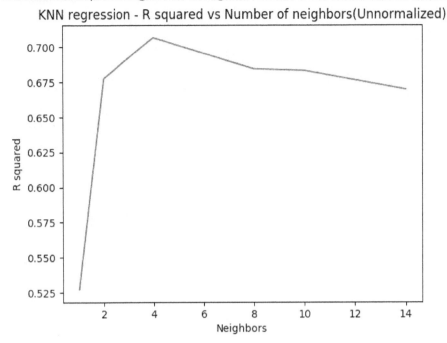

KNN regression - R squared vs Number of neighbors(Unnormalized)

1.4c K Nearest Neighbors Regression – R(Normalized)

In the code below the input features are normalized before using KNN regression in R. Clearly R squared improves when the features are normalized.

```
# Read the auto data
df=read.csv("auto_mpg.csv",stringsAsFactors = FALSE) # Data from UCI

#Convert to dataframe
df1 <- as.data.frame(sapply(df,as.numeric))

# Select specific columns
df2 <- df1 %>% select(cylinder,displacement, horsepower,weight,
acceleration, year,mpg)

#Choose only complete cases
df3 <- df2[complete.cases(df2),]

# Split the dataframe as train and test
train_idx <- trainTestSplit(df3,trainPercent=75,seed=5)
train <- df3[train_idx, ]
test <- df3[-train_idx, ]
```

```
#  Select the feature variables
train.X=train[,1:6]
# Set the target for training
train.Y=train[,7]

# Set the feature variables and target for the test data
test.X=test[,1:6]
test.Y=test[,7]


# Perform MinMaxScaling of feature variables on the train and test
sets
train.X.scaled=MinMaxScaler(train.X)
test.X.scaled=MinMaxScaler(test.X)

# Create a list of neighbors
rsquared <- NULL

#Loop through number of neighbors and compute R squared
neighbors <-c(1,2,4,6,8,10,12,15,20,25,30)
for(i in seq_along(neighbors)){
    # Fit a KNN model
    knn=knn.reg(train.X.scaled,test.X.scaled,train.Y,k=i)
    # Compute R ssquared
    rsquared[i]=knnRSquared(knn$pred,test.Y)

}

# Plot the number of knn neighbors and R squared
df <- data.frame(neighbors,Rsquared=rsquared)

# Plot the number of neighors vs the R squared
ggplot(df,aes(x=neighbors,y=Rsquared)) + geom_point()
+geom_line(color="blue") + xlab("Number of neighbors") + ylab("R
squared") + ggtitle("KNN regression - R squared vs Number of
Neighors(Normalized)")
```

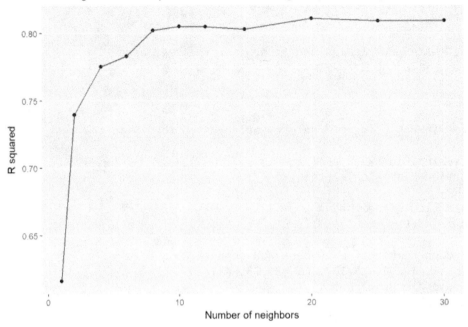

1.4d K Nearest Neighbors Regression – Python (Normalized)

In the code below the features are normalized before doing KNN regression. This improves R squared when the features are normalized with MinMaxScaling

```
import numpy as np
import pandas as pd
import os
import matplotlib.pyplot as plt
from sklearn.model_selection import train_test_split
from sklearn.linear_model import LinearRegression
from sklearn.preprocessing import PolynomialFeatures
from sklearn.neighbors import KNeighborsRegressor
from sklearn.preprocessing import MinMaxScaler

# Read the auto dataset with pandas
autoDF =pd.read_csv("auto_mpg.csv",encoding="ISO-8859-1")
autoDF.shape
autoDF.columns
#Select the necessary columns
```

```python
autoDF1=autoDF[['mpg','cylinder','displacement','horsepower','weight'
,'acceleration','year']]

# Convert all columns to numeric
autoDF2 = autoDF1.apply(pd.to_numeric, errors='coerce')

# Drop columns with NA
autoDF3=autoDF2.dropna()
autoDF3.shape

# Set the feature and target variables
X=autoDF3[['cylinder','displacement','horsepower','weight','accelerat
ion','year']]
y=autoDF3['mpg']

# Perform a train/ test  split
X_train, X_test, y_train, y_test = train_test_split(X, y,
random_state = 0)

# Perform MinMaxScaling
scaler = MinMaxScaler()

# Scale the train set
X_train_scaled = scaler.fit_transform(X_train)

# Apply scaling on test set
X_test_scaled = scaler.transform(X_test)

# Create a list of neighbors
rsquared=[]

# Loop through the KNN neighbors and compute R Squared
neighbors=[1,2,4,6,8,10,12,15,20,25,30]
for i in neighbors:
    # Fit a KNN model
    knnreg = KNeighborsRegressor(n_neighbors = i).fit(X_train_scaled,
y_train)
    # Compute R squared
    rsquared.append(knnreg.score(X_test_scaled, y_test))
    print('R-squared test score: {:.3f}'
          .format(knnreg.score(X_test_scaled, y_test)))

# Plot the number of  KNN neighors vs the R squared
fig4=plt.plot(neighbors,rsquared)
fig4=plt.title("KNN regression - R squared vs Number of
neighbors(Normalized)")
fig4=plt.xlabel("Neighbors")
fig4=plt.ylabel("R squared")
fig4.figure.savefig('foo4.png', bbox_inches='tight')
```

```
print "Finished plotting and saving"
## R-squared test score: 0.703
## R-squared test score: 0.810
## R-squared test score: 0.830
## R-squared test score: 0.838
## R-squared test score: 0.834
## R-squared test score: 0.828
## R-squared test score: 0.827
## R-squared test score: 0.826
## R-squared test score: 0.816
## R-squared test score: 0.815
## R-squared test score: 0.809
## Finished plotting and saving
```

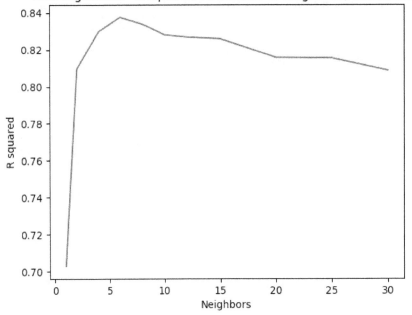

5. Classification and Cross Validation

This chapter discusses classification algorithms and cross validation. It includes the implementation of

-Logistic Regression
-K Nearest Neighbors (KNN) classification
-Leave out one Cross Validation (LOOCV)
-K Fold Cross Validation
in both R and Python.

The associated code in this chapter can be downloaded as an R Markdown file from Github at https://github.com/tvganesh/PracticalMachineLearningWithRandPython

The following classification problem is based on Logistic Regression. The data is an included data set in Scikit-Learn, which was saved as .csv file and later also used in the R implementation. The fit of a classification Machine Learning Model depends on how correctly the ML model classifies the data. There are several measures of testing a model's classification performance. They are

–**Accuracy** = TP + TN / (TP + TN + FP + FN) – Fraction of all classes correctly classified
–**Precision** = TP / (TP + FP) – Fraction of correctly classified positives among those classified as positive
– **Recall** = TP / (TP + FN) Also known as sensitivity, or True Positive Rate (True positive) – Fraction of correctly classified as positive among all positives in the data
– **F1** = 2 * Precision * Recall / (Precision + Recall)

1a. Logistic Regression – R code

The caret and e1071 package is required for invoking the confusionMatrix call in R. The code below implements Logisitic Regression in R and computes Accuracy, Sensitivity, Specificity etc.


```
source("RFunctions.R")
library(dplyr)
library(caret)
library(e1071)

# Read the data ( saved from from sklearn datasets)
cancer <- read.csv("cancer.csv")
```

```
# Rename the target variable
names(cancer) <- c(seq(1,30),"output")

# Split the dataset as training and test sets
train_idx <- trainTestSplit(cancer,trainPercent=75,seed=5)
train <- cancer[train_idx, ]
test <- cancer[-train_idx, ]

# Fit a generalized linear logistic model,
fit=glm(output~.,family=binomial,data=train,control = list(maxit =
50))

# Predict the output from the model
a=predict(fit,newdata=train,type="response")

# Set the target variable response >0.5 as 1 and <=0.5 as 0
b=ifelse(a>0.5,1,0)

# Compute the confusion matrix for training data – Accuracy,
Sensitivity, Specificity
confusionMatrix(b,train$output)
## Confusion Matrix and Statistics
##
##            Reference
## Prediction   0    1
##          0 154    0
##          1   0  272
##
##                 Accuracy : 1
##                   95% CI : (0.9914, 1)
##      No Information Rate : 0.6385
##      P-Value [Acc > NIR] : < 2.2e-16
##
##                    Kappa : 1
##   Mcnemar's Test P-Value : NA
##
##              Sensitivity : 1.0000
##              Specificity : 1.0000
##           Pos Pred Value : 1.0000
##           Neg Pred Value : 1.0000
##               Prevalence : 0.3615
##           Detection Rate : 0.3615
##     Detection Prevalence : 0.3615
##        Balanced Accuracy : 1.0000
##
##         'Positive' Class : 0
##
```

```
# Predict the target given the test data
m=predict(fit,newdata=test,type="response")

# Set the target as 1 if >0.5 and 0 if <=0
n=ifelse(m>0.5,1,0)

# Compute the confusion matrix for test output
confusionMatrix(n,test$output)
## Confusion Matrix and Statistics
##
##           Reference
## Prediction  0  1
##          0 52  4
##          1  5 81
##
##               Accuracy : 0.9366
##                 95% CI : (0.8831, 0.9706)
##    No Information Rate : 0.5986
##    P-Value [Acc > NIR] : <2e-16
##
##                  Kappa : 0.8677
##  Mcnemar's Test P-Value : 1
##
##            Sensitivity : 0.9123
##            Specificity : 0.9529
##         Pos Pred Value : 0.9286
##         Neg Pred Value : 0.9419
##             Prevalence : 0.4014
##         Detection Rate : 0.3662
##   Detection Prevalence : 0.3944
##      Balanced Accuracy : 0.9326
##
##       'Positive' Class : 0
##
```

1b. Logistic Regression – Python code

The code below implements Logistic Regression in Python and also computes the confusion matrix, accuracy, precision, recall and F1 score.

```
import numpy as np
import pandas as pd
import os
import matplotlib.pyplot as plt
from sklearn.model_selection import train_test_split
from sklearn.linear_model import LogisticRegression
from sklearn.datasets import make_classification, make_blobs
from sklearn.metrics import confusion_matrix
```

```python
from matplotlib.colors import ListedColormap
from sklearn.datasets import load_breast_cancer

# Load the cancer data
(X_cancer, y_cancer) = load_breast_cancer(return_X_y = True)

#Split the dataset as training/test
X_train, X_test, y_train, y_test = train_test_split(X_cancer,
y_cancer,
                                                    random_state = 0)

# Fit Logistic Regression function
clf = LogisticRegression().fit(X_train, y_train)

# Compute and print the Accuray scores
print('Accuracy of Logistic regression classifier on training set:
{:.2f}' .format(clf.score(X_train, y_train)))
print('Accuracy of Logistic regression classifier on test set:
{:.2f}'.format(clf.score(X_test, y_test)))

# Predict the output based on te Test data
y_predicted=clf.predict(X_test)

# Compute and print confusion matrix with the test data
confusion = confusion_matrix(y_test, y_predicted)

# Compute Accuracy, Precision, Recall and F1 scores
from sklearn.metrics import accuracy_score, precision_score,
recall_score, f1_score
print('Accuracy: {:.2f}'.format(accuracy_score(y_test, y_predicted)))
print('Precision: {:.2f}'.format(precision_score(y_test,
y_predicted)))
print('Recall: {:.2f}'.format(recall_score(y_test, y_predicted)))
print('F1: {:.2f}'.format(f1_score(y_test, y_predicted)))
## Accuracy of Logistic regression classifier on training set: 0.96
## Accuracy of Logistic regression classifier on test set: 0.96
## Accuracy: 0.96
## Precision: 0.99
## Recall: 0.94
## F1: 0.97
```

2. Dummy variables

The following R and Python code show how dummy variables are handled in R and Python. Dummy variables are categorical variables (variables which can take one of several distinct values) , which have to be converted into appropriate values before using them in Machine Learning Model. For e.g. if we had currency as 'dollar', 'rupee' and 'yen' then the dummy variable call will convert this as

```
dollar 0 0 0
rupee  0 0 1
yen    0 1 0
```

2a. Logistic Regression with dummy variables- R code

In R the 'dummies' library has to be used to convert dummy variables into appropriate values, before applying any Machine Learning algorithm. Dummy variables are categorical or factor variables where the values in the variable/column is one of several distinct values.

```
# Load the dummies library
library(dummies)

# Read the Adult data set
df <- read.csv("adult1.csv",stringsAsFactors = FALSE,na.strings =
c(""," "," ?"))

# Remove rows which have NA
df1 <- df[complete.cases(df),]
dim(df1)
## [1] 30161    16

# Select specific columns
adult <- df1 %>%
dplyr::select(age,occupation,education,educationNum,capitalGain,
capital.loss,hours.per.week,native.country,salary)

# Set the data frame with dummy data for all categorical/factor
variables
adult1 <- dummy.data.frame(adult, sep = ".")

#Split the dataset as training and test
train_idx <- trainTestSplit(adult1,trainPercent=75,seed=1111)
train <- adult1[train_idx, ]
test <- adult1[-train_idx, ]

# Fit a binomial logistic regression
fit=glm(salary~.,family=binomial,data=train)

# Predict response
a=predict(fit,newdata=train,type="response")

# If response >0.5 then it is a 1 and 0 otherwise
b=ifelse(a>0.5,1,0)
```

```
# Compute and print the confusion matrix on training data - Accuracy,
Sensitivity,
# Specificity
confusionMatrix(b,train$salary)
## Confusion Matrix and Statistics
##
##           Reference
## Prediction     0     1
##          0 16065  3145
##          1   968  2442
##
##                Accuracy : 0.8182
##                  95% CI : (0.8131, 0.8232)
##     No Information Rate : 0.753
##     P-Value [Acc > NIR] : < 2.2e-16
##
##                   Kappa : 0.4375
##  Mcnemar's Test P-Value : < 2.2e-16
##
##             Sensitivity : 0.9432
##             Specificity : 0.4371
##          Pos Pred Value : 0.8363
##          Neg Pred Value : 0.7161
##              Prevalence : 0.7530
##          Detection Rate : 0.7102
##    Detection Prevalence : 0.8492
##       Balanced Accuracy : 0.6901
##
##        'Positive' Class : 0
##


# Compute and print the confusion matrix on test data - Accuracy,
Sensitivity,
# Specificity
m=predict(fit,newdata=test,type="response")
## Warning in predict.lm(object, newdata, se.fit, scale = 1, type =
## ifelse(type == : prediction from a rank-deficient fit may be
misleading

# If value > 0.5 set as 1 else set as 0
n=ifelse(m>0.5,1,0)

confusionMatrix(n,test$salary)
## Confusion Matrix and Statistics
##
##           Reference
## Prediction     0     1
```

```
##           0 5263 1099
##           1  357  822
##
##               Accuracy : 0.8069
##                 95% CI : (0.7978, 0.8158)
##    No Information Rate : 0.7453
##    P-Value [Acc > NIR] : < 2.2e-16
##
##                  Kappa : 0.4174
##  Mcnemar's Test P-Value : < 2.2e-16
##
##            Sensitivity : 0.9365
##            Specificity : 0.4279
##         Pos Pred Value : 0.8273
##         Neg Pred Value : 0.6972
##             Prevalence : 0.7453
##         Detection Rate : 0.6979
##   Detection Prevalence : 0.8437
##       Balanced Accuracy : 0.6822
##
##        'Positive' Class : 0
##
```

2b. Logistic Regression with dummy variables-Python code

As mentioned above categorical variables have to converted before using the dataframe in Machine Learning. Pandas has a 'get_dummies' function for handling dummies before using a machine learning algorithm

```python
import numpy as np
import pandas as pd
import os
import matplotlib.pyplot as plt
from sklearn.model_selection import train_test_split
from sklearn.linear_model import LogisticRegression
from sklearn.metrics import confusion_matrix
from sklearn.metrics import accuracy_score, precision_score,
recall_score, f1_score

# Read  the adult dataset frim UCI
df =pd.read_csv("adult1.csv",encoding="ISO-8859-1",na_values=["",","," ?"])

# Drop rows with NA
df1=df.dropna()
print(df1.shape)
```

133

```
# Select specific columns in the dataframe
adult = df1[['age', 'occupation', 'education', 'educationNum',
'capitalGain','capital-loss', 'hours-per-week','native-
country','salary']]

X=adult[['age','occupation','education','educationNum','capitalGain',
'capital-loss', 'hours-per-week','native-country']]

# Set dummy  values for  factor variables
X_adult=pd.get_dummies(X,columns=['occupation','education','native-
country'])
# Set the target variable
y=adult['salary']

# Split the data set into training and test sets
X_adult_train, X_adult_test, y_train, y_test =
train_test_split(X_adult, y, random_state = 0)

#Fit a Logistic Regression
clf = LogisticRegression().fit(X_adult_train, y_train)

# Compute and display Accuracy and Confusion matrix
print('Accuracy of Logistic regression classifier on training set:
{:.2f}'.format(clf.score(X_adult_train, y_train)))
print('Accuracy of Logistic regression classifier on test set:
{:.2f}'.format(clf.score(X_adult_test, y_test)))

# Predict the target values with the test data
y_predicted=clf.predict(X_adult_test)

# Compute and print the confusion matrix - Accuracy, precision,
recall, F1 scores
confusion = confusion_matrix(y_test, y_predicted)
print('Accuracy: {:.2f}'.format(accuracy_score(y_test, y_predicted)))
print('Precision: {:.2f}'.format(precision_score(y_test,
y_predicted)))
print('Recall: {:.2f}'.format(recall_score(y_test, y_predicted)))
print('F1: {:.2f}'.format(f1_score(y_test, y_predicted)))
## (30161, 16)
## Accuracy of Logistic regression classifier on training set: 0.82
## Accuracy of Logistic regression classifier on test set: 0.81
## Accuracy: 0.81
## Precision: 0.68
## Recall: 0.41
## F1: 0.51
```

3a – K Nearest Neighbors Classification – R code

The R code below perform classification using KNN algorithm. The <u>Adult</u> data set is taken from **UCI Machine Learning Repository** (http://archive.ics.uci.edu/ml/index.php)

```
source("RFunctions.R")

# Read the adult data set
df <- read.csv("adult1.csv",stringsAsFactors = FALSE,na.strings =
c(""," "," ?"))

# Remove rows which have NA
df1 <- df[complete.cases(df),]
dim(df1)
## [1] 30161    16

# Select specific columns from the dataset
adult <- df1 %>%
dplyr::select(age,occupation,education,educationNum,capitalGain,
capital.loss, hours.per.week, native.country, salary)

# Set dummy variables
adult1 <- dummy.data.frame(adult, sep = ".")

#Split train and test as required by KNN classsification model
train_idx <- trainTestSplit(adult1,trainPercent=75,seed=1111)
train <- adult1[train_idx, ]
test <- adult1[-train_idx, ]
train.X <- train[,1:76]
train.y <- train[,77]
test.X <- test[,1:76]
test.y <- test[,77]

# Fit a model for 1,3,5,10 and 15 neighbors
cMat <- NULL

#Loop based on number of nearest neighbors and compute the accuracy
neighbors <-c(1,3,5,10,15)
for(i in seq_along(neighbors)){
    fit =knn(train.X,test.X,train.y,k=i)
    table(fit,test.y)
    a<-confusionMatrix(fit,test.y)
    cMat[i] <- a$overall[1]
    print(a$overall[1])
}
##  Accuracy
## 0.7835831
##  Accuracy
## 0.8162047
##  Accuracy
## 0.8089113
##  Accuracy
```

```
## 0.8209787
##   Accuracy
## 0.8184591
```

```
#Plot the Accuracy for each of the KNN models based on number of
neighbors
df <- data.frame(neighbors,Accuracy=cMat)
ggplot(df,aes(x=neighbors,y=Accuracy)) + geom_point()
+geom_line(color="blue") + xlab("Number of neighbors") +
ylab("Accuracy") + ggtitle("KNN regression - Accuracy vs Number of
Neighors (Unnormalized)")
```

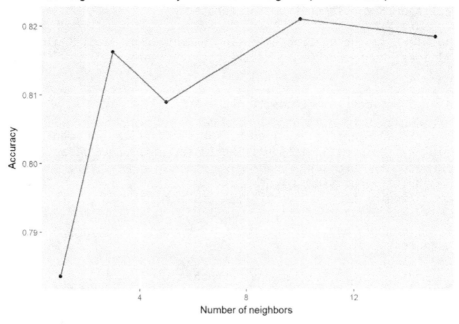

3b – K Nearest Neighbors Classification – Python code

KNN classification is performed on the Adult data set using Python. The confusion matrix is computed and displayed.

```
import numpy as np
import pandas as pd
import os
import matplotlib.pyplot as plt
from sklearn.model_selection import train_test_split
from sklearn.metrics import confusion_matrix
```

```python
from sklearn.metrics import accuracy_score, precision_score,
recall_score, f1_score
from sklearn.neighbors import KNeighborsClassifier
from sklearn.preprocessing import MinMaxScaler

# Read the adult dataset
df =pd.read_csv("adult1.csv",encoding="ISO-8859-1",na_values=[""," 
"," ?"])

# Drop rows with NAs
df1=df.dropna()
print(df1.shape)

# Select specific columns
adult =
df1[['age','occupation','education','educationNum','capitalGain','cap
ital-loss', 'hours-per-week','native-country','salary']]

X=adult[['age', 'occupation', 'education','educationNum',
'capitalGain','capital-loss', 'hours-per-week','native-country']]

#Set values for dummy variables
X_adult=pd.get_dummies(X,columns=['occupation','education','native-
country'])
# Set the target variable
y=adult['salary']

#Split the dataset as training and test sets
X_adult_train, X_adult_test, y_train, y_test =
train_test_split(X_adult, y, random_state = 0)

# Before performing KNN classification with Python  the data has to
be normalized
# Normalize the data using MinMaxScaler
scaler = MinMaxScaler()
X_train_scaled = scaler.fit_transform(X_adult_train)

# Normalize the test set also
X_test_scaled = scaler.transform(X_adult_test)

# Compute the accuracy for KNN model with 1,3,5,10 & 15 neighbors
accuracy=[]
neighbors=[1,3,5,10,15]
for i in neighbors:
    knn = KNeighborsClassifier(n_neighbors = i)
    knn.fit(X_train_scaled, y_train)
    accuracy.append(knn.score(X_test_scaled, y_test))
    print('Accuracy test score: {:.3f}'
        .format(knn.score(X_test_scaled, y_test)))
```

```
# Plot the models with the Accuracy attained for each of these KNN
models
fig1=plt.plot(neighbors,accuracy)
fig1=plt.title("KNN regression - Accuracy vs Number of neighbors")
fig1=plt.xlabel("Neighbors")
fig1=plt.ylabel("Accuracy")
fig1.figure.savefig('foo1.png', bbox_inches='tight')
## (30161, 16)
## Accuracy test score: 0.749
## Accuracy test score: 0.779
## Accuracy test score: 0.793
## Accuracy test score: 0.804
## Accuracy test score: 0.803
```

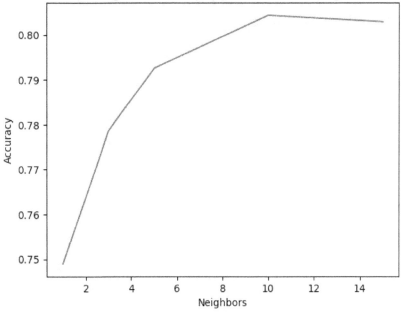

4 MPG vs Horsepower

The following scatter plot shows the non-linear relation between mpg and horsepower. This will be used as the data input for computing K-Fold Cross Validation Error

4a MPG vs Horsepower scatter plot – R Code

```
# Read the auto dataset from UCI
df=read.csv("auto_mpg.csv",stringsAsFactors = FALSE) # Data from UCI
```

```
# Convert all columns to numeric
df1 <- as.data.frame(sapply(df,as.numeric))

# Select specific columns
df2 <- df1 %>% dplyr::select(cylinder,displacement,
horsepower,weight, acceleration, year,mpg)

# Filter out rows with incomplete data
df3 <- df2[complete.cases(df2),]
ggplot(df3,aes(x=horsepower,y=mpg)) + geom_point() +
xlab("Horsepower") +   ylab("Miles Per gallon") + ggtitle("Miles per
Gallon vs Hosrsepower")
```

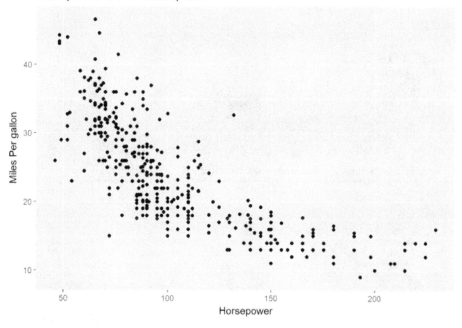

Miles per Gallon vs Hosrsepower

4b MPG vs Horsepower scatter plot – Python Code

```
import numpy as np
import pandas as pd
import os
import matplotlib.pyplot as plt

# Read the auto data set
autoDF =pd.read_csv("auto_mpg.csv",encoding="ISO-8859-1")
autoDF.shape
```

```
autoDF.columns

# Select specific columns
autoDF1=autoDF[['mpg','cylinder','displacement','horsepower','weight'
,'acceleration','year']]

# Convert all columns to numeric
autoDF2 = autoDF1.apply(pd.to_numeric, errors='coerce')

# Drop incomplete rows with NAs
autoDF3=autoDF2.dropna()
autoDF3.shape
#X=autoDF3[['cylinder','displacement','horsepower','weight']]

# Set the feature and target variables
X=autoDF3[['horsepower']]
y=autoDF3['mpg']

# Create a scatter plot
fig11=plt.scatter(X,y)
fig11=plt.title("KNN regression - Accuracy vs Number of neighbors")
fig11=plt.xlabel("Neighbors")
fig11=plt.ylabel("Accuracy")
fig11.figure.savefig('foo11.png', bbox_inches='tight')
```

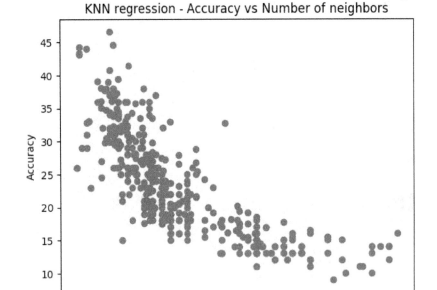

5 K-Fold Cross Validation

K-Fold Cross Validation is a technique in which the data set is divided into K Folds or K partitions. The Machine Learning model is trained on K-1 folds and tested on the Kth fold i.e. we will have K-1 folds for training data and 1 for testing the ML model. Since we can partition this as C_1^K or K choose 1, there will be K such partitions. The K-Fold Cross Validation estimates the average validation error that we can expect on a new unseen test data.

The formula for K-Fold Cross validation is as follows

$$MSE_K = \frac{\sum(y - yhat)^2}{n_K}$$

and

$$n_K = \frac{N}{K}$$

and

$$CV_K = \sum_{K=1}^{K} \left(\frac{n_K}{N}\right) MSE_K$$

where n_K is the number of elements in partition 'K' and N is the total number of elements

$$CV_K = \sum_{K=1}^{K} MSE_K$$

$$CV_K = \frac{\sum_{K=1}^{K} MSE_K}{K}$$

Leave Out one Cross Validation (LOOCV) is a special case of K-Fold Cross Validation where N-1 data points are used to train the model and 1 data point is used to test the model. There are N such paritions of N-1 & 1 that are possible. The mean error is measured The Cross Valifation Error for LOOCV is

$$CV_N = \frac{1}{n} * \frac{\sum_1^n (y - yhat)^2}{1 - h_i}$$

where h_i is the diagonal hat matrix

It took me a day and a half to implement the K Fold Cross Validation formula. In any case do let me know if you think it is off

5a. Leave out one cross validation (LOOCV) – R Code

R uses the package 'boot' for performing Cross Validation error computation. In the following code it can be seen the lowest LOOCV error is for the polynomial of degree 7.

```
library(boot)
library(reshape2)

# Read the auto dataset
df=read.csv("auto_mpg.csv",stringsAsFactors = FALSE) # Data from UCI

# Convert all columns to numeric
df1 <- as.data.frame(sapply(df,as.numeric))

# Select specific columns
df2 <- df1 %>% dplyr::select(cylinder,displacement,
horsepower,weight, acceleration, year,mpg)

# Pick only rows with complete cases
df3 <- df2[complete.cases(df2),]

# Create a random seed
set.seed(17)

# Create a vector for cross-validation error
cv.error=rep(0,10)

# Fit regression models for polynomials from 1,2,..10 and compute the
LOOCV
# error
for (i in 1:10){
    # Fit a regression model of degree 'i'
    glm.fit=glm(mpg~poly(horsepower,i),data=df3)
    # Compute the Leave Out One Cross Validation Error for the model
    cv.error[i]=cv.glm(df3,glm.fit)$delta[1]

}
cv.error
## [1] 24.23151 19.24821 19.33498 19.42443 19.03321 18.97864
18.83305
## [8] 18.96115 19.06863 19.49093

# Create and display a plot between the degree of the model and the
LOOCV error
folds <- seq(1,10)
df <- data.frame(folds,cvError=cv.error)
ggplot(df,aes(x=folds,y=cvError)) + geom_point()
+geom_line(color="blue") + xlab("Degree of Polynomial") + ylab("Cross
Validation Error") + ggtitle("Leave one out Cross Validation - Cross
Validation Error vs Degree of Polynomial")
```

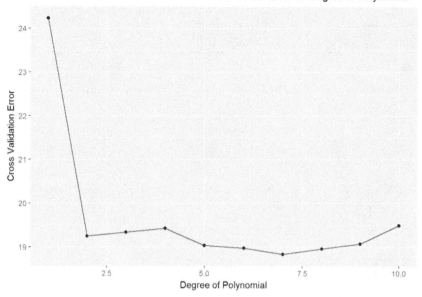

Leave one out Cross Validation - Cross Validation Error vs Degree of Polynomial

5b. Leave out one cross validation (LOOCV) – Python Code

In Python there is no available function to compute Cross Validation error and we have to compute the above formula. For LOOCV I use the K-Fold Cross Validation with K=N

```
import numpy as np
import pandas as pd
import os
import matplotlib.pyplot as plt
from sklearn.linear_model import LinearRegression
from sklearn.cross_validation import train_test_split, KFold
from sklearn.preprocessing import PolynomialFeatures
from sklearn.metrics import mean_squared_error

# Read the auto dataset
autoDF =pd.read_csv("auto_mpg.csv",encoding="ISO-8859-1")
autoDF.shape
autoDF.columns

# Select specific columns
autoDF1=autoDF[['mpg','cylinder','displacement','horsepower','weight','acceleration','year']]
# Convert all columns to numeric
```

```python
autoDF2 = autoDF1.apply(pd.to_numeric, errors='coerce')

# Remove rows with NAs
autoDF3=autoDF2.dropna()
autoDF3.shape

# Set feature and target variables
X=autoDF3[['horsepower']]
y=autoDF3['mpg']

# Compute Leave Out One Cross Validation Error for polynomial of
# degree 1,2,3... 10
def computeCVError(X,y,folds):
    deg=[]
    mse=[]
    degree1=[1,2,3,4,5,6,7,8,9,10]

    nK=len(X)/float(folds)
    xval_err=0

    # Loop over degree 'j'
    for j in degree1:

        # Split the data as 'folds'
        kf = KFold(len(X),n_folds=folds)

        # Loop over the  fold indices
        for train_index, test_index in kf:

            # Create the appropriate train and test partitions from
the fold index
            X_train, X_test = X.iloc[train_index], X.iloc[test_index]
            y_train, y_test = y.iloc[train_index], y.iloc[test_index]

            # For the polynomial degree 'j'
            poly = PolynomialFeatures(degree=j)

            # Transform the X_train and X_test with polynomial
            X_train_poly = poly.fit_transform(X_train)
            X_test_poly = poly.fit_transform(X_test)

            # Fit a model on the transformed data
            linreg = LinearRegression().fit(X_train_poly, y_train)

            # Compute yhat or ypred
            y_pred = linreg.predict(X_test_poly)

                # Compute MSE * n_K/N
```

```
                test_mse = mean_squared_error(y_test,  y_pred)*
float(len(X_train))/ float(len(X))

            # Add the test_mse for this partition of the data
            mse.append(test_mse)

        # Compute the mean of all folds for degree 'j'
        deg.append(np.mean(mse))
    return(deg)

# Create an empty  data frame
df=pd.DataFrame()

# Call the function once. For LOOCV K=N. hence len(X) is passed as
number of folds
cvError=computeCVError(X,y,len(X))

# Create and plot LOOCV error  for each degree of polynomial 1,2,..10
df=pd.DataFrame(cvError)
fig3=df.plot()
fig3=plt.title("Leave one out Cross Validation - Cross Validation
Error vs Degree of Polynomial")
fig3=plt.xlabel("Degree of Polynomial")
fig3=plt.ylabel("Cross validation Error")
fig3.figure.savefig('foo3.png', bbox_inches='tight')
```

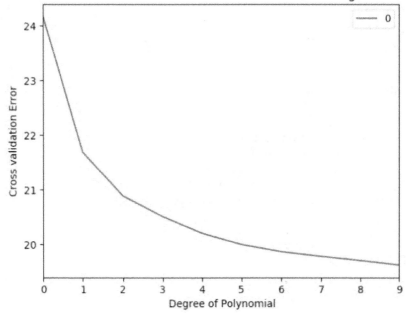

6a K-Fold Cross Validation – R code

Here K-Fold Cross Validation is done for 4, 5 and 10 folds using the R package boot and the glm package. The Cross Validation error for 4, 5, 10 folds are then plotted to see which gives the lowest error

```r
library(boot)
library(reshape2)
set.seed(17)

#Read the auto dataset
df=read.csv("auto_mpg.csv",stringsAsFactors = FALSE) # Data from UCI

# Convert all columns to numeric
df1 <- as.data.frame(sapply(df,as.numeric))

# Select specific columns
df2 <- df1 %>% dplyr::select(cylinder,displacement,
horsepower,weight, acceleration, year,mpg)

# Filter only complete rows
df3 <- df2[complete.cases(df2),]
a=matrix(rep(0,30),nrow=3,ncol=10)
set.seed(17)

# Set the folds as 4,5 and 10
folds<-c(4,5,10)

# Loop over the folds
for(i in seq_along(folds)){

    #Initialize to 0
    cv.error.10=rep(0,10)
    for (j in 1:10){

        # Fit a generalized linear model
        glm.fit=glm(mpg~poly(horsepower,j),data=df3)

        # Compute K Fold Validation error
        a[i,j]=cv.glm(df3,glm.fit,K=folds[i])$delta[1]

    }

}

# Create and display the K Fold Cross Validation Error for polynomial
4,5,10
```

```
# Create a datafranme
b <- t(a)
df <- data.frame(b)
df1 <- cbind(seq(1,10),df)

names(df1) <- c("PolynomialDegree","4-fold","5-fold","10-fold")

# Melt the dataframe
df2 <- melt(df1,id="PolynomialDegree")

# Display multiple plots.
ggplot(df2) + geom_line(aes(x=PolynomialDegree, y=value,
colour=variable),size=2) + xlab("Degree of Polynomial") + ylab("Cross
Validation Error") + ggtitle("K Fold Cross Validation - Cross
Validation Error vs Degree of Polynomial")
```

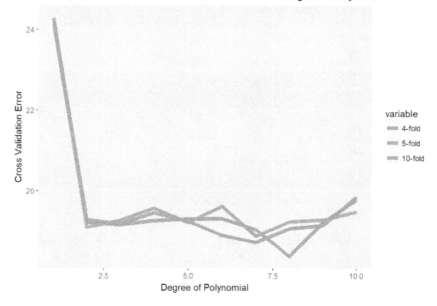

6b. K Fold Cross Validation – Python code

Python does not seem to have a library for performing K-Fold crossvalidation. The implementation of K-Fold Cross Validation Error can be implemented easily and I have done this below. K-Fold cross validation is done for 4,5 and 10 folds and the cross validation error is plotted. **Note:** This is exactly the same implementation as done for LOOCV. In this case case the number of folder is 'K' instead of 'N' which was used in LOOCV

```
import numpy as np
import pandas as pd
```

```
import os
import matplotlib.pyplot as plt
from sklearn.linear_model import LinearRegression
from sklearn.cross_validation import train_test_split, KFold
from sklearn.preprocessing import PolynomialFeatures
from sklearn.metrics import mean_squared_error

# Read the auto dataset
autoDF =pd.read_csv("auto_mpg.csv",encoding="ISO-8859-1")
autoDF.shape
autoDF.columns

# Select specific columns
autoDF1=autoDF[['mpg','cylinder','displacement','horsepower','weight'
,'acceleration','year']]

#Convert all columns to numeric
autoDF2 = autoDF1.apply(pd.to_numeric, errors='coerce')

# Drop NA rows
autoDF3=autoDF2.dropna()
autoDF3.shape

# Set the feature and target variables
#X=autoDF3[['cylinder','displacement','horsepower','weight']]
X=autoDF3[['horsepower']]
y=autoDF3['mpg']

# Create Cross Validation function
def computeCVError(X,y,folds):

    # Create empty lists for degree of polynomial and to hold the K-
Fold CV error
    deg=[]
    mse=[]

    # For degree 1,2,3,..10
    degree1=[1,2,3,4,5,6,7,8,9,10]

    # Set the number of folds
    nK=len(X)/float(folds)
    xval_err=0

    # Loop over the degree 'j' of polynomial
    for j in degree1:

        # Split the data into 'folds'
        kf = KFold(len(X),n_folds=folds)
```

```python
        # Loop over fold indices
        for train_index, test_index in kf:

                # Partition the data acccording the fold indices
generated
                X_train, X_test = X.iloc[train_index], X.iloc[test_index]
                y_train, y_test = y.iloc[train_index], y.iloc[test_index]

                # Transform the X_train and X_test as per the polynomial
degree 'j'
                poly = PolynomialFeatures(degree=j)
                X_train_poly = poly.fit_transform(X_train)
                X_test_poly = poly.fit_transform(X_test)

                # Fit a polynomial regression model
                linreg = LinearRegression().fit(X_train_poly, y_train)

                # Compute yhat or ypred
                y_pred = linreg.predict(X_test_poly)

                # Compute MSE *(nK/N)
                test_mse = mean_squared_error(y_test,
y_pred)*float(len(X_train))/float(len(X))

                # Append to list for different folds
                mse.append(test_mse)

        # Compute the mean for poylnomial 'j'
        deg.append(np.mean(mse))
    return(deg)

# Create and display a plot of K -Folds
#Create an empty dataframe
df=pd.DataFrame()

# Loop over number of folds
for folds in [4,5,10]:

    # Compute K-Fold Cross validation error
    cvError=computeCVError(X,y,folds)
    #print(cvError)
    # Create a new dataframe
    df1=pd.DataFrame(cvError)
    # Concatenate the dataframes
    df=pd.concat([df,df1],axis=1)
    #print(cvError)

# Plot the K-Fold cross validation error vs degree of polynomial
df.columns=['4-fold','5-fold','10-fold']
```

```
df=df.reindex([1,2,3,4,5,6,7,8,9,10])
df
fig2=df.plot()
fig2=plt.title("K Fold Cross Validation - Cross Validation Error vs
Degree of Polynomial")
fig2=plt.xlabel("Degree of Polynomial")
fig2=plt.ylabel("Cross validation Error")
fig2.figure.savefig('foo2.png', bbox_inches='tight')
output
```

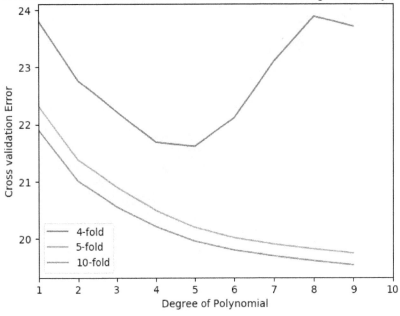

6.   Regression techniques and regularization

While applying Machine Learning techniques on real world data we will find that the data set to include a large number of predictors for a target variable. It is quite likely, that not all the predictors or feature variables will have an impact on the output. Hence it is becomes necessary to choose only those features which will influence the output variable, thus simplifying to a reduced feature set on which to train the ML model on. The techniques that are used for feature selection and to identify the reduced feature set which have an impact on the target variable are the following

- Best fit
- Forward fit
- Backward fit
- Ridge Regression or L2 regularization
- Lasso or L1 regularization

This post includes the equivalent Machine Learning (ML) code in R and Python.

All these methods remove those features, which do not sufficiently influence the output and hence the final ML model will only contain those predictors that actually influence the target variable.

You can download the associated code in this chapter as a R Markdown file from Github at https://github.com/tvganesh/PracticalMachineLearningWithRandPython

1.1 Best Fit

For a dataset with features f1, f2, f3...fn, the 'Best fit' approach, chooses all possible combinations of features and creates separate ML models for each of the different combinations. The best fit algorithm, then uses some filtering criteria based on Adjusted Rsquared, Cp, BIC or AIC to pick out the best model among all models. (Rsquared, Cp, BIC or AIC are measures that are used to determine the relative quality of different models. They help us to pick the best model)

Since the Best-Fit, approach searches the entire solution space, it is computationally infeasible. The number of models that have to be searched increase exponentially as the number of predictors increase. For 'p' predictors a total of 2^p ML models have to be searched. This can be shown as follows

There are C_1 ways to choose single feature ML models among 'n' features, C_2 ways to choose 2 feature models among 'n' models and so on, or

$1 + C_1 + C_2 + ... + C_n$

= Total number of models in Best Fit. Since from Binomial theorem we have

$(1 + x)^n = 1 + C_1 x + C_2 x^2 + ... + C_n x^n$

When x=1 in the equation (1) above, this becomes

$2^n = 1 + C_1 + C_2 + ... + C_n$

Hence, there are 2^n models to search amongst in Best Fit. For 10 features this is 2^{10} or ~1000 models and for 40 features this becomes 2^{40} which almost 1 trillion. Usually there are datasets with 1000 or maybe even 100000 features and Best fit becomes computationally infeasible.

Anyways, I have included the Best Fit approach as I use the Boston crime datasets, which is available both in the MASS package in R and Sklearn in Python and it has 13 features. Even this small feature set takes a bit of time since the Best-fit needs to search among ~ $2^{13} = 8192$ models

Initially I perform a simple Linear Regression Fit to determine statistically insignificant features. By looking at the p-values of the features it can be seen that 'indus' and 'age' features have high p-values and are not significant

1.1a Linear Regression – R code

The R code below implements simple multi-variate regression between the features in the Boston data set and the median value of the house as the target variable. After the fit is done, a summary of the fit is dumped to check the degree of influence of the different feature variables on the target output using the p-values. Best-fit, forward-fit, backward-fit then demonstrate how to select the best set of features for the Machine Learning model.

```
source('RFunctions-1.R')

#Read the Boston crime data
df=read.csv("Boston.csv",stringsAsFactors = FALSE) # Data from MASS -
SL

# Rename the columns to more readable names
names(df) <-c("no", "crimeRate", "zone", "indus", "charles","nox",
"rooms", "age", "distances", "highways","tax", "teacherRatio",
"color", "status", "cost")

# Select specific columns
```

```
df1 <- df %>%
dplyr::select("crimeRate","zone","indus","charles","nox","rooms","age
", "distances", "highways", "tax", "teacherRatio", "color", "status",
"cost")

dim(df1)
## [1] 506  14

# Linear Regression fit
fit <- lm(cost~. ,data=df1)

# Display a summary of all features and their influence p-value
summary(fit)
##
## Call:
## lm(formula = cost ~ ., data = df1)
##
## Residuals:
##     Min      1Q  Median      3Q     Max
## -15.595  -2.730  -0.518   1.777  26.199
##
## Coefficients:
##                 Estimate Std. Error t value Pr(>|t|)
## (Intercept)    3.646e+01  5.103e+00   7.144 3.28e-12 ***
## crimeRate     -1.080e-01  3.286e-02  -3.287 0.001087 **
## zone           4.642e-02  1.373e-02   3.382 0.000778 ***
## indus          2.056e-02  6.150e-02   0.334 0.738288
## charles        2.687e+00  8.616e-01   3.118 0.001925 **
## nox           -1.777e+01  3.820e+00  -4.651 4.25e-06 ***
## rooms          3.810e+00  4.179e-01   9.116  < 2e-16 ***
## age            6.922e-04  1.321e-02   0.052 0.958229
## distances     -1.476e+00  1.995e-01  -7.398 6.01e-13 ***
## highways       3.060e-01  6.635e-02   4.613 5.07e-06 ***
## tax           -1.233e-02  3.760e-03  -3.280 0.001112 **
## teacherRatio  -9.527e-01  1.308e-01  -7.283 1.31e-12 ***
## color          9.312e-03  2.686e-03   3.467 0.000573 ***
## status        -5.248e-01  5.072e-02 -10.347  < 2e-16 ***
## ---
## Signif. codes:  0 '***' 0.001 '**' 0.01 '*' 0.05 '.' 0.1 ' ' 1
##
## Residual standard error: 4.745 on 492 degrees of freedom
## Multiple R-squared:  0.7406, Adjusted R-squared:  0.7338
## F-statistic: 108.1 on 13 and 492 DF,  p-value: < 2.2e-16
```

From the above summary(fit) call, it can be seen that 'indus' and 'age' features have high p-values and are not significant. Next we apply the different feature selection models to automatically remove features that are not significant below

1.1a Best Fit – R code

Best Fit is one of the feature selection methods. The Best Fit requires the 'leaps' R package. The Best fit takes all possible combinations of features to identify the set of features that provide the best fit.

```
library(leaps)
source('RFunctions-1.R')

#Read the Boston crime data - UCI repository
df=read.csv("Boston.csv",stringsAsFactors = FALSE) # Data from MASS -
SL

# Rename the columns to more readable names
names(df) <-c("no", "crimeRate", "zone", "indus", "charles", "nox",
"rooms", "age", "distances", "highways", "tax", "teacherRatio",
"color", "status", "cost")

# Select specific columns
df1 <- df %>% dplyr::select("crimeRate", "zone", "indus", "charles",
"nox", "rooms", "age", "distances", "highways", "tax",
"teacherRatio", "color", "status", "cost")

# Perform a best fit
bestFit=regsubsets(cost~.,df1,nvmax=13)

# Generate a summary of the fit
bfSummary=summary(bestFit)

# Plot the Residual Sum of Squares vs number of variables
plot(bfSummary$rss,xlab="Number of Variables", ylab="RSS", type="l",
main="Best fit RSS vs No of features")

# Get the index of the  model which has the least residual sum of
squares (rss)
a=which.min(bfSummary$rss)

# Mark this in red
points(a,bfSummary$rss[a],col="red",cex=2,pch=20)
```

The plot below shows that the Best fit occurs with all 13 features included. Notice that there is no significant change in RSS from 11 features onward.

Best fit RSS vs No of features

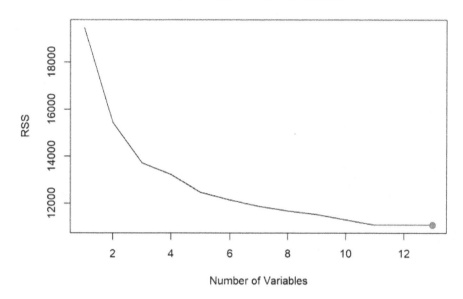

```
# Plot the Cp statistic vs Number of variables for all models
plot(bfSummary$cp,xlab="Number of
Variables",ylab="Cp",type='l',main="Best fit Cp vs No of features")

# Find the model which has  lowest Cp value
b=which.min(bfSummary$cp)

# Mark this in red
points(b,bfSummary$cp[b],col="red",cex=2,pch=20)
```

Based on 'Cp' metric the best fit occurs at 11 features as seen below. The values of the coefficients are also included below

Best fit Cp vs No of features

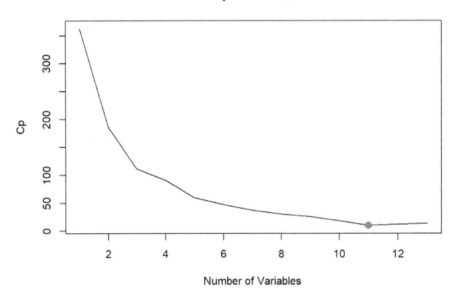

```
# Display the set of features which provide the best fit
coef(bestFit,b)
##   (Intercept)      crimeRate             zone         charles
nox
##  36.341145004   -0.108413345     0.045844929    2.718716303  -
17.376023429
##         rooms      distances         highways             tax
teacherRatio
##   3.801578840   -1.492711460     0.299608454   -0.011777973   -
0.946524570
##         color         status
##   0.009290845   -0.522553457


#  Plot the BIC values of all the models
plot(bfSummary$bic,xlab="Number of
Variables",ylab="BIC",type='l',main="Best fit BIC vs No of Features")
# Find and mark the model with lowest BIC value
c=which.min(bfSummary$bic)

# Mark this model point in red
points(c,bfSummary$bic[c],col="red",cex=2,pch=20)
```

Best fit BIC vs No of Features

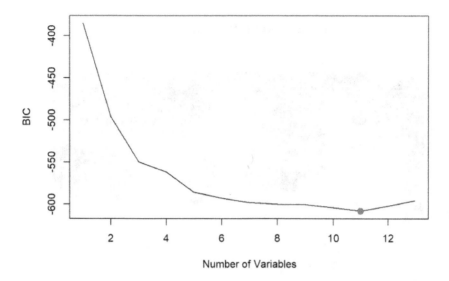

```
# R has some other good plots for best fit
plot(bestFit,scale="r2",main="Rsquared vs No Features")
```

R has the following set of really nice visualizations. The plot below shows the Rsquared for a set of predictor variables. It can be seen when Rsquared starts at 0.74-

indus, charles and age have not been included.

Rsquared vs No Features

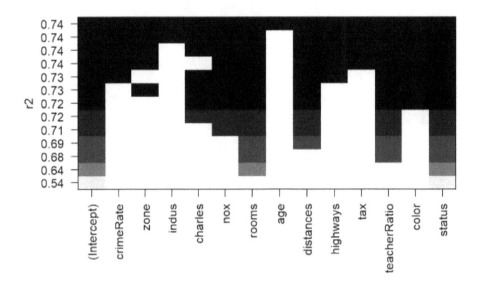

```
plot(bestFit,scale="Cp",main="Cp vs NoFeatures")
```

The Cp plot below for value shows indus, charles and age as not included in the Best fit

Cp vs NoFeatures

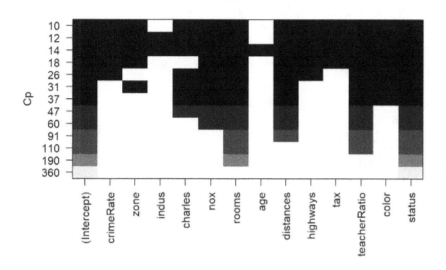

plot(bestFit,scale="bic",main="BIC vs Features")

BIC vs Features

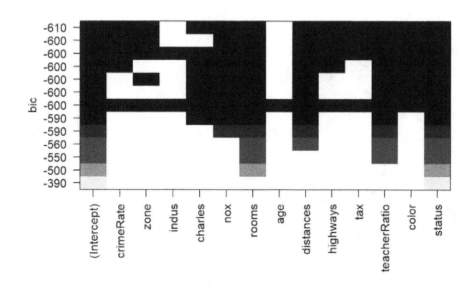

1.1b Best fit (Exhaustive Search) – Python code

The Python package for performing a Best Fit is the Exhaustive Feature Selector (EFS)

```python
import numpy as np
import pandas as pd
import os
import matplotlib.pyplot as plt
from sklearn.model_selection import train_test_split
from sklearn.linear_model import LinearRegression
from mlxtend.feature_selection import ExhaustiveFeatureSelector as
EFS

# Read the Boston crime data
df = pd.read_csv("Boston.csv",encoding = "ISO-8859-1")

#Rename the columns
df.columns=["no","crimeRate", "zone", "indus", "chasRiver", "NO2",
"rooms", "age", "distances", "idxHighways", "taxRate",
"teacherRatio", "color", "status", "cost"]

# Set feature and target variables
X=df[["crimeRate", "zone", "indus", "chasRiver", "NO2",
"rooms","age","distances", "idxHighways", "taxRate", "teacherRatio",
"color", "status"]]
y=df['cost']

# Perform an Exhaustive Search. The EFS and SFS packages use
'neg_mean_squared_error'. The 'mean_squared_error' seems to have been
deprecated. I think this is just the MSE with the a negative sign.
Set the min and max features

lr = LinearRegression()
efs1 = EFS(lr,
           min_features=1,
           max_features=13,
           scoring='neg_mean_squared_error',
           print_progress=True,
           cv=5)

# Create a efs fit
efs1 = efs1.fit(X.as_matrix(), y.as_matrix())

print('Best negtive mean squared error: %.2f' % efs1.best_score_)

## Print the index of  of the best features
print('Best subset:', efs1.best_idx_)
Features: 8191/8191Best negtive mean squared error: -28.92
## ('Best subset:', (0, 1, 4, 6, 7, 8, 9, 10, 11, 12))
```

The indices for the best subset are shown above.

1.2 Forward fit

Forward fit is a greedy algorithm that tries to optimize the features selected, by minimizing the selection criteria (adj R Squared, Cp, AIC or BIC) at every step. For a dataset with features f1, f2, f3...fn, the forward fit starts with the NULL set. It then picks the ML model with a single feature from n features which has the highest adj Rsquared, or minimum Cp, BIC or some such criteria. After picking the 1st feature from n features, which satisfies the criteria the most, the next feature from the remaining n-1 features is chosen. When the 2-feature model that satisfies the selection criteria the best is chosen, another feature from the remaining n-2 features are added and so on. The forward fit is a sub-optimal algorithm. There is no guarantee that the final list of features chosen will be the best among the lot. The computation required for this is of

$n + n - 1 + n - 2 + ..1 = n(n + 1)/2$ which is of the order of n^2. Though forward fit is a sub optimal solution, it is far more computationally efficient than best fit

1.2a Forward fit – R code

Forward fit is another feature selection method. Forward fit in R determines that 11 features are required for the best fit. The features are shown below

```
library(leaps)
# Read the data
df=read.csv("Boston.csv",stringsAsFactors = FALSE) # Data from MASS -
SL
# Rename the columns
names(df) <-c("no", "crimeRate", "zone", "indus","charles", "nox",
"rooms", "age", "distances", "highways", "tax", "teacherRatio",
"color", "status", "cost")

# Select columns
df1 <- df %>% dplyr::select("crimeRate", "zone", "indus", "charles",
"nox", "rooms", "age","distances", "highways", "tax", "teacherRatio",
"color", "status","cost")

#Split as training and test
train_idx <- trainTestSplit(df1,trainPercent=75,seed=5)
train <- df1[train_idx, ]
test <- df1[-train_idx, ]

# Find the best forward fit
fitFwd=regsubsets(cost~.,data=train,nvmax=13,method="forward")
```

```
# Compute the Mean Squared Error (MSE)
valErrors=rep(NA,13)
test.mat=model.matrix(cost~.,data=test)

# Loop through all the features
for(i in 1:13){
    coefi=coef(fitFwd,id=i)

    # Predict the target value
    pred=test.mat[,names(coefi)]%*%coefi

    # Compute the mean squared error
    valErrors[i]=mean((test$cost-pred)^2)
}

# Plot the Residual Sum of Squares vs number of features in the model
plot(valErrors,xlab="Number of Variables",ylab="Validation
Error",type="l", main="Forward fit RSS vs No of features")

# Find the index of the model with the lowest Mean Squared Error
a<-which.min(valErrors)
print(a)
## [1] 11

# Highlight the smallest value
points(c,valErrors[a],col="blue",cex=2,pch=20)
```

Forward fit R selects 11 predictors as the best ML model to predict the 'cost' output variable. The values for these 11 predictors are included below

Forward fit RSS vs No of features

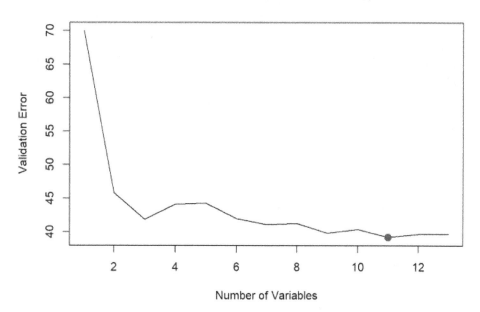

```
#Print the 11 ccoefficients
coefi=coef(fitFwd,id=i)
coefi
##   (Intercept)      crimeRate           zone          indus
charles
##  2.397179e+01 -1.026463e-01  3.118923e-02  1.154235e-04
3.512922e+00
##           nox          rooms            age      distances
highways
## -1.511123e+01  4.945078e+00 -1.513220e-02 -1.307017e+00
2.712534e-01
##           tax    teacherRatio          color         status
## -1.330709e-02 -8.182683e-01  1.143835e-02 -3.750928e-01
```

1.2b Forward fit with Cross Validation – R code

The Python package, SFS, includes N Fold Cross Validation errors for forward and backward fit, so I decided to add this code to R. This is not available in the 'leaps' R package, however the implementation is quite simple.

```r
library(dplyr)
df=read.csv("Boston.csv",stringsAsFactors = FALSE) # Data from MASS -
SL
names(df) <-c("no", "crimeRate", "zone", "indus", "charles", "nox",
"rooms", "age", "distances", "highways", "tax", "teacherRatio",
"color", "status", "cost")

# Select specific columns
df1 <- df %>% dplyr::select("crimeRate", "zone", "indus", "charles",
"nox", "rooms", "age", "distances", "highways", "tax",
"teacherRatio", "color", "status", "cost")

set.seed(6)
# Set max number of features
nvmax<-13

# Initialize cvError toNULL
cvError <- NULL

# Loop through each features
for(i in 1:nvmax){

    # Set no of folds
    noFolds=5

    # Create the rows which fall into different folds from 1..noFolds
    folds = sample(1:noFolds, nrow(df1), replace=TRUE)

    #Initialize cross validation to 0
    cv<-0

    # Loop through the folds
    for(j in 1:noFolds){

        # The training is all rows for which the row is != j (k-1
folds -> training)
        train <- df1[folds!=j,]

        # The rows which have j as the index become the test set
        test <- df1[folds==j,]

        # Create a forward fitting model on the training data
        fitFwd=regsubsets(cost~.,data=train,nvmax=13,method="forward")

        # Select the number of features and get the feature
coefficients
        coefi=coef(fitFwd,id=i)

        #Get the value of the test data
```

```
        test.mat=model.matrix(cost~.,data=test)

        # Multiply the tes data with the fitted coefficients to get
the predicted value
        # pred = b0 + b1x1+b2x2... b13x13
        pred=test.mat[,names(coefi)]%*%coefi

        # Compute Mean Squared Error (MSE)
        rss=mean((test$cost - pred)^2)

        # Add all the Cross Validation errors
        cv=cv+rss
    }
    # Compute the average of MSE for K folds for number of features
'i'
    cvError[i]=cv/noFolds
}

# Create a sequence from 1,2,..13
a <- seq(1,13)

# Create a dataframe with the sequence and the cross validation error
d <- as.data.frame(t(rbind(a,cvError)))
names(d) <- c("Features","CVError")

#Plot the CV Error vs No of Features
ggplot(d,aes(x=Features,y=CVError),color="blue") + geom_point() +
geom_line(color="blue") + xlab("No of features") + ylab("Cross
Validation Error") + ggtitle("Forward Selection - Cross Valdation
Error vs No of Features")
```

Forward fit with 5 fold cross validation indicates that all 13 features are required

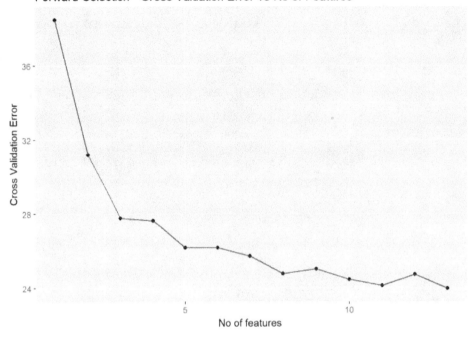

Forward Selection - Cross Valdation Error vs No of Features

```
# Find the the index of the model which gives the least MSE
a=which.min(cvError)
print(a)
## [1] 13

#Print the 13 coefficients of these features
coefi=coef(fitFwd,id=a)
coefi
##   (Intercept)       crimeRate            zone           indus
charles
##  36.650645380    -0.107980979    0.056237669     0.027016678
4.270631466
##           nox           rooms             age       distances
highways
## -19.000715500     3.714720418     0.019952654    -1.472533973
0.326758004
##           tax     teacherRatio           color          status
##  -0.011380750    -0.972862622     0.009549938    -0.582159093
```

1.2c Forward fit – Python code

The Forwatd Fit in Python uses the Sequential Feature Selection (SFS) package (SFS)(https://rasbt.github.io/mlxtend/user_guide/feature_selection/SequentialFeatureSelector/)

Note: The Cross validation error for SFS in sklearn is negative, possibly because it computes the 'neg_mean_squared_error'. The earlier 'mean_squared_error' in the package seems to have been deprecated. I have taken the -ve of this neg_mean_squared_error. I think this would give mean_squared_error.

```python
import numpy as np
import pandas as pd
import os
import matplotlib.pyplot as plt
from sklearn.model_selection import train_test_split
from sklearn.linear_model import LinearRegression
from sklearn.datasets import load_boston
from mlxtend.plotting import plot_sequential_feature_selection as plot_sfs
import matplotlib.pyplot as plt
from mlxtend.feature_selection import SequentialFeatureSelector as SFS
from sklearn.linear_model import LinearRegression

# Read the Boston data
df = pd.read_csv("Boston.csv",encoding = "ISO-8859-1")

#Rename the columns to readable values
df.columns=["no", "crimeRate", "zone", "indus", "chasRiver", "NO2",
"rooms", "age","distances", "idxHighways", "taxRate", "teacherRatio",
"color", "status", "cost"]

# Set the features and the target variables
X=df[["crimeRate", "zone", "indus", "chasRiver", "NO2", "rooms",
"age", "distances", "idxHighways", "taxRate", "teacherRatio",
"color", "status"]]
y=df['cost']

# Fit a Linear Regression model
lr = LinearRegression()

# Create a forward fit model
sfs = SFS(lr,
          k_features=(1,13),
          forward=True, # Forward fit
          floating=False,
          scoring='neg_mean_squared_error',
          cv=5)

# Fit this on the data
sfs = sfs.fit(X.as_matrix(), y.as_matrix())
```

```
# Get all the details of the forward fits
a=sfs.get_metric_dict()

# Create empty lists for storing the cross validation errors
n=[]
o=[]

# Compute the mean cross validation scores
for i in np.arange(1,13):
    n.append(-np.mean(a[i]['cv_scores']))

# Create a sequence of 13 integers
m=np.arange(1,13)

# Plot the CV scores vs the number of features
fig1=plt.plot(m,n)
fig1=plt.title('Mean CV Scores vs No of features')
fig1.figure.savefig('fig1.png', bbox_inches='tight')

print(pd.DataFrame.from_dict(sfs.get_metric_dict(confidence_interval=
0.90)).T)

# Get the index of the model features with the lowest cross
validation error
idx = np.argmin(n)
print "No of features=",idx

#Get the features indices for the best forward fit and convert to
list
b=list(a[idx]['feature_idx'])
print(b)

# Index the column names.
# Features from forward fit
print("Features selected in forward fit")
print(X.columns[b])
##     avg_score ci_bound
cv_scores  \
## 1    -42.6185  19.0465  [-23.5582499971, -41.8215743748, -
73.993608929...
## 2    -36.0651  16.3184  [-18.002498199, -40.1507894517, -
56.5286659068...
## 3    -34.1001   20.87   [-9.43012884381, -25.9584955394, -
36.184188174...
## 4    -33.7681  20.1638  [-8.86076528781, -28.650217633, -
35.7246353855...
## 5    -33.6392  20.5271  [-8.90807628524, -28.0684679108, -
35.827463022...
```

```
## 6    -33.6276   19.0859   [-9.549485942, -30.9724602876, -
32.6689523347,...
## 7    -32.4082   19.1455   [-10.0177149635, -28.3780298492, -
30.926917231...
## 8    -32.3697    18.533   [-11.1431684243, -27.5765510172, -
31.168994094...
## 9    -32.4016   21.5561   [-10.8972555995, -25.739780653, -
30.1837430353...
## 10   -32.8504   22.6508   [-12.3909282079, -22.1533250755, -
33.385407342...
## 11   -34.1065   24.7019   [-12.6429253721, -22.1676650245, -
33.956999528...
## 12   -35.5814    25.693   [-12.7303397453, -25.0145323483, -
34.211898373...
## 13   -37.1318   23.2657   [-12.4603005692, -26.0486211062, -
33.074137979...
##
##                                      feature_idx   std_dev   std_err
## 1                                           (12,)   18.9042   9.45212
## 2                                        (10, 12)   16.1965   8.09826
## 3                                     (10, 12, 5)   20.7142   10.3571
## 4                                  (10, 3, 12, 5)   20.0132   10.0066
## 5                               (0, 10, 3, 12, 5)   20.3738   10.1869
## 6                            (0, 3, 5, 7, 10, 12)   18.9433   9.47167
## 7                         (0, 2, 3, 5, 7, 10, 12)   19.0026   9.50128
## 8                      (0, 1, 2, 3, 5, 7, 10, 12)   18.3946   9.19731
## 9                  (0, 1, 2, 3, 5, 7, 10, 11, 12)   21.3952   10.6976
## 10              (0, 1, 2, 3, 4, 5, 7, 10, 11, 12)   22.4816   11.2408
## 11           (0, 1, 2, 3, 4, 5, 6, 7, 10, 11, 12)   24.5175   12.2587
## 12        (0, 1, 2, 3, 4, 5, 6, 7, 9, 10, 11, 12)   25.5012   12.7506
## 13     (0, 1, 2, 3, 4, 5, 6, 7, 8, 9, 10, 11, 12)   23.0919    11.546
## No of features= 7
## [0, 2, 3, 5, 7, 10, 12]
##
#######################################################################
############
## Features selected in forward fit
## Index([u'crimeRate', u'indus', u'chasRiver', u'rooms',
u'distances',
##        u'teacherRatio', u'status'],
##      dtype='object')
```

The table above shows the average score, 10 fold CV errors, the features included at every step, std. deviation and std. error

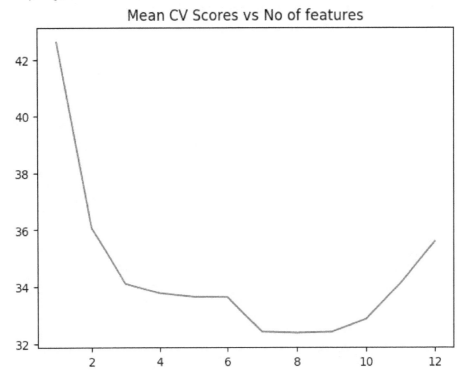

The above plot indicates that 8 features provide the lowest Mean CV error

1.3 Backward Fit

Backward fit belongs to the class of greedy algorithms which tries to optimize the feature set, by dropping a feature at every stage which results in the worst performance for a given criteria of Adj R Squared, Cp, BIC or AIC. For a dataset with features f1, f2, f3...fn, the backward fit starts with the all the features f1, f2.. fn to begin with. It then pick the ML model with a n-1 features by dropping the feature, f_j, for e.g., the inclusion of which results in the worst performance in adj R Squared, or minimum Cp, BIC or some such criteria. At every step, 1 feature is dropped. There is no guarantee that the final list of features chosen will be the best among the lot. The computation required for this is of $n + n - 1 + n - 2 + ..1 = n(n + 1)/2$ which is of the order of n^2. Though backward fit is a sub optimal solution, it is far more computationally efficient than best fit and is the third feature selection technique.

1.3a Backward fit – R code

The code below implements the Backward fit, feature selection technique

```r
library(dplyr)

# Read the Boston data
df=read.csv("Boston.csv",stringsAsFactors = FALSE) # Data from MASS -
SL

# Rename the columns
names(df) <-c("no", "crimeRate", "zone", "indus", "charles","nox",
"rooms", "age", "distances", "highways", "tax", "teacherRatio",
"color", "status", "cost")

# Select columns
df1 <- df %>% dplyr::select("crimeRate", "zone", "indus", "charles",
"nox", "rooms", "age", "distances", "highways", "tax",
"teacherRatio", "color", "status", "cost")

set.seed(6)

# Set max number of features
nvmax<-13

cvError <- NULL
# Loop through each features
for(i in 1:nvmax){

    # Set no of folds
    noFolds=5

    # Create the rows which fall into different folds from 1..noFolds
    folds = sample(1:noFolds, nrow(df1), replace=TRUE)

    #Initialize cross validation error to 0
    cv<-0

    # Loop through the number of folds
    for(j in 1:noFolds){

        # The training is all rows for which the row is != j
        train <- df1[folds!=j,]

        # The rows which have j as the index become the test set
        test <- df1[folds==j,]

        # Create a backward fitting model on the training dataset
```

```r
        fitFwd=regsubsets(cost~., data=train, nvmax=13,
method="backward")

        # Select the number of features and get the feature
coefficients
        coefi=coef(fitFwd,id=i)

        #Get the value of the test data
        test.mat=model.matrix(cost~.,data=test)

        # Multiply the tes data with teh fitted coefficients to get
the predicted value
        # pred = b0 + b1x1+b2x2... b13x13
        pred=test.mat[,names(coefi)]%*%coefi

        # Compute Mean Squared Error (MSE)
        rss=mean((test$cost - pred)^2)

        # Add the Residual sum of square
        cv=cv+rss
    }
    # Compute the average of MSE for K folds for number of features
'i'
    cvError[i]=cv/noFolds
}

# Create a sequence of integers
a <- seq(1,13)

# Create a dataframe with the cross validation error
d <- as.data.frame(t(rbind(a,cvError)))

# Rename the columns
names(d) <- c("Features","CVError")

# Plot the Cross Validation Error vs Number of features
ggplot(d,aes(x=Features,y=CVError),color="blue") + geom_point() +
geom_line(color="blue") + xlab("No of features") + ylab("Cross
Validation Error") + ggtitle("Backward Selection - Cross Valdation
Error vs No of Features")
```

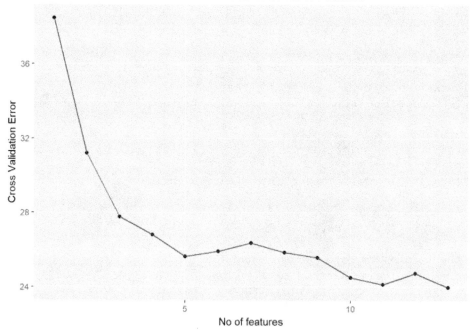

Backward Selection - Cross Valdation Error vs No of Features

```
# Get the index of  model with the lowest cross validation
a=which.min(cvError)
print(a)
## [1] 13

#Print the 13 coefficients of these features
coefi=coef(fitFwd,id=a)
coefi
##   (Intercept)      crimeRate           zone            indus
charles
##   36.650645380   -0.107980979    0.056237669     0.027016678
4.270631466
##            nox          rooms            age        distances
highways
## -19.000715500    3.714720418    0.019952654   -1.472533973
0.326758004
##            tax    teacherRatio          color           status
##   -0.011380750   -0.972862622    0.009549938   -0.582159093
```

Backward selection in R also indicates the 13 features and the corresponding coefficients as providing the best fit

1.3b Backward fit – Python code

The Backward Fit in Python uses the Sequential feature selection (SFS) package
(SFS)(https://rasbt.github.io/mlxtend/user_guide/feature_selection/SequentialFeatureS
elector/)

```python
import numpy as np
import pandas as pd
import os
import matplotlib.pyplot as plt
from sklearn.model_selection import train_test_split
from sklearn.linear_model import LinearRegression
from mlxtend.plotting import plot_sequential_feature_selection as
plot_sfs
import matplotlib.pyplot as plt
from mlxtend.feature_selection import SequentialFeatureSelector as
SFS
from sklearn.linear_model import LinearRegression

# Read the Boston data
df = pd.read_csv("Boston.csv",encoding = "ISO-8859-1")

#Rename the columns to more readable names
df.columns=["no", "crimeRate", "zone", "indus", "chasRiver", "NO2",
"rooms", "age", "distances", "idxHighways", "taxRate",
"teacherRatio", "color", "status", "cost"]

# Set the feature and target variables
X=df[["crimeRate","zone", "indus", "chasRiver", "NO2", "rooms",
"age", "distances", "idxHighways", "taxRate", "teacherRatio",
"color", "status"]]
y=df['cost']

# Create a linear regression model
lr = LinearRegression()

# Create the SFS model
sfs = SFS(lr,
         k_features=(1,13),
         forward=False, # Backward
         floating=False,
         scoring='neg_mean_squared_error',
         cv=5)

# Fit the model
sfs = sfs.fit(X.as_matrix(), y.as_matrix())
a=sfs.get_metric_dict()

# Create an empty list for storing  MSE
n=[]
o=[]
```

```
# Compute the mean of the validation scores
for i in np.arange(1,13):
    # Append the cross validation scores
    n.append(-np.mean(a[i]['cv_scores']))

# Create a sequence of 12 integers
m=np.arange(1,13)
# Plot the Validation scores vs number of features
fig2=plt.plot(m,n)
fig2=plt.title('Mean CV Scores vs No of features')
fig2.figure.savefig('fig2.png', bbox_inches='tight')

print(pd.DataFrame.from_dict(sfs.get_metric_dict(confidence_interval=
0.90)).T)

# Get the index of the model with the least cross validation error
idx = np.argmin(n)
print "No of features=",idx
#Get the features indices for the best forward fit and convert to
list
b=list(a[idx]['feature_idx'])

# Index the column names.
# Features from backward fit
print("Features selected in bacward fit")
print(X.columns[b])
##      avg_score ci_bound
cv_scores  \
## 1    -42.6185  19.0465  [-23.5582499971, -41.8215743748, -
73.993608929...
## 2    -36.0651  16.3184  [-18.002498199, -40.1507894517, -
56.5286659068...
## 3    -35.4992  13.9619  [-17.2329292677, -44.4178648308, -
51.633177846...
## 4     -33.463  12.4081  [-20.6415333292, -37.3247852146, -
47.479302977...
## 5    -33.1038  10.6156  [-20.2872309863, -34.6367078466, -
45.931870352...
## 6    -32.0638  10.0933  [-19.4463829372, -33.460638577, -
42.726257249,...
## 7    -30.7133  9.23881  [-19.4425181917, -31.1742902259, -
40.531266671...
## 8    -29.7432  9.84468  [-19.445277268, -30.0641187173, -
40.2561247122...
## 9    -29.0878  9.45027  [-19.3545569877, -30.094768669, -
39.7506036377...
## 10   -28.9225  9.39697  [-18.562171585, -29.968504938, -
39.9586835965,...
```

```
## 11  -29.4301  10.8831  [-18.3346152225, -30.3312847532, -
45.065432793...
## 12  -30.4589  11.1486  [-18.493389527, -35.0290639374, -
45.1558231765...
## 13  -37.1318  23.2657  [-12.4603005692, -26.0486211062, -
33.074137979...
##
##                                 feature_idx  std_dev  std_err
## 1                                    (12,)   18.9042  9.45212
## 2                                  (10, 12)  16.1965  8.09826
## 3                                (10, 12, 7) 13.8576  6.92881
## 4                              (12, 10, 4, 7) 12.3154  6.15772
## 5                           (4, 7, 8, 10, 12) 10.5363  5.26816
## 6                         (4, 7, 8, 9, 10, 12) 10.0179  5.00896
## 7                      (1, 4, 7, 8, 9, 10, 12) 9.16981  4.58491
## 8                  (1, 4, 7, 8, 9, 10, 11, 12) 9.77116  4.88558
## 9               (0, 1, 4, 7, 8, 9, 10, 11, 12) 9.37969  4.68985
## 10           (0, 1, 4, 6, 7, 8, 9, 10, 11, 12)  9.3268   4.6634
## 11        (0, 1, 3, 4, 6, 7, 8, 9, 10, 11, 12) 10.8018  5.40092
## 12     (0, 1, 2, 3, 4, 6, 7, 8, 9, 10, 11, 12) 11.0653  5.53265
## 13  (0, 1, 2, 3, 4, 5, 6, 7, 8, 9, 10, 11, 12) 23.0919   11.546
## No of features= 9
## Features selected in bacward fit
## Index([u'crimeRate', u'zone', u'NO2', u'distances',
u'idxHighways', u'taxRate',
##        u'teacherRatio', u'color', u'status'],
##       dtype='object')
```

The table above shows the average score, 10 fold CV errors, the features included at every step, std. deviation and std. error

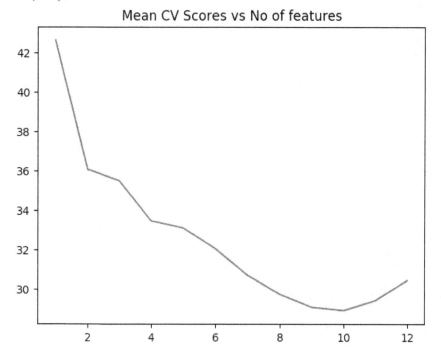

Backward fit in Python indicate that 10 features provide the best fit

1.3c Sequential Floating Forward Selection (SFFS) – Python code

The Sequential Feature search also includes 'floating' variants, which include or exclude features conditionally, once they were excluded or included. The SFFS can conditionally include features, which were excluded from the previous step, if it results in a better fit. This option will tend to a better solution, than plain simple SFS. These variants are included below

```
import numpy as np
import pandas as pd
import os
import matplotlib.pyplot as plt
from sklearn.model_selection import train_test_split
from sklearn.linear_model import LinearRegression
from sklearn.datasets import load_boston
```

```python
from mlxtend.plotting import plot_sequential_feature_selection as
plot_sfs
import matplotlib.pyplot as plt
from mlxtend.feature_selection import SequentialFeatureSelector as
SFS
from sklearn.linear_model import LinearRegression

# Read the Boston data set
df = pd.read_csv("Boston.csv",encoding = "ISO-8859-1")

#Rename the columns to more readable names
df.columns=["no", "crimeRate", "zone" ,"indus", "chasRiver", "NO2",
"rooms", "age","distances", "idxHighways", "taxRate", "teacherRatio",
"color", "status", "cost"]

# Set the feature and target variables
X=df[["crimeRate", "zone", "indus", "chasRiver", "NO2", "rooms",
"age",  "distances", "idxHighways", "taxRate", "teacherRatio",
"color","status"]]
y=df['cost']

# Fit a linear regression model
lr = LinearRegression()

# Create a SFFS model with forward=True
sffs = SFS(lr,
          k_features=(1,13),
          forward=True,  # Forward
          floating=True, #Floating
          scoring='neg_mean_squared_error',
          cv=5)

# Fit a SFFS model
sffs = sffs.fit(X.as_matrix(), y.as_matrix())
a=sffs.get_metric_dict()

# Initialize lists for storing the MSE
n=[]
o=[]
# Compute mean validation scores
for i in np.arange(1,13):
    # Append the CV scores to the list
    n.append(-np.mean(a[i]['cv_scores']))

# Create a sequence of 13
m=np.arange(1,13)

# Plot the cross validation score vs number of features
fig3=plt.plot(m,n)
```

```
fig3=plt.title('SFFS:Mean CV Scores vs No of features')
fig3.figure.savefig('fig3.png', bbox_inches='tight')

print(pd.DataFrame.from_dict(sffs.get_metric_dict(confidence_interval
=0.90)).T)

# Get the index of the model with least CV score
idx = np.argmin(n)
print "No of features=",idx

#Get the features indices for the best forward floating fit and
convert to list
b=list(a[idx]['feature_idx'])
print(b)
print("##################################################################
####################")
# Index the column names.
# Features from forward fit
print("Features selected in forward fit")
print(X.columns[b])
##      avg_score ci_bound
cv_scores  \
## 1   -42.6185  19.0465  [-23.5582499971, -41.8215743748, -
73.993608929...
## 2   -36.0651  16.3184  [-18.002498199, -40.1507894517, -
56.5286659068...
## 3   -34.1001   20.87   [-9.43012884381, -25.9584955394, -
36.184188174...
## 4   -33.7681  20.1638  [-8.86076528781, -28.650217633, -
35.7246353855...
## 5   -33.6392  20.5271  [-8.90807628524, -28.0684679108, -
35.827463022...
## 6   -33.6276  19.0859  [-9.549485942, -30.9724602876, -
32.6689523347,...
## 7   -32.1834  12.1001  [-17.9491036167, -39.6479234651, -
45.470227740...
## 8   -32.0908  11.8179  [-17.4389015788, -41.2453629843, -
44.247557798...
## 9   -31.0671  10.1581  [-17.2689542913, -37.4379370429, -
41.366372300...
## 10  -28.9225  9.39697  [-18.562171585, -29.968504938, -
39.9586835965,...
## 11  -29.4301  10.8831  [-18.3346152225, -30.3312847532, -
45.065432793...
## 12  -30.4589  11.1486  [-18.493389527, -35.0290639374, -
45.1558231765...
## 13  -37.1318  23.2657  [-12.4603005692, -26.0486211062, -
33.074137979...
##
```

179

```
##                               feature_idx  std_dev  std_err
## 1                                   (12,)  18.9042  9.45212
## 2                                (10, 12)  16.1965  8.09826
## 3                             (10, 12, 5)  20.7142  10.3571
## 4                          (10, 3, 12, 5)  20.0132  10.0066
## 5                       (0, 10, 3, 12, 5)  20.3738  10.1869
## 6                    (0, 3, 5, 7, 10, 12)  18.9433  9.47167
## 7                  (0, 1, 2, 3, 7, 10, 12)  12.0097  6.00487
## 8               (0, 1, 2, 3, 7, 8, 10, 12)  11.7297  5.86484
## 9            (0, 1, 2, 3, 7, 8, 9, 10, 12)  10.0822  5.04111
## 10        (0, 1, 4, 6, 7, 8, 9, 10, 11, 12)   9.3268   4.6634
## 11        (0, 1, 3, 4, 6, 7, 8, 9, 10, 11, 12)  10.8018  5.40092
## 12     (0, 1, 2, 3, 4, 6, 7, 8, 9, 10, 11, 12)  11.0653  5.53265
## 13  (0, 1, 2, 3, 4, 5, 6, 7, 8, 9, 10, 11, 12)  23.0919   11.546
## No of features= 9
## [0, 1, 2, 3, 7, 8, 9, 10, 12]
##
###########################################################################
############
## Features selected in forward fit
## Index([u'crimeRate', u'zone', u'indus', u'chasRiver',
u'distances',
##         u'idxHighways', u'taxRate', u'teacherRatio', u'status'],
##       dtype='object')
```

The table above shows the average score, 10 fold CV errors, the features included at every step, std. deviation and std. error

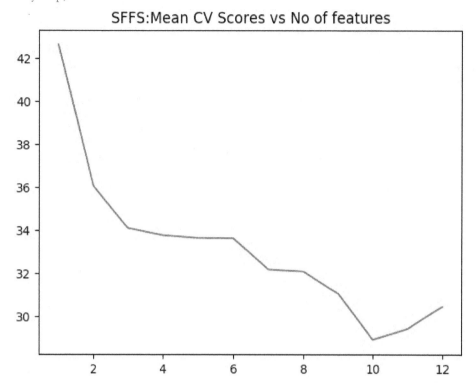

SFFS provides the best fit with 10 predictors

1.3d Sequential Floating Backward Selection (SFBS) – Python code

The SFBS is an extension of the SBS. Here features that are excluded at any stage can be conditionally included if the resulting feature set gives a better fit. The implementation is in Python below

```
import numpy as np
import pandas as pd
import os
import matplotlib.pyplot as plt
from sklearn.model_selection import train_test_split
from sklearn.linear_model import LinearRegression
from sklearn.datasets import load_boston
```

```python
from mlxtend.plotting import plot_sequential_feature_selection as
plot_sfs
import matplotlib.pyplot as plt
from mlxtend.feature_selection import SequentialFeatureSelector as
SFS
from sklearn.linear_model import LinearRegression

# Read the Boston data set
df = pd.read_csv("Boston.csv",encoding = "ISO-8859-1")

#Rename the columns to readable names
df.columns=["no", "crimeRate", "zone","indus", "chasRiver",
"NO2","rooms", "age", "distances", "idxHighways", "taxRate",
"teacherRatio", "color", "status", "cost"]

# Set the feature and target variables
X=df[["crimeRate", "zone", "indus", "chasRiver", "NO2", "rooms",
"age", "distances", "idxHighways", "taxRate", "teacherRatio",
"color", "status"]]
y=df['cost']

# Fit a linear regression model
lr = LinearRegression()

# Perform a SFBS model with forward =False
sffs = SFS(lr,
          k_features=(1,13),
          forward=False, # Backward
          floating=True, # Floating
          scoring='neg_mean_squared_error',
          cv=5)

# Fit a SFBS model
sffs = sffs.fit(X.as_matrix(), y.as_matrix())
a=sffs.get_metric_dict()

# Create a list for storing CV Errors
n=[]
o=[]

# Compute the mean cross validation score
for i in np.arange(1,13):
    # Append CV scores to list
    n.append(-np.mean(a[i]['cv_scores']))

# Create a sequence of 13 integers
m=np.arange(1,13)

#Plot CV Scores for SFBS model vs number of features
```

```
fig4=plt.plot(m,n)
fig4=plt.title('SFBS: Mean CV Scores vs No of features')
fig4.figure.savefig('fig4.png', bbox_inches='tight')

print(pd.DataFrame.from_dict(sffs.get_metric_dict(confidence_interval
=0.90)).T)

# Get the index of the model with least CV score
idx = np.argmin(n)
print "No of features=",idx
#Get the features indices for the best backward floating fit and
convert to list
b=list(a[idx]['feature_idx'])
print(b)

print("################################################################
###################")
# Index the column names.
# Features from forward fit
print("Features selected in backward floating fit")
print(X.columns[b])
##      avg_score ci_bound
cv_scores  \
## 1   -42.6185  19.0465  [-23.5582499971, -41.8215743748, -
73.993608929...
## 2   -36.0651  16.3184  [-18.002498199, -40.1507894517, -
56.5286659068...
## 3   -34.1001   20.87   [-9.43012884381, -25.9584955394, -
36.184188174...
## 4    -33.463  12.4081  [-20.6415333292, -37.3247852146, -
47.479302977...
## 5   -32.3699  11.2725  [-20.8771078371, -34.9825657934, -
45.813447203...
## 6   -31.6742  11.2458  [-20.3082500364, -33.2288990522, -
45.535507868...
## 7   -30.7133  9.23881  [-19.4425181917, -31.1742902259, -
40.531266671...
## 8   -29.7432  9.84468  [-19.445277268, -30.0641187173, -
40.2561247122...
## 9   -29.0878  9.45027  [-19.3545569877, -30.094768669, -
39.7506036377...
## 10  -28.9225  9.39697  [-18.562171585, -29.968504938, -
39.9586835965,...
## 11  -29.4301  10.8831  [-18.3346152225, -30.3312847532, -
45.065432793...
## 12  -30.4589  11.1486  [-18.493389527, -35.0290639374, -
45.1558231765...
## 13  -37.1318  23.2657  [-12.4603005692, -26.0486211062, -
33.074137979...
```

183

```
##
##                                     feature_idx  std_dev  std_err
## 1                                        (12,)   18.9042  9.45212
## 2                                     (10, 12)   16.1965  8.09826
## 3                                  (10, 12, 5)   20.7142  10.3571
## 4                               (4, 10, 7, 12)   12.3154  6.15772
## 5                           (12, 10, 4, 1, 7)   11.1883  5.59417
## 6                        (4, 7, 8, 10, 11, 12)  11.1618  5.58088
## 7                     (1, 4, 7, 8, 9, 10, 12)   9.16981  4.58491
## 8                  (1, 4, 7, 8, 9, 10, 11, 12)  9.77116  4.88558
## 9               (0, 1, 4, 7, 8, 9, 10, 11, 12)  9.37969  4.68985
## 10          (0, 1, 4, 6, 7, 8, 9, 10, 11, 12)   9.3268   4.6634
## 11        (0, 1, 3, 4, 6, 7, 8, 9, 10, 11, 12)  10.8018  5.40092
## 12     (0, 1, 2, 3, 4, 6, 7, 8, 9, 10, 11, 12)  11.0653  5.53265
## 13  (0, 1, 2, 3, 4, 5, 6, 7, 8, 9, 10, 11, 12)  23.0919   11.546
## No of features= 9
## [0, 1, 4, 7, 8, 9, 10, 11, 12]
##
###########################################################################
############
## Features selected in backward floating fit
## Index([u'crimeRate', u'zone', u'NO2', u'distances',
u'idxHighways', u'taxRate',
##         u'teacherRatio', u'color', u'status'],
##       dtype='object')
```

The table above shows the average score, 10 fold CV errors, the features included at every step, std. deviation and std. error

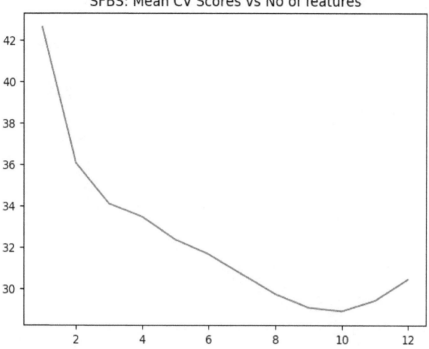

SFBS: Mean CV Scores vs No of features

SFBS indicates that 10 features are needed for the best fit

1.4 Ridge regression

In Linear Regression the Residual Sum of Squares (RSS) is given as

$$RSS = \sum_{i=1}^{n}\left(y_i - \beta_0 - \sum_{j=1}^{p}\beta_j x_{ij}\right)^2$$

Ridge regularization $= \sum_{i=1}^{n}\left(y_i - \beta_0 - \sum_{j=1}^{p}\beta_j x_{ij}\right)^2 + \lambda \sum_{j=1}^{p}\beta^2$

where λ is the regularization or tuning parameter. Increasing λ increases the penalty on the coefficients thus shrinking them. However, in Ridge Regression features that do not influence the target variable will shrink closer to zero, but never become zero except for very large values of λ. Ridge regression does automatic feature selection.

1.4a Ridge Regression – R code

Ridge regression in R requires the 'glmnet' package . The code below implements Ridge regression in R. The plot below shows how changing the value of λ results in coefficient shrinkage

```
library(glmnet)
library(dplyr)

# Read the Boston data
df=read.csv("Boston.csv",stringsAsFactors = FALSE) # Data from MASS -
SL

#Rename the columns to more readable names
names(df) <-c("no", "crimeRate", "zone", "indus", "charles", "nox",
"rooms", "age", "distances", "highways", "tax", "teacherRatio",
"color", "status", "cost")

# Select specific columns
df1 <- df %>% dplyr::select("crimeRate", "zone", "indus", "charles",
"nox", "rooms", "age", "distances", "highways", "tax",
"teacherRatio", "color", "status", "cost")

# Set X and y as matrices - feature and target variables
X=as.matrix(df1[,1:13])
y=df1$cost

# Fit a Ridge model. Note : alpha=0 for ridge regression
fitRidge <-glmnet(X,y,alpha=0)

#Plot the model where the coefficient shrinkage is plotted vs log
lambda
plot(fitRidge, xvar="lambda", label=TRUE,main= "Ridge regression
coefficient shrikage vs log lambda")
```

The plot below shows how the 13 coefficients for the 13 predictors vary when lambda is increased. The x-axis includes log (lambda). We can see that increasing lambda from 10^2 to 10^6 significantly shrinks the coefficients. We can draw a vertical line from

186

the x-axis and read the values of the 13 coefficients. Some of them will be close to zero

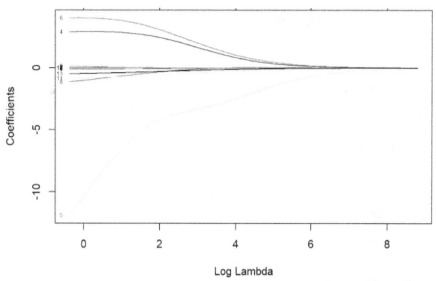

Ridge regression coefficient shrikage vs log lambda

```
# Compute the cross validation error
cvRidge=cv.glmnet(X,y,alpha=0)

#Plot the cross validation error
plot(cvRidge, main="Ridge regression Cross Validation Error (10
fold)")
```

This gives the 10 fold Cross Validation Error with respect to log (lambda).As lambda increase, the MSE increases

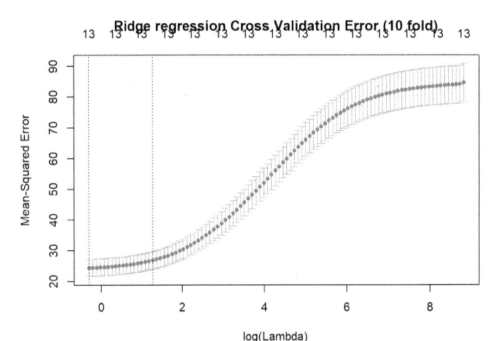

1.4a Ridge Regression – Python code

The coefficient shrinkage for Python can be plotted like R using Least Angle Regression model a.k.a. LARS package. This is included below

```python
import numpy as np
import pandas as pd
import os
import matplotlib.pyplot as plt
from sklearn.model_selection import train_test_split

# Read the Boston data set
df = pd.read_csv("Boston.csv",encoding = "ISO-8859-1")

#Rename the columns to more readable names
df.columns=["no", "crimeRate", "zone", "indus", "chasRiver", "NO2",
"rooms", "age", "distances", "idxHighways", "taxRate",
"teacherRatio", "color", "status","cost"]
```

```python
# Set the feature and target variables
X=df[["crimeRate", "zone", "indus", "chasRiver", "NO2", "rooms",
"age","distances", "idxHighways", "taxRate", "teacherRatio", "color",
"status"]]
y=df['cost']

from sklearn.preprocessing import MinMaxScaler
scaler = MinMaxScaler()

from sklearn.linear_model import Ridge
X_train, X_test, y_train, y_test = train_test_split(X, y,
                                                    random_state = 0)

# Scale and transform the X_train and X_test
X_train_scaled = scaler.fit_transform(X_train)
X_test_scaled = scaler.transform(X_test)

# Fit a ridge regression with alpha=20
linridge = Ridge(alpha=20.0).fit(X_train_scaled, y_train)

# Print the training R squared
print('R-squared score (training): {:.3f}'
    .format(linridge.score(X_train_scaled, y_train)))

# Print the test Rsquared
print('R-squared score (test): {:.3f}'
    .format(linridge.score(X_test_scaled, y_test)))
print('Number of non-zero features: {}'
    .format(np.sum(linridge.coef_ != 0)))

# Create empty lists for computing training and test R squared
trainingRsquared=[]
testRsquared=[]

# Plot the effect of alpha on the test Rsquared
print('Ridge regression: effect of alpha regularization parameter\n')
# Choose a list of alpha values
for this_alpha in [0.001,.01,.1,0, 1, 10, 20, 50, 100, 1000]:
    linridge = Ridge(alpha = this_alpha).fit(X_train_scaled, y_train)

    # Compute training rsquared
    r2_train = linridge.score(X_train_scaled, y_train)

    # Compute test rsqaured
    r2_test = linridge.score(X_test_scaled, y_test)
    num_coeff_bigger = np.sum(abs(linridge.coef_) > 1.0)


    # Append the training  R squared
```

```python
    trainingRsquared.append(r2_train)

    # Append the test  R squared
    testRsquared.append(r2_test)

# Create a dataframe with the different alphas
alpha=[0.001,.01,.1,0, 1, 10, 20, 50, 100, 1000]
trainingRsquared=pd.DataFrame(trainingRsquared,index=alpha)
testRsquared=pd.DataFrame(testRsquared,index=alpha)

# Plot training and test R squared as a function of alpha after
concatenating
df3=pd.concat([trainingRsquared,testRsquared],axis=1)
df3.columns=['trainingRsquared','testRsquared']

# Plot and compare training and test r squared
fig5=df3.plot()
fig5=plt.title('Ridge training and test squared error vs Alpha')
fig5.figure.savefig('fig5.png', bbox_inches='tight')

# Plot the coefficient shrinage using the LARS package
from sklearn import linear_model
#
#####################################################################
########
# Compute paths
n_alphas = 200
# Set alphas in log space
alphas = np.logspace(0, 8, n_alphas)

coefs = []
for a in alphas:
    # Fit ridge regression
    ridge = linear_model.Ridge(alpha=a, fit_intercept=False)
    ridge.fit(X_train_scaled, y_train)
    coefs.append(ridge.coef_)

#
#####################################################################
########
# Display results
ax = plt.gca()
fig6=ax.plot(alphas, coefs)
fig6=ax.set_xscale('log')
fig6=ax.set_xlim(ax.get_xlim()[::-1])  # reverse axis
fig6=plt.xlabel('alpha')
fig6=plt.ylabel('weights')
fig6=plt.title('Ridge coefficients as a function of the
regularization')
```

```
fig6=plt.axis('tight')
plt.savefig('fig6.png', bbox_inches='tight')
## R-squared score (training): 0.620
## R-squared score (test): 0.438
## Number of non-zero features: 13
## Ridge regression: effect of alpha regularization parameter
```

The plot below shows the training and test error when increasing the tuning or regularization parameter 'alpha'

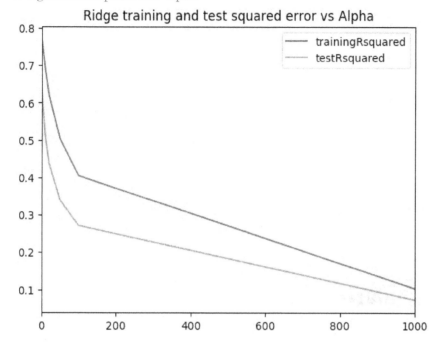

For Python the coefficient shrinkage with LARS must be viewed from right to left, where you have increasing alpha. As alpha increases,the coefficients shrink to 0.

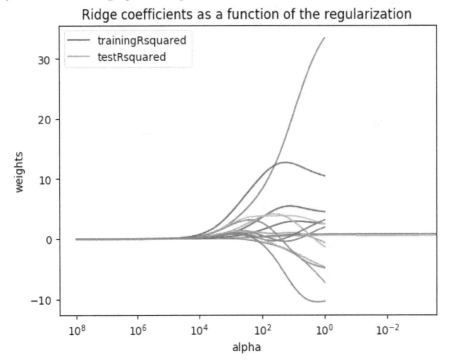

1.5 Lasso regularization

The Lasso is another form of regularization, also known as L1 regularization and can be used for automatic feature selection. Unlike the Ridge Regression where the coefficients of features, which do not influence the target, tend to zero, in the lasso regularization the coefficients become 0. The general form of Lasso is as follows

$$\sum_{i=1}^{n}(y_i - \beta_0 - \sum_{j=1}^{p}\beta_j x_{ij})^2 + \lambda \sum_{j=1}^{p}|\beta|$$

1.5a Lasso regularization – R code

```
library(glmnet)
library(dplyr)

# Read the Boston data set
df=read.csv("Boston.csv",stringsAsFactors = FALSE) # Data from MASS -
SL
```

```
# Rename columns to more readable values
names(df) <-c("no", "crimeRate", "zone", "indus", "charles", "nox",
"rooms", "age", "distances", "highways", "tax", "teacherRatio",
"color", "status", "cost")

# Select specific columns
df1 <- df %>% dplyr::select("crimeRate", "zone", "indus", "charles",
"nox", "rooms", "age","distances", "highways", "tax", "teacherRatio",
"color", "status", "cost")

# Set X and y as matrices - features and target variables
X=as.matrix(df1[,1:13])
y=df1$cost

# Fit the lasso model
fitLasso <- glmnet(X,y)

# Plot the coefficient shrinkage as a function of log(lambda)
plot(fitLasso,xvar="lambda",label=TRUE,main="Lasso regularization -
Coefficient shrinkage vs log lambda")
```

The plot below shows that in L1 regularization the coefficients actually become zero with increasing lambda

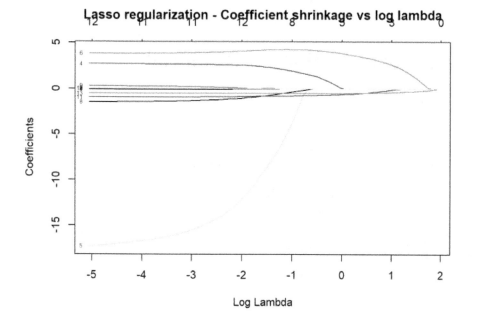

```
# Compute the cross validation error (10 fold)
cvLasso=cv.glmnet(X,y,alpha=0)
```

```
# Plot the cross validation error
plot(cvLasso)
```

This gives the MSE for the lasso model

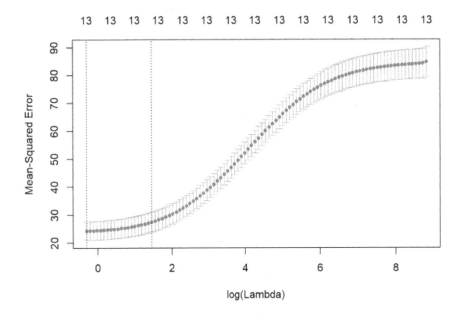

1.5 b Lasso regularization – Python code

```python
import numpy as np
import pandas as pd
import os
import matplotlib.pyplot as plt
from sklearn.model_selection import train_test_split
from sklearn.linear_model import Lasso
from sklearn.preprocessing import MinMaxScaler
from sklearn import linear_model
scaler = MinMaxScaler()

# Read the Boston data set
df = pd.read_csv("Boston.csv",encoding = "ISO-8859-1")

#Rename the columns to more readable names
df.columns=["no","crimeRate", "zone", "indus", "chasRiver", "NO2",
"rooms", "age","distances", "idxHighways", "taxRate", "teacherRatio",
"color", "status", "cost"]

# Set feature and target variables
```

```python
X=df[["crimeRate", "zone", "indus", "chasRiver", "NO2", "rooms",
"age","distances", "idxHighways", "taxRate", "teacherRatio", "color",
"status"]]
y=df['cost']

# Split train and test sets
X_train, X_test, y_train, y_test = train_test_split(X, y,
                                                    random_state = 0)

# Scale and transform the training and test data
X_train_scaled = scaler.fit_transform(X_train)
X_test_scaled = scaler.transform(X_test)

# Fit a Lasso model. Alpha is a constant that multiplies the L1 term
linlasso = Lasso(alpha=0.1, max_iter = 10).fit(X_train_scaled,
y_train)

# Print Rsquared
print('Non-zero features: {}'
    .format(np.sum(linlasso.coef_ != 0)))
print('R-squared score (training): {:.3f}'
    .format(linlasso.score(X_train_scaled, y_train)))
print('R-squared score (test): {:.3f}\n'
    .format(linlasso.score(X_test_scaled, y_test)))
print('Features with non-zero weight (sorted by absolute
magnitude):')

for e in sorted (list(zip(list(X), linlasso.coef_)),  key = lambda e:
-abs(e[1])):
    if e[1] != 0:
        print('\t{}, {:.3f}'.format(e[0], e[1]))


print('Lasso regression: effect of alpha regularization\n\
parameter on number of features kept in final model\n')

# Create empty lists for training and test R squared
trainingRsquared=[]
testRsquared=[]

# Loop through different values of alpha
for alpha in [0.01,0.07,0.05, 0.1, 1,2, 3, 5, 10]:
    linlasso = Lasso(alpha, max_iter = 10000).fit(X_train_scaled,
y_train)

    # Compute score on training data
    r2_train = linlasso.score(X_train_scaled, y_train)

    # Compute score on test data
```

```
    r2_test = linlasso.score(X_test_scaled, y_test)

    # Append the training and test rsquared to the respective lists
    trainingRsquared.append(r2_train)
    testRsquared.append(r2_test)

# Create a list with values for alpha
alpha=[0.01,0.07,0.05, 0.1, 1,2, 3, 5, 10]

#Create a dataframe  for training and test R squared
trainingRsquared=pd.DataFrame(trainingRsquared,index=alpha)
testRsquared=pd.DataFrame(testRsquared,index=alpha)

# Concatenate the dataframes
df3=pd.concat([trainingRsquared,testRsquared],axis=1)

#Rename the columns
df3.columns=['trainingRsquared','testRsquared']

# Plot the data frame with the training and test R squared
fig7=df3.plot()
fig7=plt.title('LASSO training and test squared error vs Alpha')
fig7.figure.savefig('fig7.png', bbox_inches='tight')

## Non-zero features: 7
## R-squared score (training): 0.726
## R-squared score (test): 0.561
##
## Features with non-zero weight (sorted by absolute magnitude):
##   status, -18.361
##   rooms, 18.232
##   teacherRatio, -8.628
##   taxRate, -2.045
##   color, 1.888
##   chasRiver, 1.670
##   distances, -0.529
## Lasso regression: effect of alpha regularization
## parameter on number of features kept in final model
##
## Computing regularization path using the LARS ...
## .C:\Users\Ganesh\ANACON~1\lib\site-
packages\sklearn\linear_model\coordinate_descent.py:484:
```

The plot below gives the training and test R squared error

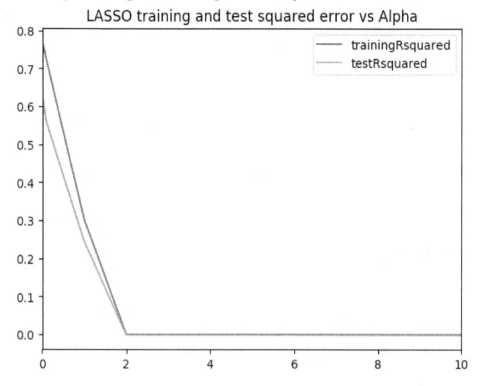

LASSO training and test squared error vs Alpha

1.5c Lasso coefficient shrinkage – Python code

To plot the coefficient shrinkage for Lasso the Least Angle Regression model a.k.a. LARS package. This is shown below

```
import numpy as np
import pandas as pd
import os
import matplotlib.pyplot as plt
from sklearn.model_selection import train_test_split
from sklearn.linear_model import Lasso
from sklearn.preprocessing import MinMaxScaler
from sklearn import linear_model
scaler = MinMaxScaler()

# Read the Boston data
df = pd.read_csv("Boston.csv",encoding = "ISO-8859-1")

#Rename the columns
```

```python
df.columns=["no", "crimeRate", "zone", "indus", "chasRiver", "NO2",
"rooms", "age", "distances", "idxHighways", "taxRate",
"teacherRatio", "color", "status", "cost"]

# Set the feature and target variables
X=df[["crimeRate","zone", "indus","chasRiver", "NO2", "rooms", "age",
"distances", "idxHighways", "taxRate","teacherRatio", "color",
status"]]
y=df['cost']

# Split as  training and test sets
X_train, X_test, y_train, y_test = train_test_split(X, y,
                                                    random_state = 0)

# Scale and transform the training and test data
X_train_scaled = scaler.fit_transform(X_train)
X_test_scaled = scaler.transform(X_test)

print("Computing regularization path using the LARS ...")
alphas, _, coefs = linear_model.lars_path(X_train_scaled, y_train,
method='lasso', verbose=True)

xx = np.sum(np.abs(coefs.T), axis=1)
xx /= xx[-1]

#Plot the Lasso coefficient shrinkage
fig8=plt.plot(xx, coefs.T)
ymin, ymax = plt.ylim()
fig8=plt.vlines(xx, ymin, ymax, linestyle='dashed')
fig8=plt.xlabel('|coef| / max|coef|')
fig8=plt.ylabel('Coefficients')
fig8=plt.title('LASSO Path - Coefficient Shrinkage vs L1')
fig8=plt.axis('tight')
plt.savefig('fig8.png', bbox_inches='tight')
```

This plot show the coefficient shrinkage for lasso.

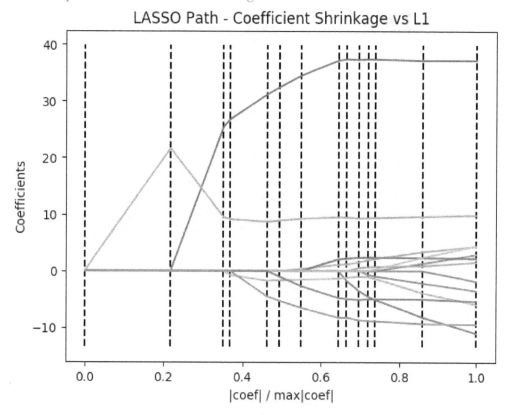

7. SVMs, Decision Trees and Validation curves

This chapter deals with Support Vector Machines (SVMs), using both a Linear and a Radial basis kernel, and Decision Trees. Further, a closer look is taken at some of the metrics associated with binary classification, namely accuracy vs precision and recall. I also touch upon Validation curves, Precision-Recall, ROC curves and AUC with equivalent code in R and Python

Download the associated code in this chapter as an R Markdown file from Github at https://github.com/tvganesh/PracticalMachineLearningWithRandPython

Support Vector Machines (SVM) is another useful Machine Learning model that can be used for both regression and classification problems. SVMs used in classification, computes the hyperplane, that separates the 2 classes with the maximum margin. To do this, the features may need to be transformed into a larger multi-dimensional feature space. SVMs can be used with different kernels namely linear, polynomial or radial basis to determine the best fitting model for a given classification problem.

For classification measures such as Accuracy, Precision, Recall and F1 score are used. Accuracy gives the fraction of data that were correctly classified as belonging to the +ve or -ve class. However, 'accuracy' in itself is not a good enough measure because it does not take into account the fraction of the data that were incorrectly classified. This issue becomes even more critical in different domains. For e.g. a surgeon who would like to detect cancer, would like to err on the side of caution, and classify even a possibly non-cancerous patient as possibly having cancer, rather than mis-classifying a malignancy as benign. Here we would like to increase recall or sensitivity, which is given by Recall= TP/(TP+FN) or we try reduce mis-classification by either increasing the (true positives) TP or reducing (false negatives) FN.

On the other hand, search algorithms would like to increase precision, which tries to reduce the number of irrelevant results in the search result. Precision= TP/ (TP+FP). In other words we do not want 'false positives' or irrelevant results to come in the search results and there is a need to reduce the false positives.

When we try to increase 'precision', we do so at the cost of 'recall', and vice-versa. One way to clarify this concept is to define precision and recall as follows

Precision: The number of times a cancer detection test correctly identifies cancer tissues as cancerous. It does not incorrectly classify non-cancerous tissues as cancerous i.e. the test keeps the number of 'false positives' in the denominator low.

Recall : Recall denotes the number of times cancer detection test actually classifies all those tissues which are actually cancerous i.e. the test does not incorrectly classify a cancerous tissue as non-cancerous. In other words, recall requires that 'false negatives' be kept to a minimum.

1.1a. Linear SVM – R code

In R code below, I use SVM on the cancer dataset with a linear kernel. The confusion matrix alongwith accuracy, sensitivy and specificity is computed and printed.

```
source('RFunctions-1.R')
library(dplyr)
library(e1071)
library(caret)
library(reshape2)
library(ggplot2)

# Read the cancer dataset (data from sklearn)
cancer <- read.csv("cancer.csv")

# Set the target variable
cancer$target <- as.factor(cancer$target)

# Split dataset into training and test sets
train_idx <- trainTestSplit(cancer,trainPercent=75,seed=5)
train <- cancer[train_idx, ]
test <- cancer[-train_idx, ]

# Use SVM to fit a model, using a linear kernel- target vs all other
variables.
# Do not scale the data
svmfit=svm(target~., data=train, kernel="linear",scale=FALSE)

# Predict the target for test set
ypred=predict(svmfit,test)

#Print a confusion matrix and display  Accuracy, Sensitivity,
Specificity
confusionMatrix(ypred,test$target)
## Confusion Matrix and Statistics
##
##           Reference
## Prediction  0  1
##          0 54  3
##          1  3 82
##
##               Accuracy : 0.9577
```

```
##                  95% CI : (0.9103, 0.9843)
##     No Information Rate : 0.5986
##     P-Value [Acc > NIR] : <2e-16
##
##                   Kappa : 0.9121
##  Mcnemar's Test P-Value : 1
##
##             Sensitivity : 0.9474
##             Specificity : 0.9647
##          Pos Pred Value : 0.9474
##          Neg Pred Value : 0.9647
##              Prevalence : 0.4014
##          Detection Rate : 0.3803
##    Detection Prevalence : 0.4014
##       Balanced Accuracy : 0.9560
##
##        'Positive' Class : 0
##
```

1.1b Linear SVM – Python code

The code below creates a SVM with linear basis in Python, and also dumps the corresponding classification metrics like accuracy, precision, recall and F1 score.

```python
import numpy as np
import pandas as pd
import os
import matplotlib.pyplot as plt
from sklearn.model_selection import train_test_split
from sklearn.svm import LinearSVC
from sklearn.datasets import make_classification, make_blobs
from sklearn.metrics import confusion_matrix
from matplotlib.colors import ListedColormap
from sklearn.datasets import load_breast_cancer

# Load the cancer data
(X_cancer, y_cancer) = load_breast_cancer(return_X_y = True)

# Split into training and test data
X_train, X_test, y_train, y_test = train_test_split(X_cancer,
y_cancer, random_state = 0)

# Fir a SVM model using linear basis kernel
clf = LinearSVC().fit(X_train, y_train)

# Print the Accuracy of the Linear classifier in the training and
test data set
```

```
print('Breast cancer dataset')
print('Accuracy of Linear SVC classifier on training set: {:.2f}'
    .format(clf.score(X_train, y_train)))
print('Accuracy of Linear SVC classifier on test set: {:.2f}'
    .format(clf.score(X_test, y_test)))
## Breast cancer dataset
## Accuracy of Linear SVC classifier on training set: 0.92
## Accuracy of Linear SVC classifier on test set: 0.94
```

1.2 Dummy classifier

Often when we perform classification tasks using any ML model namely logistic regression, SVM, neural networks etc. it is very useful to determine how well the ML model performs against a 'dummy classifier'. A dummy classifier uses some simple computation like frequency of majority class, instead of fitting and ML model. It is essential that a ML model do much better that the dummy classifier. This problem is even more important in imbalanced classes where we have only about 10% of +ve samples. If any ML model we create has an accuracy of about 0.90, then it is evident that our classifier is not doing any better than a dummy classsfier, which can just take a majority count of this imbalanced class and also come up with 0.90. We need to be able to do better than that.

In the examples below (1.3a & 1.3b) it can be seen that SVMs with 'radial basis' kernel with unnormalized data, for both R and Python, do not perform any better than the dummy classifier.

1.2a Dummy classifier – R code

R does not seem to have an explicit dummy classifier. I created a simple dummy classifier that predicts the majority class. sklearn in Python also includes other strategies like uniform, stratified etc. but this should be possible to create in R also.

```
# Create a simple dummy classifier that computes the ratio of the
majority class to the total

# Compute the Accuracy of a dummy classifier
DummyClassifierAccuracy <- function(train,test,type="majority"){
  if(type=="majority"){
    # Compute ratio of  class '1' with the total
      count <- sum(train$target==1)/dim(train)[1]
  }
  count
}
```

```
# Read the cancer data (from sklearn)
cancer <- read.csv("cancer.csv")

# Set the target variable
cancer$target <- as.factor(cancer$target)

# Split data into training and test sets
train_idx <- trainTestSplit(cancer,trainPercent=75,seed=5)
train <- cancer[train_idx, ]
test <- cancer[-train_idx, ]


#Run the dummy classifier majority class
acc=DummyClassifierAccuracy(train,test)

# Print the accuracy of the dummy classifier
sprintf("Accuracy is %f",acc)
## [1] "Accuracy is 0.638498"
```

1.2b Dummy classifier – Python code

Python includes DummyClassifier in the sklearn library. This dummy classifier uses the majority class.

```
import numpy as np
import pandas as pd
import os
import matplotlib.pyplot as plt
from sklearn.datasets import load_breast_cancer
from sklearn.model_selection import train_test_split
from sklearn.dummy import DummyClassifier
from sklearn.metrics import confusion_matrix

# Load the cancer data set
(X_cancer, y_cancer) = load_breast_cancer(return_X_y = True)

# Split as training and test set
X_train, X_test, y_train, y_test = train_test_split(X_cancer,
y_cancer, random_state = 0)

# Use the dummy classifier on the most frequent class.
# Negative class (0) is most frequent and fit on the training data
dummy_majority = DummyClassifier(strategy =
'most_frequent').fit(X_train, y_train)

# Predict on the test set
y_dummy_predictions = dummy_majority.predict(X_test)
```

```
# Compute and print the accuracy of the dummy classifier
print('Dummy classifier accuracy on test set: {:.2f}'
    .format(dummy_majority.score(X_test, y_test)))
## Dummy classifier accuracy on test set: 0.63
```

1.3a – Radial SVM (un-normalized) – R code

SVMs perform better when the data is normalized or scaled. The 2 examples below show that SVM with radial basis kernel does not perform any better than the dummy classifier The confusion matrix, accuracy, sensitivity and specificity are computed and displayed.

```
library(dplyr)
library(e1071)
library(caret)
library(reshape2)
library(ggplot2)

# Read the cancer dataset (data from sklearn)
cancer <- read.csv("cancer.csv")

# Set the target variable
cancer$target <- as.factor(cancer$target)

# Split the cancer data set into training and test set
train_idx <- trainTestSplit(cancer,trainPercent=75,seed=5)
train <- cancer[train_idx, ]
test <- cancer[-train_idx, ]

# Fit a SVM model on the unnormalized data. Use a radial basis kernel
svmfit=svm(target~., data=train, kernel="radial",cost=10,scale=FALSE)

# Predict the target based on test data
ypred=predict(svmfit,test)

# Compute and print the confusion matrix - Accuracy, Sensitivity,
Specificity
confusionMatrix(ypred,test$target)
## Confusion Matrix and Statistics
##
##          Reference
## Prediction  0  1
##          0  0  0
##          1 57 85
##
##             Accuracy : 0.5986
##               95% CI : (0.5131, 0.6799)
```

```
##      No Information Rate : 0.5986
##      P-Value [Acc > NIR] : 0.5363
##
##                    Kappa : 0
##  Mcnemar's Test P-Value : 1.195e-13
##
##              Sensitivity : 0.0000
##              Specificity : 1.0000
##           Pos Pred Value :    NaN
##           Neg Pred Value : 0.5986
##               Prevalence : 0.4014
##           Detection Rate : 0.0000
##     Detection Prevalence : 0.0000
##        Balanced Accuracy : 0.5000
##
##         'Positive' Class : 0
##
```

1.4b – Radial SVM (un-normalized) – Python code

Using a radial basis kernel in SVM to classify the data results in much better accuracy, precision, recall and F1 score.

```python
import numpy as np
import pandas as pd
import os
import matplotlib.pyplot as plt
from sklearn.datasets import load_breast_cancer
from sklearn.model_selection import train_test_split
from sklearn.svm import SVC

# Load the cancer data
(X_cancer, y_cancer) = load_breast_cancer(return_X_y = True)

# Split the data into training and test set
X_train, X_test, y_train, y_test = train_test_split(X_cancer,
y_cancer, random_state = 0)

# Fit a SVM model on the unnormalized data using the radial basis
kernel
clf = SVC(C=10).fit(X_train, y_train)

# Print the Accuracy on the training and test data
print('Breast cancer dataset (unnormalized features)')
print('Accuracy of RBF-kernel SVC on training set: {:.2f}'
    .format(clf.score(X_train, y_train)))
```

```
print('Accuracy of RBF-kernel SVC on test set: {:.2f}'
    .format(clf.score(X_test, y_test)))
## Breast cancer dataset (unnormalized features)
## Accuracy of RBF-kernel SVC on training set: 1.00
## Accuracy of RBF-kernel SVC on test set: 0.63
```

1.5a – Radial SVM (Normalized) -R Code

The data is scaled (normalized) before using the SVM model. The SVM model has 2 parameters a) C – Large C (less regularization), more regularization b) gamma – Small gamma has larger decision boundary with more misclassfication, and larger gamma has tighter decision boundary

The R code below computes the accuracy as the regularization parameter is changed

```
trainingAccuracy <- NULL
testAccuracy <- NULL

# Create a vector of costs C1
# kernel - radial basis
# Cost - cost
# scale - indicate whether the features should be scaled/normalized

# Initialize a vector of costs
C1 <- c(.01,.1, 1, 10, 20)

# Loop through the costs
for(i in  C1){
    # Fit a SVM model with radial basis kernel, with cost 'i'  and
with normalized features
    svmfit=svm(target~., data=train,
kernel="radial",cost=i,scale=TRUE)

    # Predict the target value from the training data
    ypredTrain <-predict(svmfit,train)

    # Predict the target value from the test data
    ypredTest=predict(svmfit,test)

    #Compute and print the confusion matrix on training and test data
    a <-confusionMatrix(ypredTrain,train$target)
    b <-confusionMatrix(ypredTest,test$target)

    # Append the training and test accuracy
    trainingAccuracy <-c(trainingAccuracy,a$overall[1])
    testAccuracy <-c(testAccuracy,b$overall[1])
```

```
}

# Print the training accuracy
print(trainingAccuracy)
##  Accuracy  Accuracy  Accuracy  Accuracy  Accuracy
## 0.6384977 0.9671362 0.9906103 0.9976526 1.0000000

# Print the test accuracy
print(testAccuracy)
##  Accuracy  Accuracy  Accuracy  Accuracy  Accuracy
## 0.5985915 0.9507042 0.9647887 0.9507042 0.9507042

# Plot the training and test accuracy as a function of the cost
parameter
a <-rbind(C1,as.numeric(trainingAccuracy),as.numeric(testAccuracy))
b <- data.frame(t(a))

names(b) <- c("C1","trainingAccuracy","testAccuracy")
df <- melt(b,id="C1")
ggplot(df) + geom_line(aes(x=C1, y=value, colour=variable),size=2) +
    xlab("C (SVC regularization)value") + ylab("Accuracy") +
    ggtitle("Training and test accuracy vs C(regularization)")
```

1.5b – Radial SVM (normalized) – Python

The Radial basis kernel is used on normalized data for a range of 'C' values and the result is plotted.

```python
import numpy as np
import pandas as pd
import os
import matplotlib.pyplot as plt
from sklearn.datasets import load_breast_cancer
from sklearn.model_selection import train_test_split
from sklearn.svm import SVC
from sklearn.preprocessing import MinMaxScaler
scaler = MinMaxScaler()

# Load the cancer data
(X_cancer, y_cancer) = load_breast_cancer(return_X_y = True)

# Split the data into training and test sets
X_train, X_test, y_train, y_test = train_test_split(X_cancer,
y_cancer, random_state = 0)

# Scale and transform the data
X_train_scaled = scaler.fit_transform(X_train)
X_test_scaled = scaler.transform(X_test)

print('Breast cancer dataset (normalized with MinMax scaling)')

# Create empty lists for training and test accuracy
trainingAccuracy=[]
testAccuracy=[]

# Loop through the C1
for C1 in [.01,.1, 1, 10, 20]:

    # Fit a SVM model with a radial basis kernel with penalty
parameter 'C1'
    # C - penalty parameter
    clf = SVC(C=C1).fit(X_train_scaled, y_train)

    # Compute the training and test accuracy
    acctrain=clf.score(X_train_scaled, y_train)
    accTest=clf.score(X_test_scaled, y_test)

    # Append the training and test accuracy for the different values
of C1
    trainingAccuracy.append(acctrain)
    testAccuracy.append(accTest)

# Create a dataframe
C1=[.01,.1, 1, 10, 20]
trainingAccuracy=pd.DataFrame(trainingAccuracy,index=C1)
testAccuracy=pd.DataFrame(testAccuracy,index=C1)
```

```
# Plot training and test Accuracy as a function  C1
df=pd.concat([trainingAccuracy,testAccuracy],axis=1)
df.columns=['trainingAccuracy','trainingAccuracy']
fig1=df.plot()
fig1=plt.title('Training and test accuracy vs C (SVC)')
fig1.figure.savefig('fig1.png', bbox_inches='tight')
## Breast cancer dataset (normalized with MinMax scaling)
```

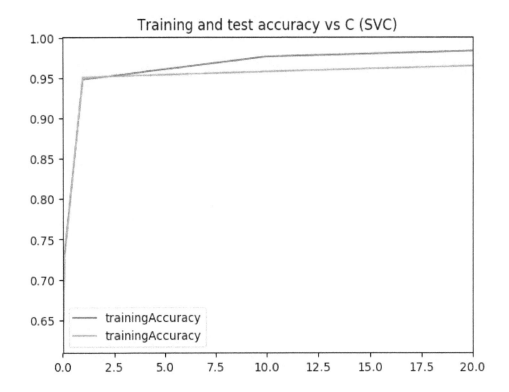

1.6a Validation curve – R code

Sklearn includes code for creating validation curves by varying parameters while computing, and plotting accuracy as gamma or C are changed. I did not find this R but I think this is a useful function and so I have created the R equivalent of this.

```
# The R equivalent of np.logspace
seqLogSpace <- function(start,stop,len){
  a=seq(log10(10^start),log10(10^stop),length=len)
  10^a
}
```

```r
# Read the data. This is taken the sklearn cancer data
cancer <- read.csv("cancer.csv")

# Set the target varaible
cancer$target <- as.factor(cancer$target)

set.seed(6)

# Create the range of C1 in log space
param_range = seqLogSpace(-3,2,20)

# Initialize the overall training and test accuracy to NULL
overallTrainAccuracy <- NULL
overallTestAccuracy <- NULL

# Loop over the parameter range of Gamma
for(i in param_range){
    # Set no of folds
    noFolds=5
    # Create the rows which fall into different folds from 1..noFolds
    folds = sample(1:noFolds, nrow(cancer), replace=TRUE)

    # Initialize the training and test accuracy of folds to 0
    trainingAccuracy <- 0
    testAccuracy <- 0

    # Loop through the folds
    for(j in 1:noFolds){

        # The training is all rows for which the row is != j (k-1
folds -> training)
        train <- cancer[folds!=j,]

        # The rows which have j as the index become the test set
        test <- cancer[folds==j,]

        # Fir a SVM model with radial basis and with scaling
        svmfit=svm(target~., data=train, kernel="radial",
gamma=i,scale=TRUE)

        # Add up all the fold accuracy for training and test
separately
        ypredTrain <-predict(svmfit,train)
        ypredTest=predict(svmfit,test)

        # Create confusion matrix
        a <-confusionMatrix(ypredTrain,train$target)
        b <-confusionMatrix(ypredTest,test$target)
```

```
      # Get the accuracy
      trainingAccuracy <-trainingAccuracy + a$overall[1]
      testAccuracy <-testAccuracy+b$overall[1]


  }
  # Compute the average of accuracy for K folds for number of
features 'i'

overallTrainAccuracy=c(overallTrainAccuracy,trainingAccuracy/noFolds)
  overallTestAccuracy=c(overallTestAccuracy,testAccuracy/noFolds)
}

#Create a dataframe
a <- rbind(param_range,as.numeric(overallTrainAccuracy),
            as.numeric(overallTestAccuracy))
b <- data.frame(t(a))

# Set the columns
names(b) <- c("C1","trainingAccuracy","testAccuracy")

# Melt the data
df <- melt(b,id="C1")
#Plot in log axis
ggplot(df) + geom_line(aes(x=C1, y=value, colour=variable),size=2) +
      xlab("C (SVC regularization)value") + ylab("Accuracy") +
      ggtitle("Training and test accuracy vs C(regularization)") +
scale_x_log10()
```

Training and test accuracy vs C(regularization)

1.6b Validation curve – Python

Validation curves can be used to measure the accuracy of training and test data as parameters are changed. In the code below validation curves are computed and plotted as gamma is varied.

```python
import numpy as np
import pandas as pd
import os
import matplotlib.pyplot as plt
from sklearn.datasets import load_breast_cancer
from sklearn.model_selection import train_test_split
from sklearn.preprocessing import MinMaxScaler
from sklearn.svm import SVC
from sklearn.model_selection import validation_curve


# Load the cancer data
(X_cancer, y_cancer) = load_breast_cancer(return_X_y = True)

# Transform and scale the data
scaler = MinMaxScaler()
X_scaled = scaler.fit_transform(X_cancer)

# Create a gamma values from 10^-3 to 10^2 with 20 equally spaced
intervals
param_range = np.logspace(-3, 2, 20)

# Compute the validation curve
train_scores, test_scores = validation_curve(SVC(), X_scaled,
y_cancer,
                                  param_name='gamma',
                                  param_range=param_range,
cv=10)

#Plot the figure
fig2=plt.figure()

#Compute the mean
train_scores_mean = np.mean(train_scores, axis=1)
train_scores_std = np.std(train_scores, axis=1)
test_scores_mean = np.mean(test_scores, axis=1)
test_scores_std = np.std(test_scores, axis=1)

fig2=plt.title('Validation Curve with SVM')
fig2=plt.xlabel('$\gamma$ (gamma)')
fig2=plt.ylabel('Score')
```

```
fig2=plt.ylim(0.0, 1.1)
lw = 2

fig2=plt.semilogx(param_range, train_scores_mean, label='Training
score', color='darkorange', lw=lw)

fig2=plt.fill_between(param_range, train_scores_mean -
train_scores_std, train_scores_mean + train_scores_std, alpha=0.2,
  color='darkorange', lw=lw)

fig2=plt.semilogx(param_range, test_scores_mean, label='Cross-
validation score', color='navy', lw=lw)

fig2=plt.fill_between(param_range, test_scores_mean -
test_scores_std, test_scores_mean + test_scores_std, alpha=0.2,
color='navy', lw=lw)
fig2.figure.savefig('fig2.png', bbox_inches='tight')
```

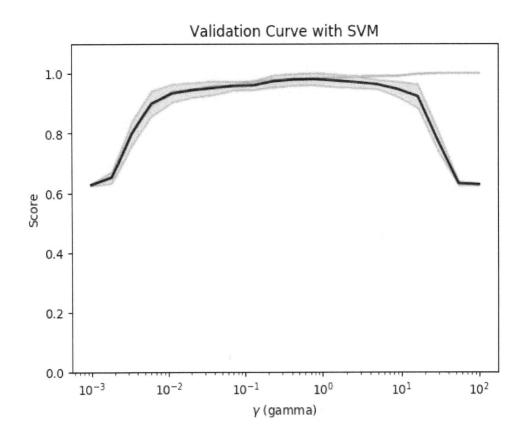

1.7a Validation Curve (Preventing data leakage) – Python code

```python
import numpy as np
import pandas as pd
import os
import matplotlib.pyplot as plt
from sklearn.datasets import load_breast_cancer
from sklearn.cross_validation import  KFold
from sklearn.preprocessing import MinMaxScaler
from sklearn.svm import SVC

# Read the cancer data
(X_cancer, y_cancer) = load_breast_cancer(return_X_y = True)

# Set the parameter range
param_range = np.logspace(-3, 2, 20)

# Set number of folds
folds=5

#Initialize overallTrain Accuracy and overallTestAccuracy
overallTrainAccuracy=[]
overallTestAccuracy=[]

# Loop over the parameter range
for c in  param_range:

    #Set trainingAccuracy & testAccuracy to 0
    trainingAccuracy=0
    testAccuracy=0

    # Get the number of folds
    kf = KFold(len(X_cancer),n_folds=folds)

    # Partition into training and test folds
    for train_index, test_index in kf:

            # Partition the data acccording the fold indices
generated
            X_train, X_test = X_cancer[train_index],
X_cancer[test_index]
            y_train, y_test = y_cancer[train_index],
y_cancer[test_index]


            # Scale and transform X_train and X_test
            scaler = MinMaxScaler()
```

```
            X_train_scaled = scaler.fit_transform(X_train)
            X_test_scaled = scaler.transform(X_test)

            # Fit a SVC model for each C=c
            clf = SVC(C=c).fit(X_train_scaled, y_train)

            #Compute the training and test score
            acctrain=clf.score(X_train_scaled, y_train)
            accTest=clf.score(X_test_scaled, y_test)

            # Sum up the  scores
            trainingAccuracy += np.sum(acctrain)
            testAccuracy += np.sum(accTest)

    # Compute the mean training and testing accuracy
    overallTrainAccuracy.append(trainingAccuracy/folds)
    overallTestAccuracy.append(testAccuracy/folds)

# Create  dataframes
overallTrainAccuracy=pd.DataFrame(overallTrainAccuracy,index=param_ra
nge)
overallTestAccuracy=pd.DataFrame(overallTestAccuracy,index=param_rang
e)

# Plot training and test R squared as a function of alpha
df=pd.concat([overallTrainAccuracy,overallTestAccuracy],axis=1)
df.columns=['trainingAccuracy','testAccuracy']

# Plot the validation curve
fig3=plt.title('Validation Curve with SVM')
fig3=plt.xlabel('$\gamma$ (gamma)')
fig3=plt.ylabel('Score')
fig3=plt.ylim(0.5, 1.1)
lw = 2

fig3=plt.semilogx(param_range, overallTrainAccuracy, label='Training
score', color='darkorange', lw=lw)

fig3=plt.semilogx(param_range, overallTestAccuracy, label='Cross-
validation score', color='navy', lw=lw)

fig3=plt.legend(loc='best')
fig3.figure.savefig('fig3.png', bbox_inches='tight')
```

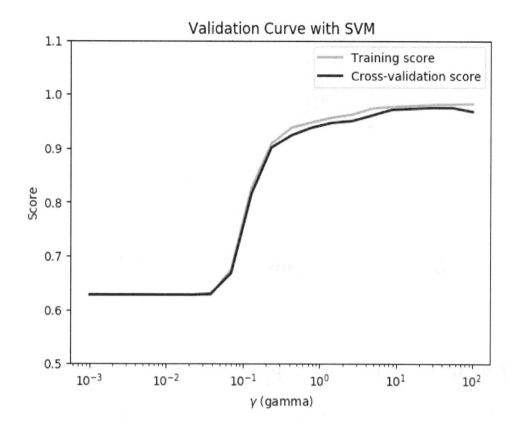

1.8 a Decision trees – R code

Decision trees in R can be plotted using the 'rpart' package. One of the main advantages of Decision Trees is that the results are very interpretable. The IRIS data is classified below using a Decision Tree

```
library(rpart)
library(rpart.plot)
rpart = NULL

# Create a decision tree
m <-rpart(Species~.,data=iris)

#Plot the decision tree
rpart.plot(m,extra=2,main="Decision Tree - IRIS")
```

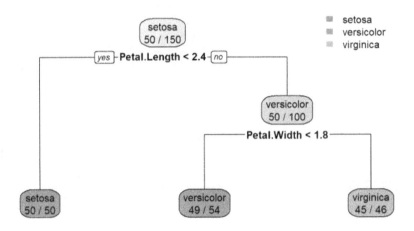

Decision Tree - IRIS

1.8   b Decision trees – Python code

A Decision Tree is used to fit the IRIS data and the resulting tree is visualized

```python
from sklearn.datasets import load_iris
from sklearn.tree import DecisionTreeClassifier
from sklearn import tree
from sklearn.model_selection import train_test_split
import graphviz

# Load the iris data
iris = load_iris()

# Split into training and test sets
X_train, X_test, y_train, y_test = train_test_split(iris.data,
iris.target, random_state = 3)

# Create a decision tree
clf = DecisionTreeClassifier().fit(X_train, y_train)

# Print the Accuracy on the training and test data
print('Accuracy of Decision Tree classifier on training set: {:.2f}'
    .format(clf.score(X_train, y_train)))
print('Accuracy of Decision Tree classifier on test set: {:.2f}'
    .format(clf.score(X_test, y_test)))
```

```
# Plot the decision tree
dot_data = tree.export_graphviz(clf, out_file=None,
                        feature_names=iris.feature_names,
                        class_names=iris.target_names,
                        filled=True, rounded=True,
                        special_characters=True)
graph = graphviz.Source(dot_data)
graph
## Accuracy of Decision Tree classifier on training set: 1.00
## Accuracy of Decision Tree classifier on test set: 0.97
```

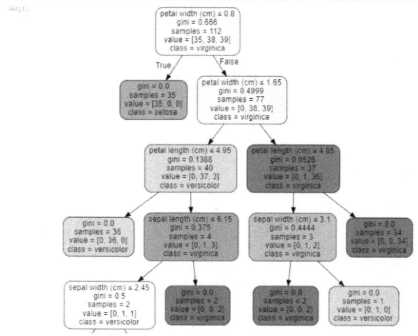

1.9a Feature importance – R code

The code below plots the feature importance of the different features while training a machine learning model.

```
set.seed(3)
# load the library
library(mlbench)
library(caret)

# Load the cancer dataset
cancer <- read.csv("cancer.csv")

# Set the target variable
cancer$target <- as.factor(cancer$target)

# $plit  data as feature variables and target variable
```

```
data <- cancer[,1:31]
target <- cancer[,32]

# Train the model
model <- train(data, target, method="rf",  preProcess="scale",
trControl= trainControl(method = "cv"))

# Compute the variable importances
importance <- varImp(model)

# Summarize variable importance
print(importance)

# Plot variable importance
plot(importance)
```

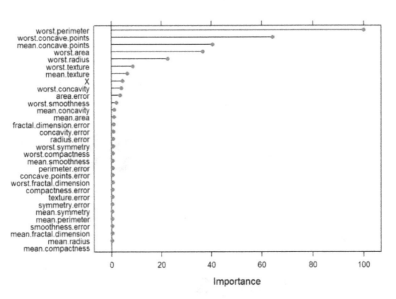

1.9b Feature importance – Python code

The feature importance of the cancer data set is plotted below

```
import numpy as np
import pandas as pd
import os
import matplotlib.pyplot as plt
from sklearn.tree import DecisionTreeClassifier
from sklearn.model_selection import train_test_split
from sklearn.datasets import load_breast_cancer
import numpy as np
```

```
# Read the cancer data
cancer= load_breast_cancer()
(X_cancer, y_cancer) = load_breast_cancer(return_X_y = True)

# Split the data as training and test sets
X_train, X_test, y_train, y_test = train_test_split(X_cancer,
y_cancer, random_state = 0)

# Use the DecisionTreClassifier
clf = DecisionTreeClassifier(max_depth = 4, min_samples_leaf = 8,
                             random_state = 0).fit(X_train, y_train)

c_features=len(cancer.feature_names)

# Compute accuracy on training and test dataset
print('Breast cancer dataset: decision tree')
print('Accuracy of DT classifier on training set: {:.2f}'
     .format(clf.score(X_train, y_train)))
print('Accuracy of DT classifier on test set: {:.2f}'
     .format(clf.score(X_test, y_test)))

# Plot the feature importances
fig4=plt.figure(figsize=(10,6),dpi=80)

fig4=plt.barh(range(c_features), clf.feature_importances_)
fig4=plt.xlabel("Feature importance")
fig4=plt.ylabel("Feature name")
fig4=plt.yticks(np.arange(c_features), cancer.feature_names)
fig4=plt.tight_layout()
plt.savefig('fig4.png', bbox_inches='tight')
## Breast cancer dataset: decision tree
## Accuracy of DT classifier on training set: 0.96
## Accuracy of DT classifier on test set: 0.94
```

Output image:

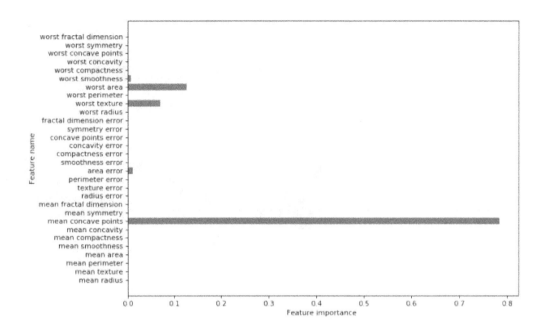

1.10a Precision-Recall, ROC curves & AUC- R code

The Precision-Recall curves show the tradeoff between precision and recall. The higher the precision, the lower the recall and vice versa. AUC curves that hug the top left corner indicate a high sensitivity, specificity and an excellent accuracy. The code below uses the library PRROC

```
source("RFunctions-1.R")
library(dplyr)
library(caret)
library(e1071)
library(PRROC)

# Read the data (this data is from sklearn!)
d <- read.csv("digits.csv")
digits <- d[2:66]
digits$X64 <- as.factor(digits$X64)

# Split as training and test sets
train_idx <- trainTestSplit(digits,trainPercent=75,seed=5)
train <- digits[train_idx, ]
test <- digits[-train_idx, ]
```

```r
# Fit a SVM model with linear basis kernel with probabilities
svmfit=svm(X64~., data=train,
kernel="linear",scale=FALSE,probability=TRUE)

# Predict the target value with the test data
ypred=predict(svmfit,test,probability=TRUE)
head(attr(ypred,"probabilities"))
##                0            1
## 6   7.395947e-01 2.604053e-01
## 8   9.999998e-01 1.842555e-07
## 12  1.655178e-05 9.999834e-01
## 13  9.649997e-01 3.500032e-02
## 15  9.994849e-01 5.150612e-04
## 16  9.999987e-01 1.280700e-06

# Store the probability of 0s and 1s
m0<-attr(ypred,"probabilities")[,1]
m1<-attr(ypred,"probabilities")[,2]

# Create a dataframe of scores
scores <- data.frame(m1,test$X64)

# Class 0 is data points of +ve class (in this case, digit 1) and -ve
class (digit 0)
#Compute Precision Recall
pr <- pr.curve(scores.class0=scores[scores$test.X64=="1",]$m1,
              scores.class1=scores[scores$test.X64=="0",]$m1,
              curve=T)

# Plot precision-recall curve
plot(pr)
```

PR curve
AUC = 0.9400659

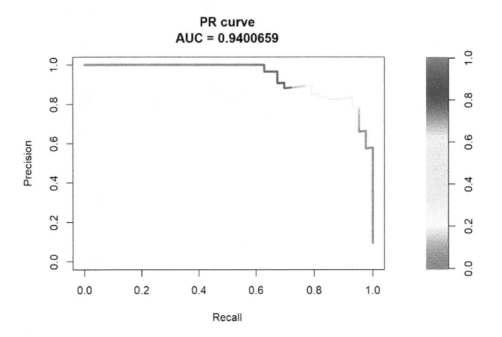

```
#Plot the ROC curve
roc<-roc.curve(m0, m1,curve=TRUE)
plot(roc)
```

ROC curve
AUC = 0.9649235

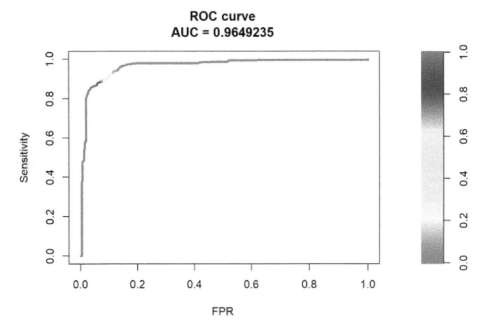

1.10b Precision-Recall, ROC curves & AUC- Python code

For Python Logistic Regression is used before plotting Precision Recall, ROC curve and compute AUC

```python
import numpy as np
import pandas as pd
import matplotlib.pyplot as plt
from sklearn.model_selection import train_test_split
from sklearn.linear_model import LogisticRegression
from sklearn.datasets import load_digits
from sklearn.metrics import precision_recall_curve
from sklearn.metrics import roc_curve, auc

#Load the digits data
dataset = load_digits()
X, y = dataset.data, dataset.target

#Create 2 classes -i) Digit 1 (from digit 1) ii) Digit 0 (from all
other digits)
# Make a copy of the target
z= y.copy()

# Replace all non 1's as 0
z[z != 1] = 0

# Split into training and test set
X_train, X_test, y_train, y_test = train_test_split(X, z,
random_state=0)

# Fit a Logistic Regression model
lr = LogisticRegression().fit(X_train, y_train)

#Compute the decision scores
y_scores_lr = lr.fit(X_train, y_train).decision_function(X_test)
y_score_list = list(zip(y_test[0:20], y_scores_lr[0:20]))

#Show the decision_function scores for first 20 instances
y_score_list

# Compute precision and recall
precision, recall, thresholds = precision_recall_curve(y_test,
y_scores_lr)
closest_zero = np.argmin(np.abs(thresholds))
closest_zero_p = precision[closest_zero]
closest_zero_r = recall[closest_zero]
```

```
#Plot the precision recall curve
plt.figure()
plt.xlim([0.0, 1.01])
plt.ylim([0.0, 1.01])
plt.plot(precision, recall, label='Precision-Recall Curve')
plt.plot(closest_zero_p, closest_zero_r, 'o', markersize = 12,
fillstyle = 'none', c='r', mew=3)
plt.xlabel('Precision', fontsize=16)
plt.ylabel('Recall', fontsize=16)
plt.axes().set_aspect('equal')
plt.savefig('fig5.png', bbox_inches='tight')

#Compute and plot the ROC
y_score_lr = lr.fit(X_train, y_train).decision_function(X_test)
fpr_lr, tpr_lr, _ = roc_curve(y_test, y_score_lr)
roc_auc_lr = auc(fpr_lr, tpr_lr)

plt.figure()
plt.xlim([-0.01, 1.00])
plt.ylim([-0.01, 1.01])
plt.plot(fpr_lr, tpr_lr, lw=3, label='LogRegr ROC curve (area =
{:0.2f})'.format(roc_auc_lr))
plt.xlabel('False Positive Rate', fontsize=16)
plt.ylabel('True Positive Rate', fontsize=16)
plt.title('ROC curve (1-of-10 digits classifier)', fontsize=16)
plt.legend(loc='lower right', fontsize=13)
plt.plot([0, 1], [0, 1], color='navy', lw=3, linestyle='--')
plt.axes()
plt.savefig('fig6.png', bbox_inches='tight')
```

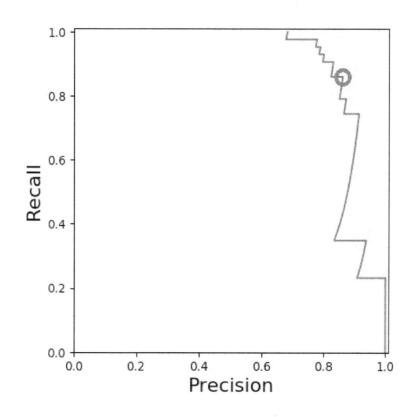

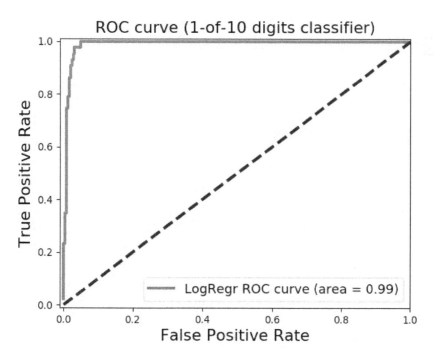

1.10c Precision-Recall, ROC curves & AUC-Python code

In the code below classification probabilities are used to compute and plot precision-recall, ROC and AUC

```python
import numpy as np
import pandas as pd
import matplotlib.pyplot as plt
from sklearn.model_selection import train_test_split
from sklearn.datasets import load_digits
from sklearn.svm import LinearSVC
from sklearn.calibration import CalibratedClassifierCV

# Load the digits data
dataset = load_digits()
X, y = dataset.data, dataset.target

# Make a copy of the target
z= y.copy()

# Replace all non 1's as 0
z[z != 1] = 0

# Split the data as training and test set
X_train, X_test, y_train, y_test = train_test_split(X, z,
random_state=0)

# Fit a Linear SVC
svm = LinearSVC()

# Need to use CalibratedClassifierSVC to redict probabilities for
LinearSVC
clf = CalibratedClassifierCV(svm)
clf.fit(X_train, y_train)

# Predict the target probabilities
y_proba_lr = clf.predict_proba(X_test)

# Compute precision recall
from sklearn.metrics import precision_recall_curve
precision, recall, thresholds = precision_recall_curve(y_test,
y_proba_lr[:,1])
closest_zero = np.argmin(np.abs(thresholds))
closest_zero_p = precision[closest_zero]
closest_zero_r = recall[closest_zero]
```

```
# Plot the precision recall curve
#plt.figure(figsize=(15,15),dpi=80)
plt.figure()
plt.xlim([0.0, 1.01])
plt.ylim([0.0, 1.01])
plt.plot(precision, recall, label='Precision-Recall Curve')
plt.plot(closest_zero_p, closest_zero_r, 'o', markersize = 12,
fillstyle = 'none', c='r', mew=3)
plt.xlabel('Precision', fontsize=16)
plt.ylabel('Recall', fontsize=16)
plt.axes().set_aspect('equal')
plt.savefig('fig7.png', bbox_inches='tight')
```

output

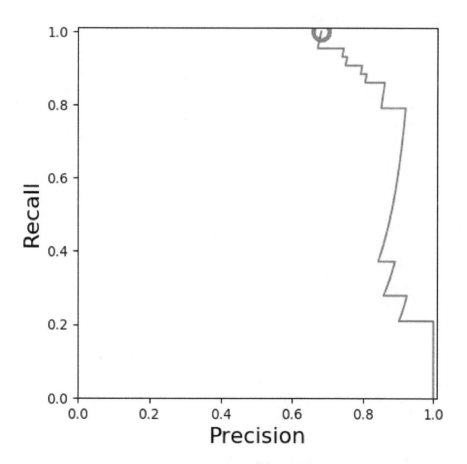

8. Splines, GAMs, Random Forests and Boosting

This chapter discusses regression with B-splines, Natural splines, Smoothing splines, Generalized Additive Models (GAMS), Bagging, Random forest and Boosting.

You can download the associated code in this chapter as a R Markdown file from Github at https://github.com/tvganesh/PracticalMachineLearningWithRandPython

1. Splines

When performing regression (continuous or logistic) between a target variable and a feature (or a set of features), a single polynomial for the entire range of the data set, usually does not give a good fit. Instead, separate regression curves could be fit for different sections of the data set.

There are several techniques, which do this for e.g. piecewise-constant functions, piecewise-linear functions, piecewise-quadratic/cubic/4th order polynomial functions etc. One such set of functions are the cubic splines, which fit cubic polynomials to successive sections of the dataset. The points where the cubic splines join are called 'knots'.

Since each section has a different cubic spline, there could be discontinuities (or breaks) at these knots. To prevent these discontinuities 'natural splines' and 'smoothing splines' ensure that the separate cubic functions have 2nd order continuity at these knots with the adjacent splines. 2nd order continuity implies that the value, 1st order derivative and 2nd order derivative at these knots are equal.

A cubic spline with knots α_k, k=1, 2, 3,..K is a piece-wise cubic polynomial with continuous derivative up to order 2 at each knot. We can write as below
For each (x_i, y_i), b_i are called 'basis' functions, where $b_1(x_i) = x_i$, $b_2(x_i) = x_i^2$, $b_3(x_i) = x_i^3$, $b_{k+3}(x_i) = (x_i - \alpha_k)^3$ where k=1,2,3... K The 1st and 2nd derivatives of cubic splines are continuous at the knots. Hence, splines provide a smooth continuous fit to the data by fitting different splines to different sections of the data

1.1a Fit a 4th degree polynomial – R code

In the code below, a non-linear function (a 4th order polynomial) is used to fit the data. Usually when we fit a single polynomial to the entire data set the tails of the fit tend to vary a lot particularly if there are fewer points at the ends. Splines help in reducing this variation at the extremities

```
library(dplyr)
library(ggplot2)
source('RFunctions-1.R')

# Read the auto dataset
df=read.csv("auto_mpg.csv",stringsAsFactors = FALSE) # Data from UCI

# Convert all columns to numeric
df1 <- as.data.frame(sapply(df,as.numeric))

#Select specific columns
df2 <- df1 %>% dplyr::select(cylinder,displacement,
horsepower,weight, acceleration, year,mpg)

# Filter only complete rows
auto <- df2[complete.cases(df2),]

# Fit a 4th degree polynomial on the dataset
fit=lm(mpg~poly(horsepower,4),data=auto)

#Display a summary of fit
summary(fit)
##
## Call:
## lm(formula = mpg ~ poly(horsepower, 4), data = auto)
##
## Residuals:
##      Min       1Q   Median       3Q      Max
## -14.8820  -2.5802  -0.1682   2.2100  16.1434
##
## Coefficients:
##                      Estimate Std. Error t value Pr(>|t|)
## (Intercept)           23.4459     0.2209 106.161   <2e-16 ***
## poly(horsepower, 4)1 -120.1377     4.3727 -27.475   <2e-16 ***
## poly(horsepower, 4)2   44.0895     4.3727  10.083   <2e-16 ***
## poly(horsepower, 4)3   -3.9488     4.3727  -0.903    0.367
## poly(horsepower, 4)4   -5.1878     4.3727  -1.186    0.236
## ---
## Signif. codes:  0 '***' 0.001 '**' 0.01 '*' 0.05 '.' 0.1 ' ' 1
##
## Residual standard error: 4.373 on 387 degrees of freedom
## Multiple R-squared:  0.6893, Adjusted R-squared:  0.6861
## F-statistic: 214.7 on 4 and 387 DF,  p-value: < 2.2e-16

#Get the range of horsepower
hp <- range(auto$horsepower)
```

```
#Create a sequence to be used for plotting
hpGrid <- seq(hp[1],hp[2],by=10)

#Predict for these values of horsepower. Set Standard error as TRUE
pred=predict(fit,newdata=list(horsepower=hpGrid),se=TRUE)

#Compute bands on either side that is 2xStandard Error (SE)
seBands=cbind(pred$fit+2*pred$se.fit,pred$fit-2*pred$se.fit)

#Plot the fit with Standard Error bands
plot(auto$horsepower,auto$mpg,xlim=hp,cex=.5,col="black",xlab="Horsep
ower", ylab="MPG", main="Polynomial of degree 4")
lines(hpGrid,pred$fit,lwd=2,col="blue")
matlines(hpGrid,seBands,lwd=2,col="blue",lty=3)
```

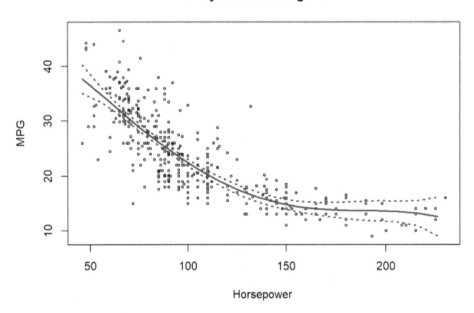

Polynomial of degree 4

1.1b Fit a 4th degree polynomial – Python code

```
import numpy as np
import pandas as pd
import os
import matplotlib.pyplot as plt
from sklearn.model_selection import train_test_split
```

```python
from sklearn.preprocessing import PolynomialFeatures
from sklearn.linear_model import LinearRegression

#Read the auto data
autoDF =pd.read_csv("auto_mpg.csv",encoding="ISO-8859-1")

# Select specific columns
autoDF1=autoDF[['mpg','cylinder','displacement','horsepower','weight'
,'acceleration','year']]

# Convert all columns to numeric
autoDF2 = autoDF1.apply(pd.to_numeric, errors='coerce')

#Drop NAs. Filter only complete rows
autoDF3=autoDF2.dropna()
autoDF3.shape

# Set the feature and target variables
X=autoDF3[['horsepower']]
y=autoDF3['mpg']

#Create a polynomial of degree 4
poly = PolynomialFeatures(degree=4)

# Scale and transform the data
X_poly = poly.fit_transform(X)

# Fit a 4th degree polynomial  to the data
linreg = LinearRegression().fit(X_poly, y)

# Create a range of values
hpGrid = np.arange(np.min(X),np.max(X),10)
hp=hpGrid.reshape(-1,1)

# Transform to 4th degree
poly = PolynomialFeatures(degree=4)
hp_poly = poly.fit_transform(hp)

#Create a scatter plot
plt.scatter(X,y)

# Compute the target value
ypred=linreg.predict(hp_poly)

# Draw the regression curve
plt.title("Poylnomial of degree 4")
fig2=plt.xlabel("Horsepower")
fig2=plt.ylabel("MPG")
plt.plot(hp,ypred,c="red")
```

```
plt.savefig('fig1.png', bbox_inches='tight')
```

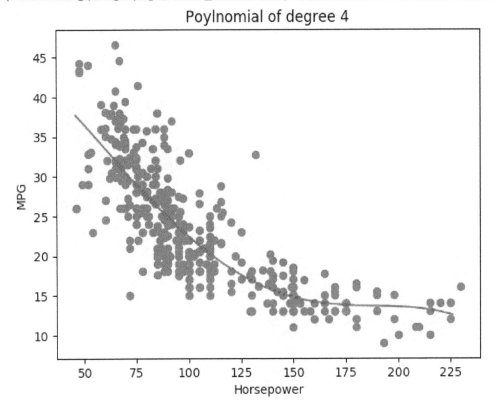

Poylnomial of degree 4

1.1c Fit a B-Spline – R Code

In the code below a B-Spline is fit on the data using R. The B-spline requires the manual selection of knots or the points at which the individual splines will join.

```
#Splines
library(splines)

# Read the auto dataset
df=read.csv("auto_mpg.csv",stringsAsFactors = FALSE) # Data from UCI

# Convert all columns to numeric
df1 <- as.data.frame(sapply(df,as.numeric))

#Select specific columns
df2 <- df1 %>% dplyr::select(cylinder, displacement, horsepower,
weight, acceleration, year,mpg)

# Filter only complete rows
```

```
auto <- df2[complete.cases(df2),]

# Fit a B-spline to the data. Select knots at 60,75,100,150.
# Knots are the points at which separate splines join
fit=lm(mpg~bs(horsepower,df=6,knots=c(60,75,100,150)),data=auto)

# Use the fitted regresion to predict
pred=predict(fit,newdata=list(horsepower=hpGrid),se=T)

# Create a scatter plot
plot(auto$horsepower,auto$mpg,xlim=hp,cex=.5,col="black",xlab="Horsep
ower", ylab="MPG", main="B-Spline with 4 knots")

#Draw predicted line  with 2 Standard Errors(SE) on either side
lines(hpGrid,pred$fit,lwd=2)
lines(hpGrid,pred$fit+2*pred$se,lty="dashed")
lines(hpGrid,pred$fit-2*pred$se,lty="dashed")
abline(v=c(60,75,100,150),lty=2,col="darkgreen")
```

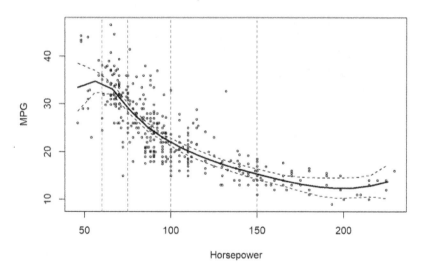

1.1d Fit a Natural Spline – R Code

Here a 'Natural Spline' is used to fit .The Natural Spline extrapolates beyond the boundary knots and the ends of the function are much more constrained than a regular spline or a global polynomial where the ends can wag a lot more. Natural splines do not require the explicit selection of knots

```r
# Read the auto dataset
df=read.csv("auto_mpg.csv",stringsAsFactors = FALSE) # Data from UCI

# Convert all columns to numeric
df1 <- as.data.frame(sapply(df,as.numeric))

#Select specific columns
df2 <- df1 %>% dplyr::select(cylinder,displacement,
horsepower,weight, acceleration, year,mpg)

# Filter only complete rows
auto <- df2[complete.cases(df2),]

# There is no need to select the knots here. There is a smoothing
parameter which
# can be specified by the degrees of freedom 'df' parameter. The
natural spline

fit2=lm(mpg~ns(horsepower,df=4),data=auto)
pred=predict(fit2,newdata=list(horsepower=hpGrid),se=T)
plot(auto$horsepower, auto$mpg, xlim=hp, cex=.5, col="black",
xlab="Horsepower", ylab="MPG", main="Natural Splines")
lines(hpGrid,pred$fit,lwd=2)
lines(hpGrid,pred$fit+2*pred$se,lty="dashed")
lines(hpGrid,pred$fit-2*pred$se,lty="dashed")
```

Natural Splines

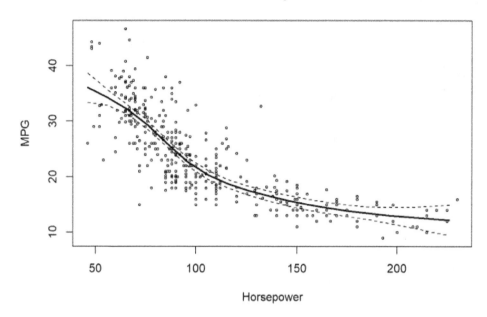

1.1.e Fit a Smoothing Spline – R code

Here a smoothing spline is used. Smoothing splines also do not require the explicit setting of knots. We can change the 'degrees of freedom (df)' parameter to get the best fit

```
# Read the auto dataset
df=read.csv("auto_mpg.csv",stringsAsFactors = FALSE) # Data from UCI

# Convert all columns to numeric
df1 <- as.data.frame(sapply(df,as.numeric))

#Select specific columns
df2 <- df1 %>% dplyr::select(cylinder, displacement, horsepower,
weight, acceleration, year,mpg)

# Filter only complete rows
auto <- df2[complete.cases(df2),]

# Smoothing spline has a smoothing parameter, the degrees of freedom
# This is too wiggly
```

237

```
plot(auto$horsepower,auto$mpg,xlim=hp,cex=.5,col="black",xlab="Horsep
ower", ylab="MPG", main="Smoothing Splines")

# Here df is set to 16. This has a lot of variance
fit=smooth.spline(auto$horsepower,auto$mpg,df=16)
lines(fit,col="red",lwd=2)

# We can use Cross Validation to allow the spline to pick the value
of this smpopothing paramter. We do not need to set the degrees of
freedom 'df'
fit=smooth.spline(auto$horsepower,auto$mpg,cv=TRUE)
lines(fit,col="blue",lwd=2)
```

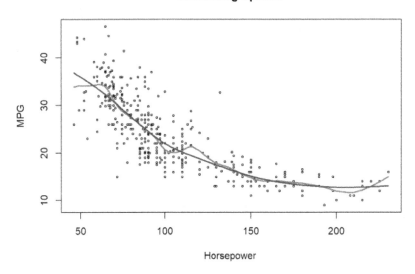

1.1e Splines – Python

There isn't as much treatment of splines in Python and SKLearn. I did find
LSQUnivariate, UnivariateSpline spline. The LSQUnivariate spline requires the explicit
setting of knots

```
import numpy as np
import pandas as pd
import os
import matplotlib.pyplot as plt
from scipy.interpolate import LSQUnivariateSpline

# Read the auto data set
autoDF =pd.read_csv("auto_mpg.csv",encoding="ISO-8859-1")
```

```
autoDF.shape
autoDF.columns

# Select specific columns
autoDF1=autoDF[['mpg','cylinder', 'displacement', 'horsepower',
'weight', 'acceleration', 'year']]
autoDF2 = autoDF1.apply(pd.to_numeric, errors='coerce')
auto=autoDF2.dropna()
auto=auto[['horsepower','mpg']].sort_values('horsepower')

# Set the knots manually
knots=[65,75,100,150]

# Create an array for X & y
X=np.array(auto['horsepower'])
y=np.array(auto['mpg'])

# Fit a LSQunivariate spline
s = LSQUnivariateSpline(X,y,knots)

#Plot the spline
xs = np.linspace(40,230,1000)
ys = s(xs)
plt.scatter(X, y)
plt.plot(xs, ys)
plt.savefig('fig2.png', bbox_inches='tight')
```

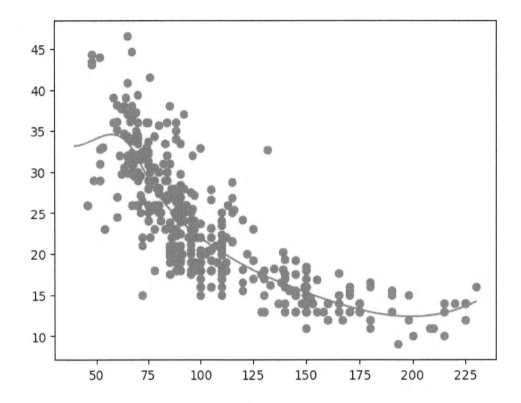

1.2 Generalized Additive models (GAMs)

Generalized Additive Models (GAMs) is a powerful ML tool.

$$y_i = \beta_0 + f_1(x_{i1}) + f_2(x_{i2}) + .. + f_p(x_{ip}) + \epsilon_i$$

In GAMs, we use a different function for each of the variables. GAMs give a much better fit since we can choose any function for the different sections

1.2a Generalized Additive Models (GAMs) – R Code

In the GAM implementation in R a smooth spline is fit for each of the features horsepower, cylinder, displacement, year and acceleration and plotted. **Note:** We can use any function for example loess, 4rd order polynomial etc.

```
library(gam)
# Read the auto dataset
```

```r
df=read.csv("auto_mpg.csv",stringsAsFactors = FALSE) # Data from UCI

# Convert all columns to numeric
df1 <- as.data.frame(sapply(df,as.numeric))

#Select specific columns
df2 <- df1 %>% dplyr::select(cylinder, displacement, horsepower,
weight, acceleration, year, mpg)

# Filter only complete rows
auto <- df2[complete.cases(df2),]

# Fit a smoothing spline for horsepower, cylinder, displacement and
acceleration
gam=gam(mpg~s(horsepower,4)+s(cylinder,5)+s(displacement,4)+s(year,4)
+s(acceleration,5),data=auto)

# Display the summary of the fit. This give the significance of each
of the parameter
# Also an ANOVA is given for each combination of the features
summary(gam)
##
## Call: gam(formula = mpg ~ s(horsepower, 4) + s(cylinder, 5) +
s(displacement,
##      4) + s(year, 4) + s(acceleration, 5), data = auto)
## Deviance Residuals:
##     Min      1Q  Median      3Q     Max
## -8.3190 -1.4436 -0.0261  1.2279 12.0873
##
## (Dispersion Parameter for gaussian family taken to be 6.9943)
##
##      Null Deviance: 23818.99 on 391 degrees of freedom
## Residual Deviance: 2587.881 on 370 degrees of freedom
## AIC: 1898.282
##
## Number of Local Scoring Iterations: 3
##
## Anova for Parametric Effects
##                      Df  Sum Sq Mean Sq  F value    Pr(>F)
## s(horsepower, 4)      1 15632.8 15632.8 2235.085 < 2.2e-16 ***
## s(cylinder, 5)        1   508.2   508.2   72.666 3.958e-16 ***
## s(displacement, 4)    1   374.3   374.3   53.514 1.606e-12 ***
## s(year, 4)            1  2263.2  2263.2  323.583 < 2.2e-16 ***
## s(acceleration, 5)    1   372.4   372.4   53.246 1.809e-12 ***
## Residuals           370  2587.9     7.0
## ---
## Signif. codes:  0 '***' 0.001 '**' 0.01 '*' 0.05 '.' 0.1 ' ' 1
##
## Anova for Nonparametric Effects
```

```
##                      Npar Df Npar F       Pr(F)
## (Intercept)
## s(horsepower, 4)          3 13.825 1.453e-08 ***
## s(cylinder, 5)            3 17.668 9.712e-11 ***
## s(displacement, 4)        3 44.573 < 2.2e-16 ***
## s(year, 4)                3 23.364 7.183e-14 ***
## s(acceleration, 5)        4  3.848  0.004453 **
## ---
## Signif. codes:  0 '***' 0.001 '**' 0.01 '*' 0.05 '.' 0.1 ' ' 1
par(mfrow=c(2,3))
plot(gam,se=TRUE)
```

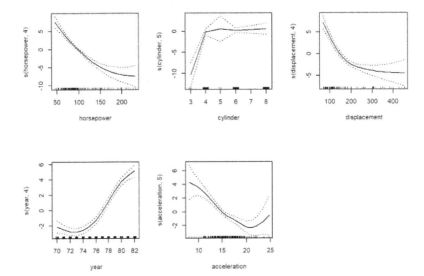

1.2b Generalized Additive Models (GAMs) – Python Code

I did not find the equivalent of GAMs in Sklearn in Python. There was an early prototype (2012) in Github. It seems that it is still work in progress or has probably been abandoned.

1.3 Tree based Machine Learning Models

Tree based Machine Learning are all based on the 'bootstrapping' technique. In bootstrapping given a sample of size N, we create datasets of size N by sampling this original dataset with replacement. Machine Learning models are built on the different bootstrapped samples and then averaged.

Decision Trees as seen above have the tendency to overfit. There are several techniques that help to avoid this namely a) Bagging b) Random Forests c) Boosting

Bagging, Random Forest and Gradient Boosting

Bagging: Bagging or Bootstrap Aggregation decreases the variance of predictions, by creating separate Decision Tree based ML models on the different samples and then averaging these ML models

Random Forests: Bagging is a greedy algorithm and tries to produce splits based on all variables, which try to minimize the error. However, the different ML models have a high correlation. Random Forests remove this shortcoming, by using a variable and random set of features to split on. Hence, the features chosen and the resulting trees are uncorrelated. When these ML models are averaged, the performance is much better.

Boosting: Gradient Boosted Decision Trees also use an ensemble of trees but they do not build Machine Learning models with random set of features at each step. Rather small and simple trees are built. Successive trees try to minimize the error from the earlier trees.

Out of Bag (OOB) Error: In Random Forest and Gradient Boosting for each bootstrap sample taken from the dataset, there will be samples left out. These are known as Out of Bag samples. Classification accuracy carried out on these OOB samples is known as OOB error

1.31a Decision Trees – R Code

The code below creates a Decision tree with the cancer training data. The summary of the fit is output. Based on the ML model, the predict function is used on test data and a confusion matrix is output.

```
library(tree)
library(caret)
library(e1071)

# Read the cancer data
cancer <- read.csv("cancer.csv",stringsAsFactors = FALSE)

# Set the feature and target variables
cancer <- cancer[,2:32]
cancer$target <- as.factor(cancer$target)

# Split the data as training and test sets
train_idx <- trainTestSplit(cancer,trainPercent=75,seed=5)
train <- cancer[train_idx, ]
test <- cancer[-train_idx, ]

# Create the Decision Tree
```

```
cancerStatus=tree(target~.,train)

# Generate and print the summary
summary(cancerStatus)
##
## Classification tree:
## tree(formula = target ~ ., data = train)
## Variables actually used in tree construction:
## [1] "worst.perimeter"      "worst.concave.points" "area.error"
## [4] "worst.texture"        "mean.texture"
"mean.concave.points"
## Number of terminal nodes:  9
## Residual mean deviance:  0.1218 = 50.8 / 417
## Misclassification error rate: 0.02347 = 10 / 426
pred <- predict(cancerStatus,newdata=test,type="class")
confusionMatrix(pred,test$target)
## Confusion Matrix and Statistics
##
##           Reference
## Prediction  0  1
##          0 49  7
##          1  8 78
##
##                  Accuracy : 0.8944
##                    95% CI : (0.8318, 0.9397)
##       No Information Rate : 0.5986
##       P-Value [Acc > NIR] : 4.641e-15
##
##                     Kappa : 0.7795
##   Mcnemar's Test P-Value : 1
##
##               Sensitivity : 0.8596
##               Specificity : 0.9176
##            Pos Pred Value : 0.8750
##            Neg Pred Value : 0.9070
##                Prevalence : 0.4014
##            Detection Rate : 0.3451
##      Detection Prevalence : 0.3944
##         Balanced Accuracy : 0.8886
##
##          'Positive' Class : 0
##
# Plot decision tree with labels
plot(cancerStatus)
text(cancerStatus,pretty=0)
```

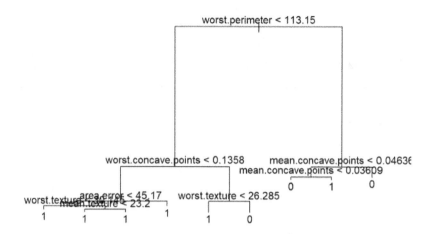

1.31b Decision Trees – Cross Validation – R Code

We can also perform a Cross Validation on the data to identify the Decision Tree, which will give the minimum deviance.

```
library(tree)
# Read the cancer data set
cancer <- read.csv("cancer.csv",stringsAsFactors = FALSE)

# Set the feature and target variables
cancer <- cancer[,2:32]
cancer$target <- as.factor(cancer$target)

# Split the data as training and test
train_idx <- trainTestSplit(cancer,trainPercent=75, seed=5)
train <- cancer[train_idx, ]
test <- cancer[-train_idx, ]

# Create Decision Tree
cancerStatus=tree(target~.,train)

# Execute 10 fold cross validation
```

```
cvCancer=cv.tree(cancerStatus)
plot(cvCancer)
```

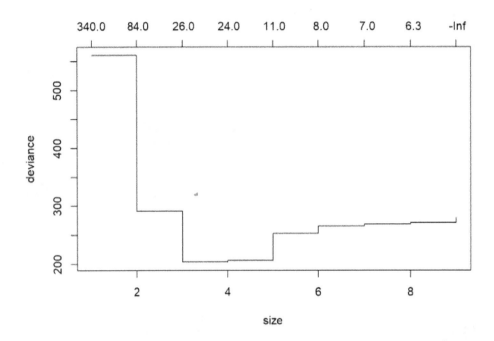

```
# Plot the deviance vs cross validation size
plot(cvCancer$size,cvCancer$dev,type='b')
```

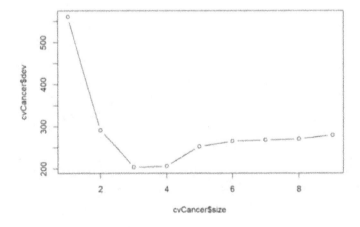

```
# Plot the decision tree
prunedCancer=prune.tree(cancerStatus,best=4)
plot(prunedCancer)
```

```
text(prunedCancer,pretty=0)
```

```
# Compute the target value for the test data
pred <- predict(prunedCancer,newdata=test,type="class")

# Compute the confusion matrix  - Accuracy, Sensitivity, Specificity
confusionMatrix(pred,test$target)
## Confusion Matrix and Statistics
##
##           Reference
## Prediction  0  1
##          0 50  7
##          1  7 78
##
##                Accuracy : 0.9014
##                  95% CI : (0.8401, 0.945)
##     No Information Rate : 0.5986
##     P-Value [Acc > NIR] : 7.988e-16
##
##                   Kappa : 0.7948
##  Mcnemar's Test P-Value : 1
##
##             Sensitivity : 0.8772
##             Specificity : 0.9176
##          Pos Pred Value : 0.8772
##          Neg Pred Value : 0.9176
##              Prevalence : 0.4014
##          Detection Rate : 0.3521
##    Detection Prevalence : 0.4014
##       Balanced Accuracy : 0.8974
##
##        'Positive' Class : 0
##
```

1.31c Decision Trees – Python Code

Below is the Python code for creating Decision Trees. The accuracy, precision, recall and F1 score is computed on the test data set.

```python
import numpy as np
import pandas as pd
import os
import matplotlib.pyplot as plt
from sklearn.metrics import confusion_matrix
from sklearn import tree
from sklearn.datasets import load_breast_cancer
from sklearn.model_selection import train_test_split
from sklearn.tree import DecisionTreeClassifier
from sklearn.datasets import make_classification, make_blobs
from sklearn.metrics import accuracy_score, precision_score,
recall_score, f1_score
import graphviz

# Load the cancer data set
cancer = load_breast_cancer()
(X_cancer, y_cancer) = load_breast_cancer(return_X_y = True)

# Split the data as training and test sets
X_train, X_test, y_train, y_test = train_test_split(X_cancer,
y_cancer, random_state = 0)

# Fit a decision tree to the data
clf = DecisionTreeClassifier().fit(X_train, y_train)

# Print the accuracy on the training and test sets
print('Accuracy of Decision Tree classifier on training set: {:.2f}'
     .format(clf.score(X_train, y_train)))
print('Accuracy of Decision Tree classifier on test set: {:.2f}'
     .format(clf.score(X_test, y_test)))

# Compute the predicted value for the test data
y_predicted=clf.predict(X_test)

# Compute the confusion matrix - Accuracy, Precision, Recall
confusion = confusion_matrix(y_test, y_predicted)
print('Accuracy: {:.2f}'.format(accuracy_score(y_test, y_predicted)))
print('Precision: {:.2f}'.format(precision_score(y_test,
y_predicted)))
print('Recall: {:.2f}'.format(recall_score(y_test, y_predicted)))
print('F1: {:.2f}'.format(f1_score(y_test, y_predicted)))

# Plot the Decision Tree
```

```
clf = DecisionTreeClassifier(max_depth=2).fit(X_train, y_train)
dot_data = tree.export_graphviz(clf, out_file=None,
                                feature_names=cancer.feature_names,
                                class_names=cancer.target_names,
                                filled=True, rounded=True,
                                special_characters=True)
graph = graphviz.Source(dot_data)
graph
## Accuracy of Decision Tree classifier on training set: 1.00
## Accuracy of Decision Tree classifier on test set: 0.87
## Accuracy: 0.87
## Precision: 0.97
## Recall: 0.82
## F1: 0.89
```

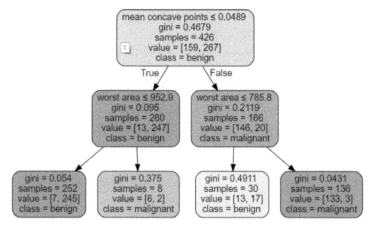

1.31d Decision Trees – Cross Validation – Python Code

In the code below 5-fold cross-validation is performed for different depths of the tree and the accuracy is computed. The accuracy on the test set seems to plateau when the depth is 8. However, it is seen to increase again from 10 to 12.

```
import numpy as np
import pandas as pd
import os
import matplotlib.pyplot as plt
from sklearn.datasets import load_breast_cancer
from sklearn.tree import DecisionTreeClassifier

# Load the cancer data set
(X_cancer, y_cancer) = load_breast_cancer(return_X_y = True)
```

```python
from sklearn.cross_validation import train_test_split, KFold

# Compute the cross validation accuracy
def computeCVAccuracy(X,y,folds):
    accuracy=[]
    foldAcc=[]

    # Set a list of tree depths
    depth=[1,2,3,4,5,6,7,8,9,10,11,12]

    # Compute number of folds
    nK=len(X)/float(folds)
    xval_err=0
    # for the tree depths
    for i in depth:
        # Get no of folds
        kf = KFold(len(X),n_folds=folds)
        for train_index, test_index in kf:
            # Partition the data
            X_train, X_test = X.iloc[train_index], X.iloc[test_index]
            y_train, y_test = y.iloc[train_index], y.iloc[test_index]

            # Create a decision tree of depth i
            clf = DecisionTreeClassifier(max_depth = i).fit(X_train,
y_train)

            # Compute score
            score=clf.score(X_test, y_test)

          # Append accuracy
          accuracy.append(score)

        #Compute the overall mean accuracy
        foldAcc.append(np.mean(accuracy))

    return(foldAcc)

# Compute the Cross Validation Accuracy
cvAccuracy=computeCVAccuracy(pd.DataFrame(X_cancer),pd.DataFrame(y_ca
ncer),folds=10)

# Create a dataframe
df1=pd.DataFrame(cvAccuracy)
df1.columns=['cvAccuracy']
df=df1.reindex([1,2,3,4,5,6,7,8,9,10,11,12])

# Plot the decision tree
df.plot()
```

```
plt.title("Decision Tree - 10-fold Cross Validation Accuracy vs Depth
of tree")
plt.xlabel("Depth of tree")
plt.ylabel("Accuracy")
plt.savefig('fig3.png', bbox_inches='tight')
```

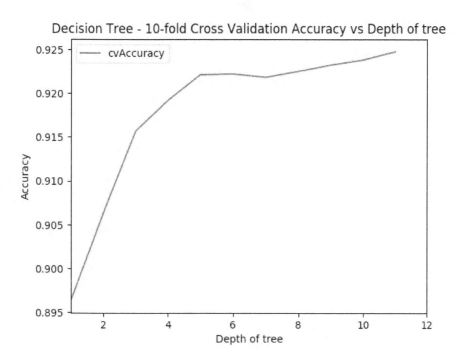

1.4a Random Forest – R code

A Random Forest is fit using the Boston data. The summary shows that 4 variables were randomly chosen at each split, and the resulting ML model explains 88.72% of the test data. Also, the variable importance is plotted. It can be seen that 'rooms' and 'status' are the most influential features in the model

```
library(randomForest)

# Read the Boston data
```

```
df=read.csv("Boston.csv",stringsAsFactors = FALSE) # Data from MASS -
SL

# Select specific columns
Boston <- df %>% dplyr::select("crimeRate", "zone", "indus",
"charles", "nox", "rooms", "age", "distances", "highways", "tax",
"teacherRatio", "color", "status","medianValue")

# Fit a Random Forest on the Boston training data
rfBoston=randomForest(medianValue~.,data=Boston)

# Display the summatu of the fit. It can be seen that the MSE is
10.88
# and the percentage variance explained is 86.14%. About 4 variables
were tried at each # #split for a maximum tree of 500.
# The MSE and percent variance is on Out of Bag trees
rfBoston
##
## Call:
##  randomForest(formula = medianValue ~ ., data = Boston)
##                Type of random forest: regression
##                      Number of trees: 500
## No. of variables tried at each split: 4
##
##          Mean of squared residuals: 9.521672
##                    % Var explained: 88.72
#List and plot the variable importances
importance(rfBoston)
##              IncNodePurity
## crimeRate        2602.1550
## zone              258.8057
## indus            2599.6635
## charles           240.2879
## nox              2748.8485
## rooms           12011.6178
## age              1083.3242
## distances        2432.8962
## highways          393.5599
## tax              1348.6987
## teacherRatio     2841.5151
## color             731.4387
## status          12735.4046

# Print the variable importances
varImpPlot(rfBoston)
```

rfBoston

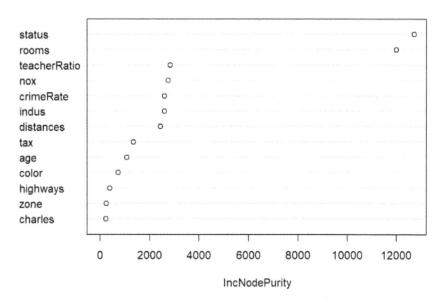

IncNodePurity

1.4b Random Forest-OOB and Cross Validation Error – R code

The figure below shows the OOB error and the Cross Validation error vs the 'mtry'. Here mtry indicates the number of random features that are chosen at each split. The lowest test error occurs when mtry = 8

```
library(randomForest)

#Read the Boston data set
df=read.csv("Boston.csv",stringsAsFactors = FALSE) # Data from MASS -
SL

# Select specific columns
Boston <- df %>% dplyr::select("crimeRate", "zone", "indus",
"charles", "nox", "rooms", "age", "distances", "highways", "tax",
"teacherRatio", "color", "status","medianValue")

# Split data as training and test sets
train_idx <- trainTestSplit(Boston,trainPercent=75,seed=5)
train <- Boston[train_idx, ]
test <- Boston[-train_idx, ]
```

```
#Initialize OOD and testError
oobError <- NULL
testError <- NULL

# In the code below the number of variables to consider at each split
is increased
# from 1 - 13(max features) and the OOB error and the MSE is computed
for(i in 1:13){
    fitRF=randomForest(medianValue~.,data=train,mtry=i,ntree=400)
    oobError[i] <-fitRF$mse[400]
    pred <- predict(fitRF,newdata=test)
    testError[i] <- mean((pred-test$medianValue)^2)
}

# Plot the number variables vs MSE for each split of tree
# We can see the OOB and Test Error. It can be seen that the Random
Forest performs
# best with the lowers MSE at mtry=6
matplot(1:13,cbind(testError,oobError),pch=19,col=c("red","blue"),
        type="b", xlab="mtry(no of varaibles at each split)", ylab=
"Mean Squared Error", main= "Random Forest - OOB and Test Error")
legend("topright",legend=c("OOB","Test"),pch=19,col=c("red","blue"))
```

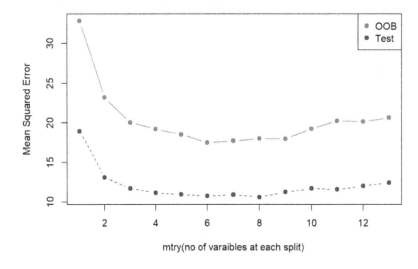

1.4c Random Forest – Python code

The python code for Random Forest Regression is shown below. The training and test score is computed. The variable importance shows that 'rooms' and 'status' are the most influential of the variables

```python
import numpy as np
import pandas as pd
import os
import matplotlib.pyplot as plt
from sklearn.model_selection import train_test_split
from sklearn.ensemble import RandomForestRegressor

# Read the Boston data set
df = pd.read_csv("Boston.csv",encoding = "ISO-8859-1")

# Set the feature and target variabls
X=df[['crimeRate', 'zone', 'indus','charles', 'nox', 'rooms', 'age',
'distances', 'highways', 'tax', 'teacherRatio','color','status']]
y=df['medianValue']

# Split the data set as training and test sets
X_train, X_test, y_train, y_test = train_test_split(X, y,
random_state = 0)

# Fit a Random forest to the data with depth of tree=4.
# random_state - seed of random number generator
regr = RandomForestRegressor(max_depth=4, random_state=0)
regr.fit(X_train, y_train)

# Compute and print the R squared for the training and test data
print('R-squared score (training): {:.3f}'
    .format(regr.score(X_train, y_train)))
print('R-squared score (test): {:.3f}'
    .format(regr.score(X_test, y_test)))

# Plot the variable importance
feature_names=['crimeRate', 'zone', 'indus', 'charles', 'nox',
'rooms', 'age', 'distances','highways', 'tax', 'teacherRatio',
'color', 'status']
print(regr.feature_importances_)
plt.figure(figsize=(10,6),dpi=80)
c_features=X_train.shape[1]
plt.barh(np.arange(c_features),regr.feature_importances_)
plt.xlabel("Feature importance")
plt.ylabel("Feature name")
```

```
plt.yticks(np.arange(c_features), feature_names)
plt.tight_layout()

plt.savefig('fig4.png', bbox_inches='tight')
## R-squared score (training): 0.917
## R-squared score (test): 0.734
## [ 0.03437382  0.           0.00580335  0.           0.00731004
0.36461548
##   0.00638577  0.03432173  0.0041244   0.01732328  0.01074148
0.0012638
##   0.51373683]
```

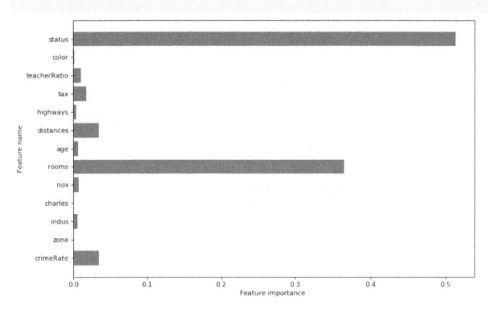

1.4d Random Forest – Cross Validation and OOB Error – Python code

As with R the 'max_features' determines the random number of features the random forest will use at each split. The plot shows that when max_features=8 the MSE is lowest

```
import numpy as np
import pandas as pd
import os
import matplotlib.pyplot as plt
from sklearn.model_selection import train_test_split
from sklearn.ensemble import RandomForestRegressor
from sklearn.model_selection import cross_val_score
```

```
# Read the Boston data set
df = pd.read_csv("Boston.csv",encoding = "ISO-8859-1")

# Set the feature and target variables
X=df[['crimeRate','zone',  'indus', 'charles','nox', 'rooms', 'age',
'distances', 'highways', 'tax', 'teacherRatio','color','status']]
y=df['medianValue']

# Initialize the cross validation error, out of bag error and out of
bag MSE
cvError=[]
oobError=[]
oobMSE=[]

# Loop through number of features
# n_estimators - no of trees in forest
# max_depth=4,
# max_features- maximum features at each split.
# oob_score - whether to generate oob_score for unseen features
# Loop through features
for i in range(1,13):
    # Fit a Random forest
    regr = RandomForestRegressor(max_depth=4, n_estimators=400,
max_features=i, oob_score=True,random_state=0)

    # Compute the MSE
    mse= np.mean(cross_val_score(regr, X, y, cv=5,scoring =
'neg_mean_squared_error'))

    # Since this is neg_mean_squared_error I have inverted the sign
to get MSE
    # Append the MSE
    cvError.append(-mse)

    # Fit on all data to compute OOB error
    regr.fit(X, y)

    # Record the OOB error for each `max_features=i` setting
    oob = 1 - regr.oob_score_
    oobError.append(oob)

    # Get the Out of Bag prediction
    oobPred=regr.oob_prediction_

    # Compute the Mean Squared Error between OOB Prediction and
target
    mseOOB=np.mean(np.square(oobPred-y))
    oobMSE.append(mseOOB)
```

```python
# Plot the CV Error and OOB Error
# Set max_features
maxFeatures=np.arange(1,13)
cvError=pd.DataFrame(cvError,index=maxFeatures)
oobMSE=pd.DataFrame(oobMSE,index=maxFeatures)

#Plot
fig8=df.plot()
fig8=plt.title('Random forest - CV Error and OOB Error vs
max_features')
fig8.figure.savefig('fig8.png', bbox_inches='tight')

#Plot the OOB Error vs max_features
plt.plot(range(1,13),oobError)
fig2=plt.title("Random Forest - OOB Error vs max_features (variable
no of features)")
fig2=plt.xlabel("max_features (variable no of features)")
fig2=plt.ylabel("OOB Error")
fig2.figure.savefig('fig7.png', bbox_inches='tight')
```

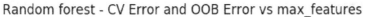

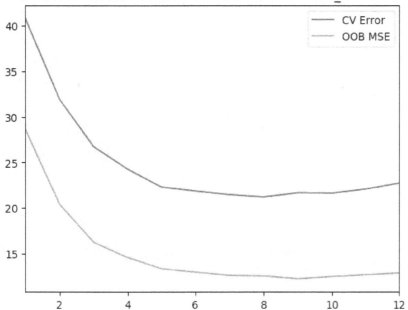

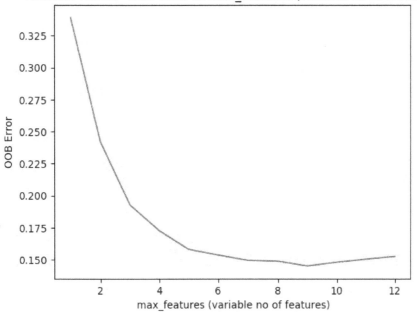

1.5a Boosting – R code

Here a Gradient Boosted ML Model is built with an n.trees=5000, with a learning rate of 0.01 and depth of 4. The feature importance plot also shows that rooms and status are the 2 most important features. The MSE vs the number of trees plateaus around 2000 trees

```
library(gbm)

# Perform gradient boosting on the Boston data set. The distribution
is gaussian since we are doing
# doing MSE. The interaction depth specifies the number of splits
boostBoston=gbm(medianValue~.,data=train,distribution="gaussian",n.tr
ees=5000, shrinkage=0.01,interaction.depth=4)

#The summary gives the variable importance. The 2 most significant
variables are
# number of rooms and lower status
summary(boostBoston)
```

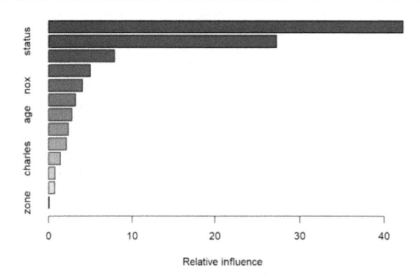

```
##                         var      rel.inf
## rooms                 rooms 42.2267200
## status               status 27.3024671
## distances         distances  7.9447972
## crimeRate         crimeRate  5.0238827
## nox                     nox  4.0616548
## teacherRatio teacherRatio  3.1991999
## age                     age  2.7909772
## color                 color  2.3436295
## tax                     tax  2.1386213
## charles             charles  1.3799109
## highways           highways  0.7644026
## indus                 indus  0.7236082
## zone                   zone  0.1001287
```

```
# The plots below show how each variable relates to the median value
of the home. As
# the number of roomd increase the median value increases and with
increase in lower status
# the median value decreases
par(mfrow=c(1,2))

#Plot the relation between the top 2 features and the target
plot(boostBoston,i="rooms")
plot(boostBoston,i="status")
```

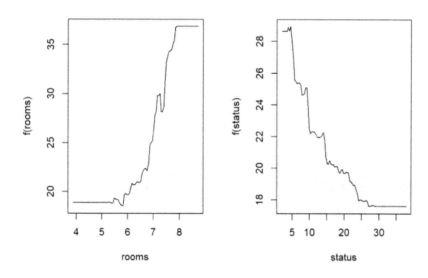

```
# Create a sequence of trees between 100-5000 incremented by 50
nTrees=seq(100,5000,by=50)

# Predict the values for the test data
pred <- predict(boostBoston,newdata=test,n.trees=nTrees)

# Compute the mean for each of the MSE for each of the number of
trees
boostError <- apply((pred-test$medianValue)^2,2,mean)

#Plot the MSE vs the number of trees
plot(nTrees,boostError,pch=19,col="blue",ylab="Mean Squared Error",
     main="Boosting Test Error")
```

Boosting Test Error

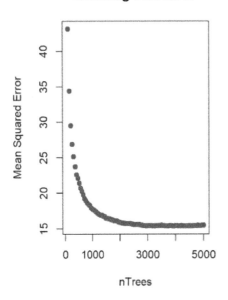

1.5b Cross Validation Boosting – R code

Included below is a cross validation error vs the learning rate. The lowest error is when learning rate = 0.09

```
cvError <- NULL
s <- c(.001,0.01,0.03,0.05,0.07,0.09,0.1)
# Set the learning rates
for(i in seq_along(s)){
    # Fit a Gradient Boosted model
    # distribution - Gaussian
    # n.trees - total number of trees to fit
    # shrinkage - learning rate or step size reduction
    # interaction.depth - maximum number of variable interaction
    #cv.folds - number of cross validation folds
    cvBoost=gbm(medianValue~., data=train, distribution="gaussian",
n.trees=5000, shrinkage=s[i], interaction.depth=4,cv.folds=5)
    cvError[i] <- mean(cvBoost$cv.error)
}

# Create a data frame for plotting
a <- rbind(s,cvError)
b <- as.data.frame(t(a))
```

```
# It can be seen that a shrinkage parameter of 0,05 gives the lowes
CV Error
ggplot(b,aes(s,cvError)) + geom_point() + geom_line(color="blue") +
    xlab("Shrinkage") + ylab("Cross Validation Error") +
    ggtitle("Gradient boosted trees - Cross Validation error vs
Shrinkage")
```

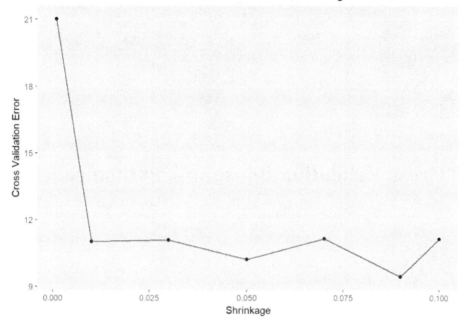

1.5c Boosting – Python code

A gradient boost ML model in Python is created below. The Rsquared score is computed on the training and test data.

```
import numpy as np
import pandas as pd
import os
import matplotlib.pyplot as plt
from sklearn.model_selection import train_test_split
from sklearn.ensemble import GradientBoostingRegressor

# Read the Boston data set
df = pd.read_csv("Boston.csv",encoding = "ISO-8859-1")

# Set the feature and target variables
X=df[['crimeRate', 'zone', 'indus','charles','nox','rooms', 'age',
'distances', 'highways', 'tax', 'teacherRatio','color','status']]
y=df['medianValue']
```

```
# Split the data as training and test set
X_train, X_test, y_train, y_test = train_test_split(X, y,
random_state = 0)

# Fit a gradient boosted model
regr = GradientBoostingRegressor()
regr.fit(X_train, y_train)

# Print the R squared for the training and test data
print('R-squared score (training): {:.3f}'
     .format(regr.score(X_train, y_train)))
print('R-squared score (test): {:.3f}'
     .format(regr.score(X_test, y_test)))
## R-squared score (training): 0.983
## R-squared score (test): 0.821
```

1.5c Cross Validation Boosting – Python code

the cross validation error is computed as the learning rate is varied. The minimum CV eror occurs when lr = 0.04

```
import numpy as np
import pandas as pd
import os
import matplotlib.pyplot as plt
from sklearn.model_selection import train_test_split
from sklearn.ensemble import RandomForestRegressor
from sklearn.ensemble import GradientBoostingRegressor
from sklearn.model_selection import cross_val_score

# Read the Boston data set
df = pd.read_csv("Boston.csv",encoding = "ISO-8859-1")

# Set the feature and target variables
X=df[['crimeRate','zone', 'indus', 'charles', 'nox','rooms', 'age',
'distances', 'highways','tax', 'teacherRatio','color','status']]
y=df['medianValue']

# Initialize the cv error
cvError=[]

# Set the learning rate
learning_rate =[.001,0.01,0.03,0.05,0.07,0.09,0.1]
for lr in learning_rate:
```

```
# Fit a Gradient Boosted model
# n_estimators - no of trees in forest
# max_depth=4,
# n_estimators - The number of boostinf stages
# learning_rate -  learning_rate
regr = GradientBoostingRegressor(max_depth=4,
n_estimators=400,learning_rate  =lr,random_state=0)

    # Compute the MSE
    mse= np.mean(cross_val_score(regr, X, y, cv=10,scoring =
'neg_mean_squared_error'))

    # Since this is neg_mean_squared_error I have inverted the sign
to get MSE
    cvError.append(-mse)

# Set the learning rates
# Plot the max_features vs CV Error
learning_rate =[.001,0.01,0.03,0.05,0.07,0.09,0.1]
plt.plot(learning_rate,cvError)
plt.title("Gradient Boosting - 5-fold CV- Mean Squared Error vs
max_features (variable no of features)")
plt.xlabel("max_features (variable no of features)")
plt.ylabel("Mean Squared Error")
plt.savefig('fig6.png', bbox_inches='tight')
```

Gradient Boosting - 5-fold CV- Mean Squared Error vs max_features (variable no of features)

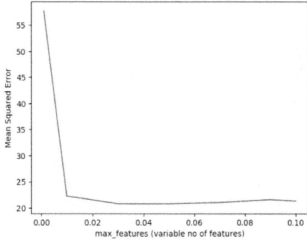

9. PCA, K-Means and Hierarchical Clustering

This chapter deals with Unsupervised Learning. Specifically, Principal Component Analysis (PCA), K-Means and Hierarchical Clustering are implemented in R and Python

Download the associated code in this chapter as a R Markdown file from Github at https://github.com/tvganesh/PracticalMachineLearningWithRandPython

1.1a Principal Component Analysis (PCA) – R code

Principal Component Analysis is used to reduce the dimensionality of the input. In the code below 8 x 8 pixel of handwritten digits is reduced into its principal components. Then a scatter plot of the first 2 principal components give a very good visual representation of the data and how the digits are distributed when displayed as a 2D plot with only the first 2 principal components

```
library(dplyr)
library(ggplot2)
#Note: This example is adapted from an the example in the book Python
Datascience handbook by
# Jake VanderPlas
(https://jakevdp.github.io/PythonDataScienceHandbook/05.09-principal-
component-analysis.html)

# Read the digits data (From sklearn datasets)
digits= read.csv("digits.csv")
# Create a digits classes target variable
digitClasses <- factor(digits$X0.000000000000000000e.00.29)

#Invoke the Principal Componsent analysis on columns 1-64
digitsPCA=prcomp(digits[,1:64])

# Create a dataframe of PCA
df <- data.frame(digitsPCA$x)

# Bind the digit classes
df1 <- cbind(df,digitClasses)

# Plot only the first 2 Principal components as a scatter plot. This
plot uses only the
# first 2 principal components
```

```
ggplot(df1,aes(x=PC1,y=PC2,col=digitClasses)) + geom_point() +
  ggtitle("Top 2 Principal Components")
```

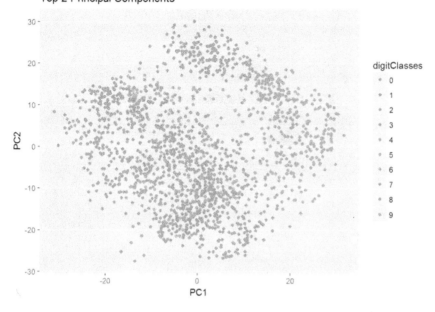

1.1 b Variance explained vs no principal components – R code

In the code below the variance explained vs, the number of principal components is plotted. It can be seen that with 20 Principal components, almost 90% of the variance is explained by this reduced dimensional model.

```
# Read the digits data (from sklearn datasets)
digits= read.csv("digits.csv")

# Digits target
digitClasses <- factor(digits$X0.000000000000000000e.00.29)
digitsPCA=prcomp(digits[,1:64])

# Get the Standard Deviation
sd=digitsPCA$sdev

# Compute the variance
digitsVar=digitsPCA$sdev^2

#Compute the percent variance explained
percentVarExp=digitsVar/sum(digitsVar)
```

```
# Plot the percent variance exlained as a function of the  number of
principal components
#plot(cumsum(percentVarExp), xlab="Principal Component",
#      ylab="Cumulative Proportion of Variance Explained",
#      main="Principal Components vs % Variance
explained",ylim=c(0,1),type='l',lwd=2,
#        col="blue")
```

Principal Components vs % Variance explained

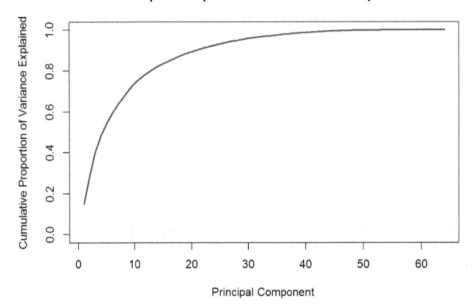

1.1c Principal Component Analysis (PCA) – Python code

```
import numpy as np
from sklearn.decomposition import PCA
from sklearn import decomposition
from sklearn import datasets
import matplotlib.pyplot as plt

from sklearn.datasets import load_digits
# Load the digits data
digits = load_digits()

# Select only the first 2 principal components
pca = PCA(2)   # project from 64 to 2 dimensions

#Compute the first 2 PCA
```

```
projected = pca.fit_transform(digits.data)

# Plot a scatter plot of the first 2 principal components
plt.scatter(projected[:, 0], projected[:, 1],
            c=digits.target, edgecolor='none', alpha=0.5,
            cmap=plt.cm.get_cmap('spectral', 10))
plt.xlabel('PCA 1')
plt.ylabel('PCA 2')
plt.colorbar();
plt.title("Top 2 Principal Components")
plt.savefig('fig1.png', bbox_inches='tight')
```

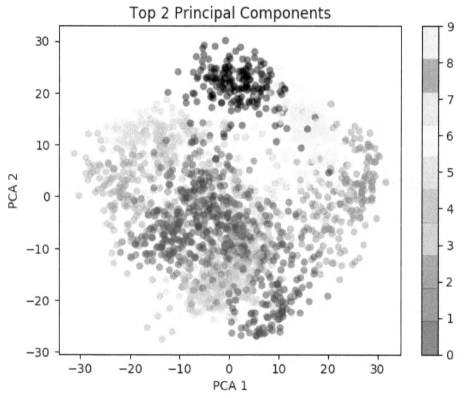

1.1 b Variance vs no principal components – Python code

```
import numpy as np
from sklearn.decomposition import PCA
from sklearn import decomposition
from sklearn import datasets
import matplotlib.pyplot as plt
from sklearn.datasets import load_digits
```

```
# Read the digits
digits = load_digits()

# Select all 64 principal components
pca = PCA(64)  # project from 64 to 2 dimensions
projected = pca.fit_transform(digits.data)

# Obtain the explained variance for each principal component
varianceExp= pca.explained_variance_ratio_

# Compute the total sum of variance
totVarExp=np.cumsum(np.round(pca.explained_variance_ratio_,
decimals=4)*100)

# Plot the variance explained as a function of the number of
principal components
plt.plot(totVarExp)
plt.xlabel('No of principal components')
plt.ylabel('% variance explained')
plt.title('No of Principal Components vs Total Variance explained')
plt.savefig('fig2.png', bbox_inches='tight')
```

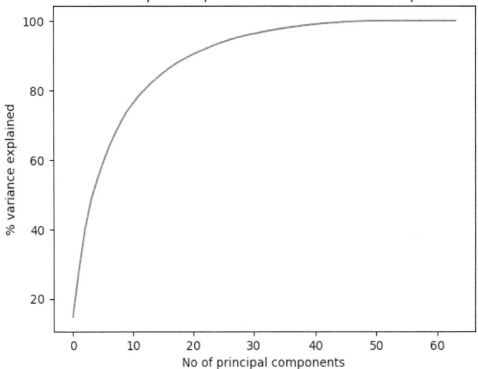

1.2a K-Means – R code

In the code below, first the scatter plot of the first 2 Principal Components of the handwritten digits is plotted as a scatter plot. Over this plot, 10 centroids of the 10 different clusters corresponding the 10 different digits is plotted over the original scatter plot.

```
library(ggplot2)

# Read the digits data
digits= read.csv("digits.csv")

# Create digit classes target variable
digitClasses <- factor(digits$X0.000000000000000000e.00.29)

# Compute the Principal COmponents
digitsPCA=prcomp(digits[,1:64])

# Create a data frame of Principal components and the digit classes
df <- data.frame(digitsPCA$x)
df1 <- cbind(df,digitClasses)

# Pick only the first 2 principal components
a<- df[,1:2]

# Compute K Means of 10 clusters and allow for 1000 iterations
k<-kmeans(a,10,1000)

# Create a dataframe of the centroids of the clusters
df2<-data.frame(k$centers)

#Plot the first 2 principal components with the K Means centroids
ggplot(df1,aes(x=PC1,y=PC2,col=digitClasses)) + geom_point() +
    geom_point(data=df2,aes(x=PC1,y=PC2),col="black",size = 4) +
    ggtitle("Top 2 Principal Components with KMeans clustering")
```

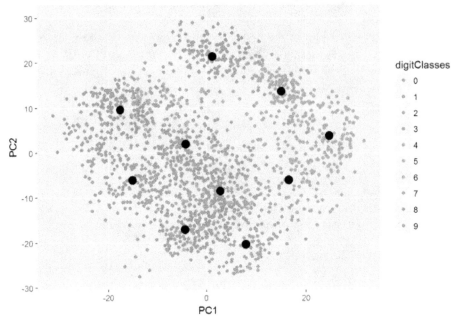

Top 2 Principal Components with KMeans clustering

1.2b K-Means – Python code

The centroids of the 10 different handwritten digits is plotted over the scatter plot of the first 2 principal components.

```
import numpy as np
from sklearn.decomposition import PCA
from sklearn import decomposition
from sklearn import datasets
import matplotlib.pyplot as plt
from sklearn.datasets import load_digits
from sklearn.cluster import KMeans
digits = load_digits()

# Select only the 1st 2 principal components
pca = PCA(2)  # project from 64 to 2 dimensions
projected = pca.fit_transform(digits.data)

# Create 10 different clusters
kmeans = KMeans(n_clusters=10)

# Compute  the clusters
kmeans.fit(projected)
y_kmeans = kmeans.predict(projected)
# Get the cluster centroids
```

```
centers = kmeans.cluster_centers_
centers

#Create a scatter plot of the first 2 principal components
plt.scatter(projected[:, 0], projected[:, 1],
            c=digits.target, edgecolor='none', alpha=0.5,
            cmap=plt.cm.get_cmap('spectral', 10))
plt.xlabel('PCA 1')
plt.ylabel('PCA 2')
plt.colorbar();
# Overlay the centroids on the scatter plot
plt.scatter(centers[:, 0], centers[:, 1], c='darkblue', s=100)
plt.savefig('fig3.png', bbox_inches='tight')
```

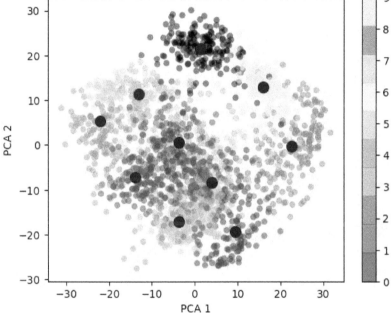

1.3a Hierarchical clusters – R code

Hierarchical clusters, is another type of unsupervised learning. It successively joins the closest pair of objects (points or clusters) in succession based on some 'distance' metric. In this type of clustering we do not have choose the number of centroids. We can cut the created dendrogram, at an appropriate height to get a desired and reasonable number of clusters. These are the following 'distance' metrics used while combining successive objects

- Ward
- Complete

273

- Single
- Average
- Centroid

```
# Read the IRIS dataset
iris <- datasets::iris
iris2 <- iris[,-5]
species <- iris[,5]

#Compute the distance matrix
d_iris <- dist(iris2)

# Use the 'average' method to for the clsuters
hc_iris <- hclust(d_iris, method = "average")

# Plot the clusters
plot(hc_iris)

# Cut tree into 3 groups
sub_grp <- cutree(hc_iris, k = 3)

# Number of members in each cluster
table(sub_grp)
## sub_grp
##  1  2  3
## 50 64 36
# Draw rectangles around the clusters
rect.hclust(hc_iris, k = 3, border = 2:5)
```

Cluster Dendrogram

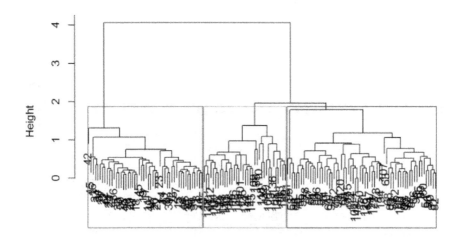

d_iris
hclust (*, "average")

1.3a Heirarchical clusters – Python code

```python
from sklearn.datasets import load_iris
import matplotlib.pyplot as plt
from scipy.cluster.hierarchy import dendrogram, linkage

# Load the IRIS data set
iris = load_iris()

# Generate the linkage matrix using the average method
Z = linkage(iris.data, 'average')

#Plot the dendrogram
dendrogram(Z)
plt.xlabel('Data')
plt.ylabel('Distance')
plt.suptitle('Samples clustering', fontweight='bold', fontsize=14);
plt.savefig('fig4.png', bbox_inches='tight')
```

Samples clustering

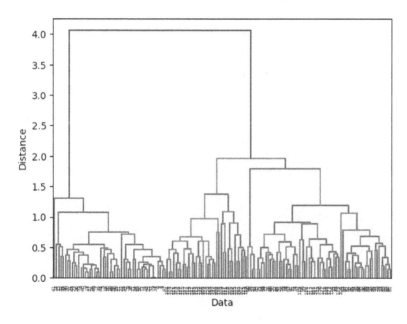

References

1. Statistical Learning, (https://lagunita.stanford.edu/courses/HumanitiesandScience/StatLearning/Winter2015/about) Prof Trevor Hastie & Prof Robert Tibesherani, Online Stanford
2. Applied Machine Learning in Python (https://www.coursera.org/learn/python-machine-learning) , Prof Kevyn-Collin Thomson, University Of Michigan, Coursera
3. I have used the (Communities and Crime and Auto MPG) data sets from UCI Machine Learning (https://archive.ics.uci.edu/ml/datasets.html)
4. The Adult data set is taken from UCI Machine Learning Repository
5. The Python package for performing a Best Fit is the Exhaustive Feature Selector(http://rasbt.github.io/mlxtend/user_guide/feature_selection/ExhaustiveFeatureSelector/)
6. The Backward Fit in Python uses the Sequential feature selection (SFS) package (SFS)(https://rasbt.github.io/mlxtend/user_guide/feature_selection/SequentialFeatureSelector/)
7. The RMarkdown file for the book can be downloaded from Github at https://github.com/tvganesh/PracticalMachineLearningWithRandPython

www.ingramcontent.com/pod-product-compliance
Lightning Source LLC
Chambersburg PA
CBHW080632060326
40690CB00021B/4905